A **SÉRIE BRASIL – Ensino Médio** oferece conteúdo completo em todos os sentidos e integra objetos digitais aos materiais impressos. Acesse o portal exclusivo da coleção e aproveite o que a Editora do Brasil preparou para você.

Portal exclusivo da coleção:
www.seriebrasilensinomedio.com.br

Instruções para acesso aos conteúdos digitais

Acesse o portal exclusivo da coleção (www.seriebrasilensinomedio.com.br) e digite seu *e-mail* e senha. Caso ainda não os tenha, faça o cadastro. Digite o código abaixo para liberar o acesso:

8499441A3068029

Esse código libera o acesso dos conteúdos digitais relativos à matéria e ao ano deste livro. Informamos que esse código é pessoal e intransferível. Guarde-o com cuidado, pois é a única forma de acesso ao conteúdo restrito do portal.

SÉRIE BRASIL
Ensino Médio

ENSINO MÉDIO
INGLÊS
Your Turn

3

Gisele Aga
Licenciada em Letras pelas Faculdades Metropolitanas Unidas (FMU). Autora de livros didáticos de Língua Inglesa para os anos finais do Ensino Fundamental, autora de materiais didáticos para programas bilíngues, editora de conteúdos didáticos, professora de Língua Inglesa para o Ensino Médio na rede particular de ensino e professora de Língua Inglesa em cursos de idiomas.

Adriana Saporito
Licenciada em Letras, com habilitação em Tradutor e Intérprete – Português e Inglês – pela Faculdade Ibero-Americana de Letras e Ciências Humanas. Professora de Literatura Brasileira, Língua Portuguesa e Língua Inglesa da rede particular de ensino, autora de livros de Língua Inglesa para Ensino Fundamental e Educação para Jovens e Adultos (EJA), editora de conteúdos didáticos.

Carla Maurício
Bacharel e licenciada em Letras pela Universidade Federal do Rio de Janeiro (UFRJ). Professora de Língua Inglesa da rede particular de ensino, editora de conteúdos didáticos, autora de livros de Língua Inglesa para os anos finais do Ensino Fundamental e do Ensino Médio.

2ª edição
São Paulo – 2016

COMPONENTE CURRICULAR
LÍNGUA ESTRANGEIRA MODERNA – INGLÊS
3º ANO
ENSINO MÉDIO

© Editora do Brasil S.A., 2016
Todos os direitos reservados

Direção geral: Vicente Tortamano Avanso
Direção adjunta: Maria Lúcia Kerr Cavalcante Queiroz

Direção editorial: Cibele Mendes Curto Santos
Gerência editorial: Felipe Ramos Poletti
Supervisão editorial: Erika Caldin
Supervisão de arte, editoração e produção digital: Adelaide Carolina Cerutti
Supervisão de direitos autorais: Marilisa Bertolone Mendes
Supervisão de controle de processos editoriais: Marta Dias Portero
Supervisão de revisão: Dora Helena Feres
Consultoria de iconografia: Tempo Composto Col. de Dados Ltda.
Licenciamentos de textos: Cinthya Utiyama, Jennifer Xavier, Paula Harue Tozaki, Renata Garbellini
Coordenação de produção CPE: Leila P. Jungstedt

Concepção, desenvolvimento e produção: Triolet Editorial e Mídias Digitais
Diretora executiva: Angélica Pizzutto Pozzani
Diretor de operações: João Gameiro
Gerente editorial: Denise Pizzutto
Editor de texto: Camilo Adorno
Assistente editorial: Tatiana Pedroso
Preparação e revisão: Amanda Andrade, Carol Gama, Érika Finati, Flávia Venezio, Flávio Frasqueti, Gabriela Damico, Juliana Simões, Leandra Trindade, Mayra Terin, Patrícia Rocco, Regina Elisabete Barbosa, Sirlei Pinochia
Projeto gráfico: Triolet Editorial/Arte
Editoras de arte: Ana Onofri, Paula Belluomini
Assistentes de arte: Beatriz Landiosi (estag.), Lucas Boniceli (estag.)
Ilustradora: Suryara Bernardi
Iconografia: Pamela Rosa (coord.), Joanna Heliszkowski
Fonografia: Maximal Estúdio
Tratamento de imagens: Fusion DG
Capa: Beatriz Marassi
Imagem de capa: John J. Klaiber Jr/Shutterstock.com

Todos os esforços foram feitos no sentido de localizar e contatar os detentores dos direitos das músicas reproduzidas no CD que integra a coleção *Your Turn*. Mediante manifestação dos interessados, a Editora do Brasil terá prazer em providenciar eventuais regularizações.

Dados Internacionais de Catalogação na Publicação (CIP)
(Câmara Brasileira do Livro, SP, Brasil)

Your Turn, 3 : ensino médio / Gisele Aga, Adriana Saporito, Carla Maurício. – 2. ed. – São Paulo : Editora do Brasil, 2016. – (Série Brasil : ensino médio)

Componente curricular: Língua estrangeira moderna – Inglês
ISBN 978-85-10-06467-5 (aluno)
ISBN 978-85-10-06468-2 (professor)

1. Inglês (Ensino médio) I. Saporito, Adriana.
II. Maurício, Carla. III. Título. IV. Série.

16-05819   CDD-420.7

Índice para catálogo sistemático:
1. Inglês : Ensino médio   420.7

Reprodução proibida. Art. 184 do Código Penal e Lei n. 9.610 de 19 de fevereiro de 1998.
Todos os direitos reservados

2016
Impresso no Brasil

2ª edição / 1ª impressão, 2016

Impressão e acabamento: Intergraf Ind. Gráfica Eireli.

Imagem de capa:
Jogo de futebol americano.

Rua Conselheiro Nébias, 887 – São Paulo/SP – CEP 01203-001
Fone: (11) 3226-0211 – Fax: (11) 3222-5583
www.editoradobrasil.com.br

APRESENTAÇÃO

Caro aluno,

É com enorme satisfação que apresentamos esta coleção. Nós a concebemos tendo em mente você como aluno e como cidadão local e global. Levamos em conta suas necessidades e expectativas em relação ao aprendizado da língua inglesa e todos os benefícios que esse conhecimento poderá trazer para sua vida social e profissional.

Sabemos que o novo milênio necessita cada vez mais de pessoas autônomas e solidárias, que tenham consciência do espaço que ocupam, do meio em que vivem e da sociedade que desejam construir. Portanto, faz-se necessário uma nova postura perante si mesmo, o outro e a realidade. A língua inglesa ocupa papel essencial nesse cenário, uma vez que é o idioma oficial dos negócios, das comunicações, das tecnologias, enfim, do mundo globalizado.

Diante disso, esta coleção oferece a você a oportunidade de entrar em contato com o inglês vivo e real por meio de textos orais e escritos sobre diversos assuntos e provenientes de várias partes do mundo. Você será convidado a refletir sobre suas experiências, suas expectativas e seus posicionamentos como cidadão da comunidade e do planeta em que vive.

Você terá também a oportunidade de produzir textos e participar de projetos que estimulam a parceria, o trabalho colaborativo e o compartilhamento de experiências e conhecimentos. Enfim, você será convidado a assumir o papel de protagonista de seu aprendizado.

Nós, autoras, acreditamos firmemente que oferecemos a você uma coleção rica em diversidade, informação, conhecimento e, especialmente, em prática da língua inglesa viva e atual. Temos plena convicção de que você se apropriará de um aprendizado que lhe trará oportunidades positivas e enriquecedoras em um futuro breve.

Agora é com você! Esperamos que aproveite ao máximo a coleção.

As autoras

Conheça o livro

As unidades do seu livro estão organizadas por seções. Conheça um pouco mais sobre elas a seguir.

Opening Pages

Seção que inicia a unidade e tem por objetivo ativar seu conhecimento prévio acerca do tema que será trabalhado, através da exploração de uma imagem. Nessas páginas você também conhecerá os objetivos da unidade.

Interdisciplinaridade

Este ícone aponta as disciplinas com as quais a unidade dialoga.

Starting Out

Esta seção tem como principais objetivos introduzir o tema que será apresentado e aprofundado ao longo da unidade, bem como ativar seu conhecimento prévio sobre o gênero textual ao qual você será exposto.

Reading Comprehension

Nesta seção, você será exposto a textos escritos de diferentes gêneros e origens, podendo desenvolver sua habilidade de leitura para compreensão geral e detalhada.

Vocabulary Study

Aqui você terá a oportunidade de estudar a língua a partir de contextos em uso presentes nos textos da seção anterior, desenvolvendo, assim, o vocabulário de maneira contextualizada.

Language in Context

Nesta seção, você poderá observar a língua e deduzir as regras gramaticais a partir do texto estudado em *Reading Comprehension*. A seção termina com a subseção *Wrapping up*, na qual você é incentivado a usar as regras gramaticais em diferentes atividades orais e escritas.

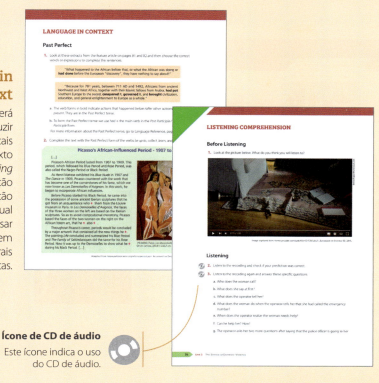

Ícone de CD de áudio
Este ícone indica o uso do CD de áudio.

Listening Comprehension

Aqui você será exposto a textos orais de diferentes gêneros e origens, podendo desenvolver sua habilidade de compreensão global e seletiva, através de variadas estratégias de audição.

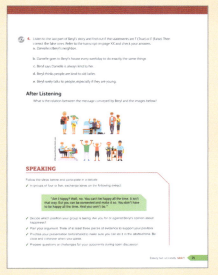

Speaking

Nesta seção, você participará de atividades que promovem a produção oral através da discussão de assuntos sobre o tema da unidade, usando o vocabulário e as estruturas gramaticais estudadas nas unidades.

Writing

Aqui você produzirá textos escritos do mesmo gênero analisado em *Reading Comprehension* e colocará em prática o vocabulário e as estruturas gramaticais estudadas na unidade, levando em consideração o propósito da produção, o público-alvo e as características do gênero.

Self-Assessment

Ao final de cada unidade, você poderá refletir e avaliar seu processo de desenvolvimento, conscientizando-se em relação aos conhecimentos adquiridos e ao que pode ser ainda aperfeiçoado.

Conheça o livro

A coleção conta ainda com os seguintes apêndices:

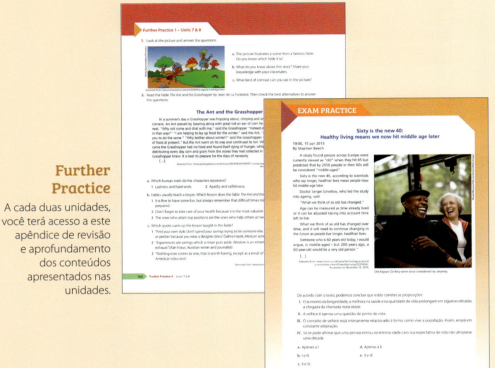

Further Practice
A cada duas unidades, você terá acesso a este apêndice de revisão e aprofundamento dos conteúdos apresentados nas unidades.

Exam Practice
Apêndice com questões semelhantes às das provas do Enem, também apresentado a cada duas unidades.

Career Planning
Aqui você poderá ler e refletir sobre algumas profissões relacionadas aos temas das unidades.

Learning from Experience
Neste apêndice, você terá a oportunidade de vivenciar experiências concretas de aprendizagem por meio de projetos interdisciplinares relacionados aos temas das unidades.

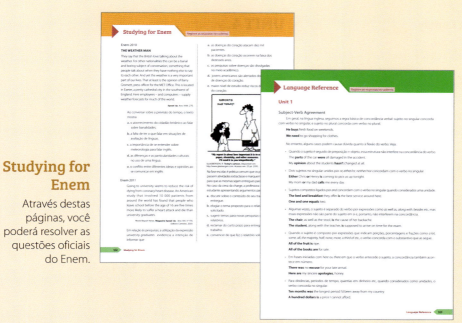

Studying for Enem

Através destas páginas, você poderá resolver as questões oficiais do Enem.

Language Reference

Apêndice de aprofundamento dos conteúdos linguísticos apresentados nas unidades, com quadros, exemplos e atividades.

Você terá acesso ainda às transcrições dos áudios, à lista de verbos irregulares e ao glossário.

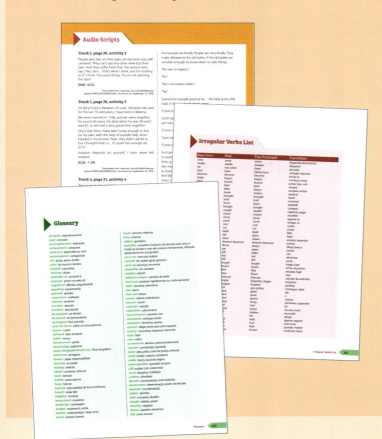

Extra Resources

Para que você possa consolidar seu aprendizado ou ainda ter acesso a novos conhecimentos além daqueles estudados em aula, recomendamos alguns artigos, vídeos, filmes etc.

Atenção!
Não escreva no livro. Todos os exercícios devem ser resolvidos no caderno.

Sumário

UNIT 1 Elderly but Not Lonely 10

Starting Out 12
Reading Comprehension 13
   Don't Abandon the Elderly 13
Vocabulary Study 16
   Prefix *un-* and other negative prefixes 16
Language in Context 17
   Subject-Verb Agreement 17
Listening Comprehension 20
Speaking 21
Writing 22
Self-Assessment 23

UNIT 2 Are You a Movie Buff? 24

Starting Out 26
Reading Comprehension 27
   Central Station 27
Vocabulary Study 30
   Movie Genres 30
Language in Context 31
   Order of Adjectives 31
   Adverbs 32
Listening Comprehension 34
Speaking 35
Writing 36
Self-Assessment 37
Further Practice 1 – Units 1 & 2 38
Exam Practice 43

UNIT 3 The Silence of Domestic Violence 44

Starting Out 46
Reading Comprehension 47
   How do we prevent violence against women? 47
Vocabulary Study 50
   Types of Domestic Abuse 50
Language in Context 51
   Conditionals 51
Listening Comprehension 54
Speaking 55
Writing 56
Self-Assessment 57

UNIT 4 Volunteering 58

Starting Out 60
Reading Comprehension 61
   An Interview with Chris Hamming, Search Gallery Volunteer 61
Vocabulary Study 64
   Adjectives Ending in *-ed* or *-ing* 64
Language in Context 65
   Past Continuous 65
   Past Continuous and Simple Past 66
Listening Comprehension 68
Speaking 69
Writing 70
Self-Assessment 71
Further Practice 2 – Units 3 & 4 72
Exam Practice 77

UNIT 5 An Eye on Africa 78

Starting Out 80
Reading Comprehension 81
   When Africa civilised Europe 81
Vocabulary Study 84
   Synonyms 84
Language in Context 85
   Past Perfect 85
Listening Comprehension 88
Speaking 89
Writing 90
Self-Assessment 91

UNIT 6 Social Media and False News 92

Starting Out 94
Reading Comprehension 95
   Putrajaya wants social media to cull 'false news' 95
Vocabulary Study 98
   Prefix *co-* 98

Language in Context 99
   Direct and Indirect Speech 99
Listening Comprehension 102
Speaking 103
Writing 104
Self-Assessment 105
Further Practice 3 – Units 5 & 6 106
Exam Practice 111

UNIT 7 Managing Your Money 112

Starting Out 114
Reading Comprehension 115
   The Money-Box 115
Vocabulary Study 118
   Idioms 118
Language in Context 119
   Reflexive Pronouns 119
   Passive Voice III 120
Listening Comprehension 122
Speaking 123
Writing 124
Self-Assessment 125

UNIT 8 High School is Over... Now What? 126

Starting Out 128
Reading Comprehension 129
   Graduation speech by Megan Lee Qi Jun 129
Vocabulary Study 132
   Borrowing 132
Language in Context 133
   Verb Tense Review 133

Listening Comprehension 136
Speaking 137
Writing 138
Self-Assessment 139
Further Practice 4 – Units 7 & 8 140
Exam Practice 145

Career Planning 146
Learning from Experience 154
Studying for Enem 162
Language Reference 169
Audio Scripts 193
Extra Resources 199
Irregular Verbs List 201
Glossary 203
Bibliography 208

Suryara Bernardi

UNIT 1

ELDERLY BUT NOT LONELY

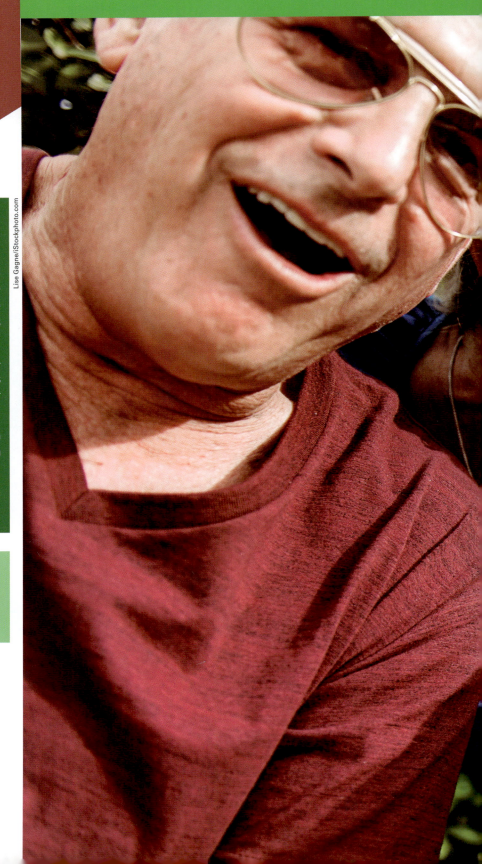

Lise Gagne/iStockphoto.com

Nesta unidade você terá oportunidade de:

- refletir e discutir sobre o papel do idoso em nossa sociedade e sobre o que pode ser feito para garantir a ele melhores condições de vida;
- reconhecer os objetivos e algumas das características das cartas dos leitores e produzir uma;
- compreender o relato de uma pessoa idosa sobre o seu dia a dia;
- participar ativamente de um debate.

- O que podemos ver na imagem?
- Podemos relacionar esta foto ao contexto social de hoje? Justifique.

STARTING OUT

1. What is portrayed in the pictures below? Share your ideas with a classmate. After that, match the pictures to their captions.

- Every second, two people around the world celebrate their sixtieth birthday.
- Fewer than one in five older people globally have access to a pension.
- Forty-seven percent of males over 60 years old and 24 percent of females over 60 years old still participate in the labour force; in some developing countries, over 90 percent of [people] over 60 work.
- In 1910, life expectancy for a Chilean female was 33 years. Today it is 82 years.
- Born in Tennessee in 1896, Besse Cooper is the world's oldest living person. On her 116th birthday this year she said, "I mind my own business. And I don't eat junk food."
- On 16 October 2011, British national Fauja Singh became the first 100-year-old to complete a marathon by running the Toronto Waterfront Marathon in Canada.
- Japan is the world's "oldest" country, with the highest concentration of people aged 60 and over.

Adapted from <www.huffingtonpost.com/2012/10/02/aging-population_n_1929464.html>. Accessed on September 20, 2015

2. Have you ever read a letter sent to a newspaper or a magazine in response to a report about how the elderly are treated in your community? How useful do you think these letters are? Discuss your answers with a classmate and report them to the whole class.

READING COMPREHENSION

Before Reading

1. Look at the banner of the online newspaper East Oregonian at the bottom of the page and answer the questions that follow.

   a. In which section of the online newspaper East Oregonian could you find letters to the editor?

   b. What other text genres could you find in this section?

   c. Why do you think people write letters to the editor?

Reading

Letter: Don't abandon the elderly

Published: September 3, 2015 5:40PM

"Were they really here?" The thought echoes around and back in Grandma's mind. These thoughts come, as she tries to process that she actually did have a visitor. Her first in 10 days. And she is one of the lucky few.

Hers are days spent alone, in the 12 x 12 room that has been her world since her family "parked" her here. She is lonely, desperately lonely. With her "history" here, how can this be?

Here, in what she knows is her hometown; where she has grown kids and half-grown grandkids. Her town, where her civic volunteering stints numbered not in days or years, but decades. Her home, where she joyously belonged to so many clubs. Where her church membership at the same house of worship was unbroken for decades. Yes, here, despite local family, friendships of years and a church "family," she is left to be lonely. Visitors are so few that this visit has left her questioning her memory, her mind, her sanity. And yet she is one of the lucky ones; she had a visitor.

As our parents and grandparents age, we have all too available "assisted living", "nursing" and "residential care" facilities where Grandma can be warehoused (female pronouns are used because elderly populations are overwhelming female). Families, all too often, seem to think: She has three meals a day, a roof over her head, someone to dispense medications. What more can she need? Thus the family can go about their business with few worries.

Em 1º de outubro de 2003, o Estatuto do Idoso foi sancionado no país. Ele define medidas de proteção para brasileiros com idade igual ou superior a 60 anos. Segundo a Secretaria de Direitos Humanos da Presidência da República e de acordo com dados do IBGE (Instituto Brasileiro de Geografia e Estatística), em 2011, a população brasileira de idosos era de 23,5 milhões de pessoas.

Baseado em: <www.sdh.gov.br/assuntos/pessoa-idosa/programas/politica-nacional-do-idoso-e-o-estatuto-do-idoso>. Acessado em: 17 de setembro de 2015.

It is true that the vast majority of our elderly are unable to travel even short distances. Mobility and vision hurdles create further difficulties. Most are even denied the ability to use a phone by hearing issues. So visitors have to come to them, rather than visits being two-way streets. Still, overwhelmingly, they don't come.

In personal observations and querying staff at local elderly care homes, the number of residents who never receive a visit from anyone is appalling. Fully half of the residents have no visitations at all. Not on holidays, weekends or birthdays. Another 30 percent receive short visits on holidays, but only then. This means that nearly 80 percent of people consigned to elder care have at most one or two visits a year. Leaving 363 days of isolation and loneliness.

Golden Age? One wonders.

Yet still one hears the echoes of Grandma's thoughts: "Was someone here? Or did I imagine it?"

Tom Marks
Hermiston

Adapted from <www.eastoregonian.com/eo/letters/20150903/letter-dont-abandon-the-elderly>.
Accessed on September 17, 2015.

1. What is the tone of the letter to the editor on pages 13 and 14?

    a. aggressive   **b.** critical   **c.** sarcastic

2. Justify your answer in the previous activity.

3. Match questions and answers according to the text. There is an extra answer.

    a. Who wrote the letter to the editor?

    b. Who do you think "Grandma" is?

    c. Why does the author mention Grandma's many activities before she was left there?

    d. Why does the author say that Grandma is a lucky person?

    e. In general, what do families think nursing homes do for the elderly?

    f. The vast majority of the elderly are unable to travel even short distances. Why?

    1. Because most of them have mobility and vision problems.

    2. Tom Marks Hermiston.

    3. Because she had a visitor while most elderly people are left alone.

    4. They think that they provide everything the elderly need.

    5. Grandma is a character that represents a typical resident of a residential care facility.

    6. Because most of them have mobility and vision problems.

    7. His intention is to show people that it is not fair being abandoned after doing so much for family, friends, and society.

4. Read the definition below. Look for rhetorical questions in the text on pages 13 and 14 and choose the best option to complete the statement that follows.

> A rhetorical question is a figure of speech in the form of a question that is asked to make a point rather than to elicit an answer. Though classically stated as a proper question, such a rhetorical device by implying a question, and therefore may not always require a question mark when written. Though a rhetorical question does not require a direct answer, in many cases it may be intended to start a discussion or at least draw an acknowledgement that the listener understands the intended message. [...]

Extracted from <http://en.wikipedia.org/wiki/Rhetorical_question>. Accessed on April 21, 2016.

The rhetorical questions presented in the letter to the editor aim mainly at...

a. expressing irony.

b. expressing agreement towards people's attitudes.

c. persuading and making readers reflect on the issue.

5. Identify the only sentence which does not convey a characteristic of the letter to the editor you have just read.

a. A person who writes letters to the editor wants to express his/her personal opinions and knowledge about a current issue.

b. The language used can be formal or informal. It depends on the target audience and where the letter is going to be published.

c. Letters to the editor are based on hypothetical facts.

d. Rhetorical questions can be asked to persuade people to see the author's point of view.

e. They are usually written in response to a magazine or newspaper article.

6. In pairs, write one more characteristic of letters to the editor.

After Reading

- Old age has much cultural and social value in Korean and Japanese societies. An elderly person's opinion is usually taken into consideration when decisions have to be made. Does this happen in our society? Explain.

- Do you think we can all benefit from the life experiences of an elderly person? Justify your answer.

- According to a study done by the World Health Organization, the number of elderly people in Brazil will almost triple by 2050. What can we do to ensure a better life for the elderly now and in the future?

- How would you like to be treated in old age? Is this the way you treat the elderly around you? Reflect and compare.

Elderly but Not Lonely **Unit 1**   15

VOCABULARY STUDY

1. Read the following extracts from the letter to the editor on pages 13 and 14 and choose the correct answer to the question that follows.

> "Hers are days spent alone, in the 12 x 12 room that has been her world since her family "parked" her here."

> "With her "history" here, how can this be?"

> "Yes, here, despite local family, friendships of years and a church "family," she is left to be lonely."

Why did the author write the words *parked*, *history*, and *family* between quotation marks?

a. To indicate that those words enclose a translation.

b. To indicate that those words have ambiguous or double meaning.

c. To indicate that those are someone's exact words.

2. Which alternative contains the words that convey the same meanings as the ones between quotation marks in the extracts above?

a. planted – past – ancestors

b. left – experiences – group

c. stationed – news – generations

d. stored – accomplishments – blood

3. Scan the text for the words *unbroken* and *unable* and infer their meanings. What meaning does the prefix *un-* convey?

4. Other prefixes such as *dis-*, *il-*, *im-*, *in-*, *ir-*, *mis-*, and *non-* convey negative meanings. Scan the text on pages 13 and 14 for the opposites of the words below and write them in your notebook. Then add one of the negative prefixes to find a synonym to the first word.

a. craziness

b. unfortunate

c. inaccessible

d. outsiders, visitors

LANGUAGE IN CONTEXT

Subject-Verb Agreement

1. Read the following extracts from the letter to the editor on pages 13 and 14 and find their subjects and verbs. Then pay attention to how they agree and match the sentences.

  I. "The thought echoes around and back in Grandma's mind."
  II. "These thoughts come, as she tries to process…"
  III. "Families, all too often, seem to think…"
  IV. "… the number of residents who never receive a visit from anyone is appalling."
  V. "Was someone here?"
  VI. "As our parents and grandparents age…"

  a. Subjects usually agree with verbs in number:

  b. Words that come between the subject and the verb,

  c. Prepositional phrases such as *of residents* and relative clauses such as *who never receive a visit from anyone* in extract IV,

  d. Indefinite pronouns like *someone* in extract V, for example,

  e. If two or more subjects that do not represent a single entity are connected by *and*,
  - take singular verb forms.
  - a singular subject agrees with a singular verb and a plural subject agrees with a plural verb.
  - when positioned between the subject and verb, do not affect their agreement.
  - such as *our parents and grandparents* in extract VI, they require a plural verb form.
  - such as *all too often* in extract III, do not interfere in their agreement.

2. Use the verbs *bother* and *drive* to complete the cartoon.

3. Now pay attention to the subject-verb agreement in these other extracts from the letter to the editor on pages 13 and 14 and complete the sentences in your notebook.

I. "It is true that the vast majority of our elderly are unable to travel even short distances."

II. "Fully half of the residents have no visitations at all."

III. "Another 30 percent receive short visits on holidays, but only then."

IV. "This means that nearly 80 percent of people consigned to elder care have at most one or two visits a year."

a. When noun or pronoun subjects indicate parts of a whole such as *the majority*, ♦ , *some*, *none*, *more,* and *all*, followed by a prepositional phrase, verbs agree with the object of the preposition.

b. Percentages and fractions need a ♦ verb form when the object of the preposition is plural, and a ♦ verb form when the object of the preposition is singular.

c. Notice that the object of a preposition may be implicit, such as in extract ♦ above.

For more information about Subject-Verb Agreement, go to Language Reference, page 169.

4. Choose between singular or plural verb forms to complete the letter to the editor below.

> ### Elderly citizens should get better pension
>
> [...]
>
> In Hong Kong, ♦ many elderly citizens living in poverty. While the government ♦ their plight, it has done little in reality to alleviate it.
>
> The Old Age Living Allowance is just HK$2,390. This is a pittance and it is not enough for people to pay for the daily necessities of life. Therefore, many elderly citizens ♦ to supplement their income by collecting material that they can sell to recycling firms, such as cardboard, newspapers and aluminium cans.
>
> The government ♦ to introduce universal retirement protection. I think such a policy would be feasible, but the administration ♦ no signs of supporting it and the elderly on low incomes ♦ to endure a poor quality of life.
>
> Christy Yeung Ho-ying, Yau Yat Chuen

Extracted from <www.scmp.com/comment/letters/article/1885918/letters-editor-december-03-2015>.
Accessed on December 2, 2015.

a. • there is • there are

b. • has recognised • have recognised

c. • is forced • are forced

d. • needs • need

e. • shows • show

f. • continues • continue

5. Use the verb forms from the box to complete the text.

> consider   includes   is   say   says   was

Over 65% of elderly face neglect and abuse in India. No country for old men?

SOURAV ROY
JULY 13, 2015

Over two-thirds of elderly people in India ♦ they are neglected by their family members while one third of the elderly claimed to have suffered physical or verbal abuse, with those in urban areas bearing the brunt more than in the rural areas, according to a study titled "Human Rights of Elderly in India: A Critical Reflection on Social Development" released recently by Agewell Foundation, which conducted interviews of 5,000 elderly people across India.

[…]

Among the elderly surveyed 22.2 per cent said a lack of gainful engagement was the most common problem in old age. 21.24 per cent of older persons think that declining health status ♦ the most common problem while 18 per cent of respondents pointed to a lack of respect and dignity.

Second in the list of problems cited by the elderly ♦ a declining health status (20.1 per cent) followed by a lack of respect in society and family (19.84 per cent). According to 25 per cent of elderly respondents, younger people ♦ elderly family members a burden on their family. An equal number of elderly (25 per cent) said that generation gap is the main reason behind violation of human rights of older persons.

In all, 20 per cent of elderly respondents admit that their younger family members are unable to take care of their elderly family members. "A comprehensive care package that ♦ promotional, preventive, curative and rehabilitative services is essential for this expanding group of population. Newer forms of services and program interventions by the government can go toward addressing the problems of the elderly," the study ♦ . Easy accessibility, continuity and good quality of care only can earn respect and satisfaction of the elderly.

Oscar Wilde once said, "Youth is wasted on the young." Makes us wonder, have the neglected, rejected and abused elderly wasted their youth on us?

saurabhpbhoyar/Shutterstock.com

Adapted from <social.yourstory.com/2015/07/elderly-in-india/>. Accessed on December 2, 2015.

WRAPPING UP

Do a classroom survey. Ask six of your classmates two questions about the elderly in their families. You can ask, for instance, "Are old people respected in your family?" or "Would you like your family to take care of you when you grow old?". Then write down the results of the survey and report them to your classmates. You can write, for example: Half / 10 percent / The majority of the classmates I interviewed…

LISTENING COMPREHENSION

Before Listening

1. Read the quote below and answer the following questions in pairs.

> "It is not how old you are, but how you are old."
> (Jules Renard, French writer)

Extracted from <www.brainyquote.com/quotes/quotes/j/julesrenar119986.html>. Accessed on September 21, 2015.

- What is the message of the quote?
- Do you agree with Renard? Why/Why not?
- What things make us old? What can we do about them?
- How do the elderly around you lead their lives?
- Are they active people? What do they do on a daily basis? Explain.
- What do you think of the way they live? Do you think they should change somehow? Explain.
- If you could give one piece of advice to an elderly person close to you, what would it be?

Listening

2. You are going to listen to Beryl Francis Newton, a 100-year-old lady, telling her story to the Australian radio program ABC Open Sunshine Coast. Listen to what she says at the very beginning of the recording and answer: What do people who live on their own suffer from? Use your own words to write about what you have inferred.

3. Put the paragraphs in order to form the second part of Beryl's story. Then listen and check your answers.

> "Since that time, I have been lucky enough to live on my own, with the help of outside help. And I handed in my license. Yeah, they didn't ask for it, but I thought that's a…it's quite fair enough uh… at 97."

> "We were married in 1938, and we were together for nearly 60 years. He died when he was 89 and I was 83, so we had a very good time together."

> "I'm Beryl Francis Newton. I'm over 100 years old, and for the last 70-odd years, I have lived in Maleny."

> "Isolation depends on yourself. I have never felt isolated."

4. Listen to the last part of Beryl's story and find out if the statements are T (True) or F (False). Then correct the false ones. Refer to the transcript on page 193 and check your answers.

- **a.** Danielle is Beryl's neighbor.
- **b.** Danielle goes to Beryl's house every weekday to do exactly the same things.
- **c.** Beryl says Danielle is always kind to her.
- **d.** Beryl thinks people are kind to old ladies.
- **e.** Beryl rarely talks to people, especially if they are young.

After Listening

What is the relation between the message conveyed by Beryl and the images below?

SPEAKING

Follow the steps below and participate in a debate.

✓ In groups of four or five, exchange ideas on the following extract.

> "Am I happy? Well, no. You can't be happy all the time. It isn't that way. But you can be contented and make it so. You don't have to be happy all the time. And you won't be."

✓ Decide which position your group is taking: Are you for or against Beryl's opinion about happiness?

✓ Plan your argument. Think of at least three pieces of evidence to support your position.

✓ Practice your presentation beforehand to make sure you can do it in the allotted time. Be clear and cohesive when you speak.

✓ Prepare questions or challenges for your opponents during open discussion.

WRITING

Write a letter to the editor in response to an article you have read which concerns you. Follow the steps below.

Planning your letter to the editor

- Choose an article you would like to express your points of view about.

- You can choose an article from newspapers, online news, or magazines, among others.

- After reading the article, reflect on the following questions: Do you agree or disagree with the arguments in the article? Why? Do you have any corrections to add to the article?

Writing and rewriting your text

- Write a draft of the letter to the editor in your notebook.

REFLECTING AND EVALUATING

Go back to your letter to the editor and make sure you paid attention to the following questions:

✓ Did you use the appropriate tone and language?

✓ Did you express your point of view clearly?

✓ Did you use strong arguments?

✓ Did you conclude the letter by restating your opinion?

✓ Did you sign your letter?

- Before showing your letter to the teacher, show it to a classmate and ask for his/her opinion.

- Finally, show it to the teacher and ask for correction.

- Write a clean copy making all the necessary adjustments.

After writing

- Exchange your letter with the letters of dfferent classmates. Which letter to the editor is the most interesting?

SELF-ASSESSMENT

Chegamos ao fim da unidade 1. Convidamos você a refletir sobre seu desempenho até aqui e responder às questões propostas abaixo, escolhendo uma das seguintes opções:

Sim.

Preciso me preparar mais.

Questões

- Você é capaz de discutir o papel social da população idosa e agir de forma a proporcionar a ela melhores condições de vida?
- Você se considera apto a ler e compreender uma carta do leitor em língua inglesa sobre fatos recentes da sociedade e reconhecer as características principais inerentes ao gênero?
- Você reúne conhecimentos linguístico-discursivos suficientes para produzir uma carta do leitor em inglês?
- Você se sente preparado para ouvir relatos sobre as experiências de vida de idosos e compreender informações específicas?
- Você se julga apto a participar de um debate, expor seus argumentos e apresentar contra-argumentação de maneira clara e coerente?

Refletindo sobre suas respostas

- De que forma suas práticas de aprendizagem no decorrer desta unidade influenciaram suas respostas?
- O que você pode fazer para aprimorar ainda mais os conhecimentos adquiridos nesta unidade?

  a. Procurar conhecer mais sobre o papel dos idosos, sobretudo em sua comunidade.

  b. Ler mais cartas do leitor publicadas em diferentes meios de comunicação para compreender pontos de vista diversos acerca de eventos atuais.

  c. Aprofundar meus conhecimentos de língua inglesa usando recursos diversos, de forma que minha participação nas atividades seja mais ativa.

  d. Outros.

UNIT 2

ARE YOU A MOVIE BUFF?

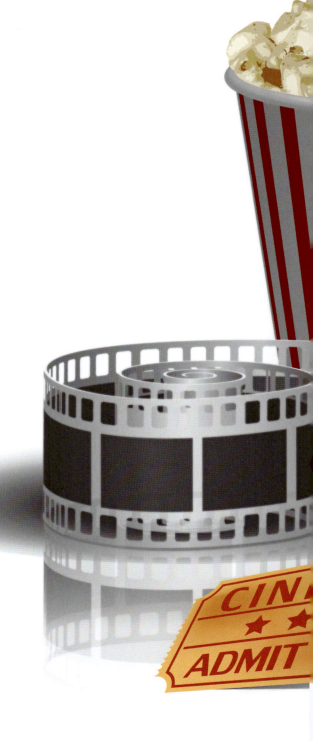

Nesta unidade você terá oportunidade de:

- refletir e discutir sobre iniciativas que promovem e dão suporte à indústria cinematográfica brasileira, bem como sobre a inserção de questões sociais em filmes e a visibilidade do cinema nacional no cenário mundial;

- reconhecer os objetivos e algumas características das resenhas de filmes e escrever uma;

- compreender uma entrevista oral dada por renomado diretor brasileiro de cinema a um canal britânico de notícias;

- discutir com os colegas sobre perguntas que gostariam de fazer a um diretor de cinema.

- O que podemos inferir da mensagem verbal contida na foto?
- Que aspectos da cultura brasileira estão representados nesta imagem?

graphit/Shutterstock.com

STARTING OUT

1. In pairs, discuss the quote and answer the following question: Why do you watch movies?

> "Movies touch our hearts, awaken our vision, and change the way we see things. They take us to other places, they open doors and minds. Movies are the memories of our lifetime; we need to keep them alive."
> (Martin Scorsese, American director and producer)

Adapted from <www.goodreads.com/author/quotes/12133.Martin_Scorsese>. Accessed on February 19, 2016.

2. Read the words and expressions in the box. Then compose the mind map in your notebook and complete it with the ones that are related to the movie industry.

> accessibility   Bollywood   face-to-face contact
> FPS   frame   motherhood   on (general) release
> rushes   slaves   tabloids   takeaway
> the big screen   special effect   studio

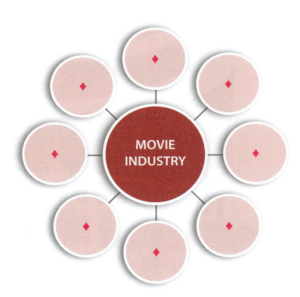

3. How do you pick out the movies you want to watch? Choose the alternatives which are true for you.

   a. I watch movie trailers.

   b. I read plot summaries.

   c. I read movie reviews.

   d. I check movie ratings.

   e. Others.

READING COMPREHENSION

Before Reading

1. Scan the movie review and find the name of the main actress in *Central Station*. Answer orally: who is she? What do you know about her?

Reading

Movie Review

Central Station (1998)
FILM REVIEW; A Journey of Hope and Self-Discovery for Two Hard-Bitten Souls
By JANET MASLIN
Published: November 20, 1998

In Walter Salles's "Central Station", a hit at Sundance and the winner of top honors at this year's Berlin Film Festival, a cynical, joyless woman crosses paths with a lonely young boy. There's plenty of room for sentimentality here, but the wonder of Mr. Salles's film is all in the telling.

Beautifully observed and featuring a bravura performance by the Brazilian actress Fernanda Montenegro, it gracefully watches these oddly paired characters develop a fractious bond that winds up profoundly changing both of them. Mr. Salles's background as a documentary filmmaker also gives this lovely, stirring film a strong sense of Brazil's impoverished rural landscape once its principals take to the road. Vinícius de Oliveira was a 10-year-old shoeshine boy when he encountered Mr. Salles at an airport and asked the man to help him buy a sandwich. Now he movingly plays the child named Josué who is foisted by fate onto this irascible older woman. Ms. Montenegro's Dora is a former schoolteacher who earns her living writing letters for the illiterate at the Rio de Janeiro railroad station of the title. She spends all day listening to the heartfelt thoughts of strangers, writes them down and then makes cruel fun of them when she gets home. After joking about the letters with her kinder friend Irene (Marilia Pera of ''Pixote''), Dora never bothers to mail them. Then a letter by Josué's mother permanently alters Dora's world.

> **FILM REVIEW**
> **FILM REVIEW; A Journey of Hope and Self-Discovery for Two Hard-Bitten Souls**
> By JANET MASLIN
> Published: November 20, 1998
>
> In Walter Salles's "Central Station," a hit at Sundance and the winner of top honors at this year's Berlin Film Festival, a cynical, joyless woman crosses paths with a lonely young boy. There's plenty of room for sentimentality here, but the wonder of Mr. Salles's film is all in the telling.

© 2016 The New York Times Company

> **TIP**
>
> Sempre que possível, assista a filmes e séries com áudio original em inglês e sem legendas. Além de ser uma forma bastante eficaz de aprender o idioma, você estará em contato com situações reais de comunicação.

Are You a Movie Buff? **Unit 2** 27

With suspicious little Josué in tow, the mother dictates a beseeching letter to her absent husband, then leaves the station and is killed by a bus. Suddenly, the boy knows no one and has no place to go. Despite her hardened bitterness and obvious loathing for children, Dora grudgingly takes him home, where Irene finds Josué adorable and is happy to help him. But Dora has other plans; she wants to sell Josué to an adoption racket and effectively trade him in for a new television set.

This scheme subsequently gets Dora into so much trouble that she abruptly decides to leave town. And she agrees to take Josué on a wild goose chase in search of his father, whom the boy says is a carpenter named Jesus. These are the events that send "Central Station" off into the countryside, and take both these hard-bitten travelers into parts unknown. […]

CENTRAL STATION
Directed by Walter Salles; written (in Portuguese, with English subtitles) by João Emanuel Carneiro and Marcos Bernstein, based on an original idea by Mr. Salles; director of photography, Walter Carvalho; edited by Isabelle Rathery and Felipe Lacerda; music by Antonio Pinto and Jaques Morelembaum; production designers, Cassio Amarante and Carla Caffe; produced by Arthur Cohn and Martine de Clermont-Tonnerre; released by Sony Pictures Classics. Running time: 115 minutes. This film is rated R.
WITH: Fernanda Montenegro (Dora), Marilia Pera (Irene), Vinícius de Oliveira (Josué), Soia Lira (Ana) and Othon Bastos (Cesar).

Adapted from <www.nytimes.com/1998/11/20/movies/film-review-a-journey-of-hope-and-self-discovery-for-two-hard-bitten-souls.html>. Accessed on September 27, 2015.

1. Who do the sentences below refer to? Read and number accordingly.

> 1. Josué   2. Irene   3. Dora   4. Josué's mother

a. He/She is happy about the possibility of helping a kid.

b. He/She meets a tragic ending.

c. He/She has no place to go to and is completely alone.

d. He/She makes money dishonestly.

2. Answer the questions.

a. What does Dora do with the letters that she writes for the illiterate?

b. What is Dora's real intention when she takes Josué to her house?

c. Where did Vinícius de Oliveira and Mr. Salles meet for the first time?

3. Pick out the only statement that is NOT true.

a. Dora is described as an insensitive woman.

b. Josué's mother is illiterate.

c. Dora doesn't have any friends.

d. Dora helps Josué find his missing father.

4. Read the definition below. Then read the movie review again and identify the best alternative to complete the sentence.

> **allusion**
>
> a statement that refers to something without mentioning it directly

Extracted from <www.merriam-webster.com/dictionary>. Accessed on February 19, 2016.

The movie *Central Station* alludes to...

a. historic Brazilian characters.

b. a Bible character.

c. a character from a fable.

5. Copy the part of the movie review that justifies your answer in the previous activity.

6. Discuss these questions in small groups.

a. Why do people read movie reviews? Where can movie reviews be found?

b. Do you think people would watch the movie after reading Janet Maslin's review? Why/Why not?

7. Identify the best answers.

a. What are the purposes of movie reviews?

- To promote the movie's sponsors, the main actors, and the director.
- To inform people about the movie, to describe, and to analyze it critically.

b. Do the authors of movie reviews express their personal opinions? Why/Why not?

- No. They tend to be impartial because they don't try to convince readers to watch the movie.
- Yes. They usually express personal opinions because they try to help readers decide whether to watch the movie or not.

After Reading

- The ANCINE (*Agência Nacional do Cinema*) promotes and supports Brazilian cinema through different programs including financial aid for independent filmmakers. In your opinion, is this kind of initiative important for the development of the Brazilian film industry? Explain your answer.

- In 1962, the Brazilian movie *O Pagador de Promessas* won the Golden Palm, the highest prize awarded at the Cannes Film Festival. Some other Brazilian movies, such as *Central do Brasil*, *Pixote*, *A Lei do Mais Fraco*, and *Tropa de Elite* have been awarded worldwide as well. How valuable is this in promoting Brazilian culture? What do these movies tell people in other countries about Brazil?

- *Central Station* addresses social issues such as illiteracy in Brazil. Should movies address social problems or should they just entertain? Justify your answer.

- Since 1998, when *Central Station* was released, many Brazilian directors, actors, and actresses have achieved international acclaim. Alice Braga, Rodrigo Santoro, José Padilha, and Wagner Moura are some examples. What qualities do these actors need to have to make it internationally?

Are You a Movie Buff? **Unit 2** 29

VOCABULARY STUDY

1. Refer to the movie review on pages 27 and 28 to infer the meaning of these words. Then match the columns.

   a. cynical
   b. joyless
   c. lonely
   d. suspicious
   e. fractious
   f. stirring
   g. impoverished
   h. irascible

   - moving, rousing
   - distrustful
   - grouchy, cross
   - unhappy
   - nonbelieving, doubtful
   - poor, exhausted
   - feeling friendless, forlorn
   - crabby

   Extracted from <www.thesaurus.com>. Accessed on September 27, 2015.

2. Choose the correct alternative to complete the movie summary below.

   > A young boy's (Oliveira) mother is killed in front of Rio de Janeiro's Central Station. Homeless and with nowhere to turn, he is reluctantly befriended by a ♦ and ♦ woman (Montenegro). Resisting her initial impulse to make a quick profit off the child, she commits to returning him to his father in Brazil's remote Northeast. The trip becomes a quest for their own identities: one boy's search for his father, and one woman's search for her heart. […]

   Extracted from <www.metacritic.com/movie/central-station>. Accessed on September 27, 2015.

   a. stirring / suspicious   b. impoverished / joyless   c. lonely / cynical

3. According to *The New York Times*, *Central Station* is classified as drama. What other movie genres do you know? Use the words from the box to label the picture.

   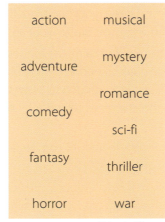
   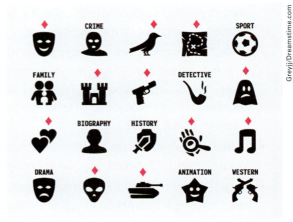

   action, musical, adventure, mystery, romance, comedy, sci-fi, fantasy, thriller, horror, war

   Extracted from <www.dreamstime.com/stock-illustration-film-genres-vector-icon-set-image42806489>. Accessed on September 27, 2015.

LANGUAGE IN CONTEXT

Order of Adjectives

1. Read these extracts from the movie review on pages 27 and 28 and find the words used to qualify or describe the nouns in bold.

"In Walter Salles's 'Central Station', a hit at Sundance and the winner of top honors at this year's Berlin Film Festival, a cynical, joyless **woman** crosses paths with a lonely young **boy**."

"Mr. Salles's background as a documentary filmmaker also gives this lovely, stirring **film** a strong sense of Brazil's impoverished rural landscape once its principals take to the road."

"Now he movingly plays the child named Josué who is foisted by fate onto this irascible older **woman**."

"With suspicious little **Josué** in tow, the mother dictates a beseeching letter to her absent husband, then leaves the station and is killed by a bus."

2. Look at the extracts in activity 1 and match the columns.

a. We can use two adjectives

b. Adjectives like *cynical, joyless, lonely, lovely,*

c. Adjectives like *young, older,*

d. When opinion and fact adjectives are used before a noun, such as in "irascible older woman",

e. When we have two opinion adjectives before a noun, such as in "lovely, stirring film",

- *stirring, irascible,* and *suspicious* express opinions. They are opinion adjectives.

- in front of the same noun.

- opinion adjectives are positioned before fact adjectives.

- the general opinion adjective comes before the specific opinion adjective.

- and *little* express facts. They are fact adjectives.

> Não se esqueça de que os adjetivos também podem ser posicionados depois de verbos, como em *That woman is cynical and joyless* ou *This film is lovely and stirring.*

For a table of Fact Adjectives Order, go to Language Reference, page 171.

3. Below are extracts from two reviews of *Central Station* by two different movie critics. Choose the alternatives that best complete them.

a. Louis B. Hobson

Jam! Movies   January 23, 2002

It's not just a ♦, ♦ drama. It's a film that transcends its national boundaries.

- heartfelt, strong
- strong, heartfelt

b. Christopher Null

Filmcritic.com   October 8, 2001

It's a ♦ ♦ tale, held together by lush photography.

- fascinating, small
- small, fascinating

Adapted from <www.rottentomatoes.com/m/central-do-brasil-central-station/reviews/>.
Accessed on September 28, 2015.

4. In pairs, discuss the questions below. Then share your opinions with the class.

   a. Reading the two reviews from activity 3, would you be interested in watching the movie if you hadn't watched it before? How do the multiple adjectives used by the critics contribute to your decision?

   b. What kind of information would you expect to find if you decided to follow the hyperlinks from the reviews in activity 3?

Adverbs

5. Read these extracts from the review of *Central Station* on pages 27 and 28 and pay attention to the words in bold. Then write down in your notebook the words that modify verbs and those that modify adjectives. Finally, complete the text.

   "**Beautifully** observed and featuring a bravura performance by the Brazilian actress Fernanda Montenegro, it **gracefully** watches these **oddly** paired characters develop a fractious bond that winds up **profoundly** changing both of them."

   ♦ are words used to modify verbs, ♦ or other adverbs. They usually indicate how, when, where, or why something happens. Although most adverbs often end in ♦ , not all words that end in *-ly* are adverbs. For instance, the words ♦ and *lovely*, which were used in the text on pages 27 and 28, are adjectives.

6. Complete this excerpt about the Indian epic sports-drama *Lagaan* with the adverbial forms derived from the following adjectives: *candid*, *entire*, *increasing*, *inevitable*, *refreshing*, and *structural*.

Art in the absence of reality

Over the past months the phenomenal success of Lagaan, a period film set in rural Awadh of the 1890's, has elicited much discussion. To the Hindi film industry much used to churning out minor variations on formulaic themes that are more commercial than artistic ventures, Lagaan represents a bold departure that borders on high art. With an indigenous theme and plot, Lagaan is ♦ at variance with the standard masala dramas ♦ shot in the West these days. But ♦ it retains much of the problematic cultural baggage of Hindi cinema. […]

This critique of Lagaan is occasioned by the hype generated by its nomination for an Oscar. If it had walked away with an Academy Award, many more breathless encomiums would have ♦ followed. One should make no mistake that the Oscars are an ♦ American affair and cannot be a barometer of world-wide artistic tastes and merit. The Oscar for foreign film category is a minor side-show, a grudging acknowledgment by Hollywood that cinema exists beyond America. Moreover, as Aamir Khan has so ♦ said on television, winning the Oscar has got more to do with mundane matters like lobbying to get the Academy members to watch the film and vote for it. That we continue to look to the West for approbation is a poor reflection on the colonised mindset of the elite in India.

[…]

colonised (UK)
colonized (US)

Adapted from <indiatogether.org/reviews/films/lagaan.htm>. Accessed on December 4, 2015.

7. Have you ever seen movies produced in Bollywood? Has the review in activity 6 aroused your curiosity about them? Justify your answer.

8. Choose the correct alternative to complete the text below.

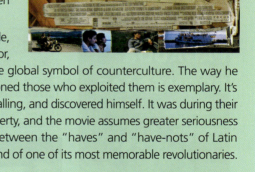

Before he changed the world, the world changed him… this was the film's punch line, and there could not have been a more apt phrase to describe the film's protagonist. Before Che Guevara became Che Guevara, he was a ♦ student, Ernesto Guevara, who undertakes a ♦ road trip with his friend Alberto Granado. But as destiny would have it, the roads take Ernesto to Latin America, Cuba, across South America, where he witnesses injustice and exploitation of the poor and takes up arms against it.

Walter Salles award-winning biopic on Che, "*The Motorcycle Diaries*" was the last film I saw. I watched it on a persistent and strong recommendation of family and friends, and this written memoir, "*The Motorcycle Diaries*", a biopic about the journey of 23-year-old Ernesto Guevara to the ♦ revolutionary Che Guevara, has been a personal journey for me.

The film recounts the 1952 journey, ♦ on motorcycle, across South America by Guevara and Granado. Author, physician, military theorist, guerrilla leader, Che's the global symbol of counterculture. The way he stood by his people, fought for the poor, and questioned those who exploited them is exemplary. It's through his adventure and travels that he found his calling, and discovered himself. It was during their expedition that Guevara and Granado encounter poverty, and the movie assumes greater seriousness once the men gain a better sense of the disparity between the "haves" and "have-nots" of Latin America. It's an exploration of identity, of a country, and of one of its most memorable revolutionaries.

[…]

Adapted from <archive.indianexpress.com/news/-the-motorcycle-diaries-is-an-exploration-of-identity/492889/>. Accessed on December 4, 2015.

a. 23-year-old medical / "fun" / iconic Marxist / initial

b. 23-year-old medical / "fun" / iconic Marxist / initially

c. 23-year-old medically / "fun" / iconic Marxist / initially

WRAPPING UP

What is your favorite movie? In your notebook, write five sentences about it using multiple adjectives before nouns and -*ly* adverbs, but do not mention the movie title. Then read your sentences to a classmate so he/she can guess which movie you are talking about. Change roles and guess your partner's favorite movie as well.

LISTENING COMPREHENSION

Before Listening

1. Look at the movie posters below and answer: what do all these movies have in common?

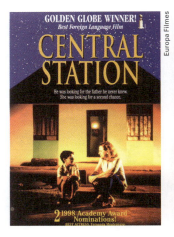 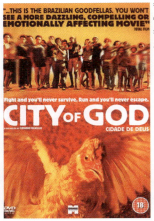 

  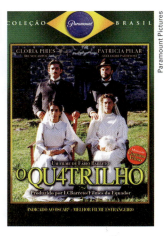

2. You are going to listen to part of an interview between the Brazilian movie director Walter Salles and Stephen Sackur from BBC News. In your opinion, what took Walter Salles to this interview?

Listening

 3. Listen to the very beginning of the interview and answer: What does Stephen Sackur say about Walter Salles's movies? Use your own words. Write it in your notebook.

4. Listen to the first part of the interview and check the true sentences.

  a. Stephen Sackur says that many Brazilian movies portray *favela* poverty and what people do to get out of it.

  b. In the interviewer's point of view, Brazil is seen abroad just the way it is due to the movies that demonstrate the country's negative points.

  c. Walter Salles claims that *Linha de Passe* is an interesting movie because it tells the story of a Brazilian young kid who breaks the line of poverty and becomes a well-known soccer player, exactly as Robinho and Ronaldo.

  d. The movie director agrees with the interviewer that *City of God*, as well as many other Brazilian movies, explore themes such as violence and corruption.

  e. He also says it is true that all the kids in the Brazilian suburbs carry guns, and that is exactly what he wanted to show in his movie.

 5. Listen to another part of the interview and answer the questions below. Use your own words.

  a. How does Stephen describe Walter Salles's movies?

  b. In the interviewer's point of view, what will happen to the director if he gets away from the clichés?

  c. Does Walter agree with the interviewer when he says his movies are depressing? What does he say? Explain.

After Listening

Have you seen any Walter Salles's movies? Which one(s)? Are his movies depressing? Share your experiences and views with the whole group.

SPEAKING

If you had the chance of asking Walter Salles only one question, which question would it be? Exchange ideas with a classmate. Then share your question with the whole group and explain why you would ask that particular question.

WRITING

Follow the steps below and write a movie review.

Planning your movie review

- Think of your favorite movie genre and your all-time favorite movie. Make notes about the plot, the main actors' performance in the movie, how suitable the soundtrack is, and other elements of the movie that you like. If necessary, do some research on the Internet and find more information about the movie you have chosen.

- If possible, watch the movie again. Watching it a second time will help you notice and absorb more details.

- Take notes of all relevant aspects.

Writing and rewriting your text

- Write a draft of the movie review in your notebook. Don't forget to take into consideration all the aspects you analyzed in the review of *Central do Brasil*.

> ### REFLECTING AND EVALUATING
>
> Go back to your movie review and make sure you paid attention to the following questions:
>
> ✓ Does the title of your movie review draw the readers' attention?
>
> ✓ Did you mention the title of the movie, its main actors, the genre, and the year it was released?
>
> ✓ Was your opinion clearly stated?
>
> ✓ Did you explain your opinion?
>
> ✓ Did you include other information that is relevant to the audience?
>
> ✓ Did you make any comments about the soundtrack, photography, or costume design?

- Exchange drafts with your classmates and decide: Is the text clear enough? Is it possible to improve it?

- After that, show the draft to the teacher.

- Write a clean copy, making all the necessary adjustments.

After writing

- Publish your review on the school newspaper or website.

- You can also publish your movie review on <www.moviequotesandmore.com/movie-reviews/>. Accessed on September 28, 2015.

- Alternatively, you and your classmates can display all movie reviews on a school wall so that everyone can read them.

SELF-ASSESSMENT

Chegamos ao fim da unidade 2. Convidamos você a refletir sobre seu desempenho até aqui e responder às questões propostas abaixo, escolhendo uma das seguintes opções:

Sim.

Preciso me preparar mais.

Questões

- Você adquiriu repertório suficiente para discutir sobre algumas ações que incentivam a indústria cinematográfica no Brasil?
- Você se sente capaz de expressar sua opinião sobre a visibilidade do cinema nacional no cenário mundial e os benefícios que isso pode trazer ao país?
- Você se considera apto a ler e compreender uma resenha de filme em língua inglesa, bem como a reconhecer as características principais inerentes ao gênero?
- Você reúne conhecimentos linguístico-discursivos suficientes para produzir uma resenha de filme em língua inglesa?
- Você se sente preparado para escutar uma entrevista em inglês e responder a perguntas específicas com suas próprias palavras?
- Você se julga apto a elaborar perguntas coerentes e interessantes para um diretor renomado de cinema?

Refletindo sobre suas respostas

- Como você analisa a evolução do seu aprendizado em relação à unidade anterior?
- De que forma suas práticas de aprendizagem no decorrer desta unidade influenciaram suas respostas?
- O que você pode fazer para aprimorar ainda mais os conhecimentos adquiridos nesta unidade?
  - **a.** Procurar conhecer mais sobre o cinema nacional, sobre as questões sociais e culturais abordadas nos filmes produzidos em meu país e sobre sua repercussão no cenário mundial.
  - **b.** Ler mais resenhas de filmes para desenvolver melhor minha capacidade de análise crítica.
  - **c.** Aprofundar meus conhecimentos de língua inglesa, usando recursos diversos, de forma que minha participação nas atividades seja mais ativa.
  - **d.** Outros.

Are you a Movie Buff? **Unit 2** 37

Further Practice 1 – Units 1 & 2

1. Read the poster and identify the option that best conveys its purpose.

World Elder Abuse Awareness Day
2015 marks 10 years of raising awareness

10 TIPS to promote respect and prevent abuse

1. Love and cherish your older relatives/whānau.
2. Speak respectfully to older people/kaumātua.
3. Include older people/kaumātua in your social activities.
4. Phone or visit your older relatives/whānau.
5. Support older people/kaumātua to spend their money how they wish.
6. Encourage and support older people/kaumātua to make their own decisions.
7. Honour older people's/kaumātua's wisdom.
8. Enable older people/kaumātua to walk at their own pace.
9. Respect older people's/kaumātua's stories.
10. Seek advice from an Elder Abuse and Neglect Prevention Service when you think an older person/kaumātua is being abused or neglected.

Stop the abuse and neglect of older people

**World Elder Abuse Awareness Day
15 June**

ageconcern.org.nz

Extracted from <www.ageconcern.org.nz/images/to%20go%20on%20website/10%20tips%20poster.png>. Accessed on December 9, 2015.

    a. It raises awareness about the rights of the elderly, such as having a comfortable life and access to different cultural activities.

    b. It aims to encourage people to appreciate the elderly and prevent mistreatment of older people.

    c. It is a form of complaint regarding the elderly's situation in New Zealand.

2. What other tips would you add to the World Elder Abuse Awareness Day poster?

3. Read the text below and look for the subjects that refer to the underlined verbs. Write them down in your notebook.

No Rest for the Elderly in India

By Neeta Lal

NEW DELHI, Apr 2 2015 (IPS) – As more and more people in India enter the 'senior citizen' category, ugly cracks are beginning to appear in a social structure that (1) <u>claims</u> to value the institution of family but in reality expresses disdain for the bonds of blood.

Recent research by HelpAge India, a leading charity dedicated to the care of seniors, (2) <u>reveals</u> that every second an elderly person in India – defined as someone above 60 years of age – (3) <u>suffers</u> abuse within their own family, a malaise that has been found to infect all social strata and all regions of the country.

The 12-city study, 'State of the Elderly in India 2014', found that one in five elderly persons (4) <u>encounters</u> physical and emotional abuse almost daily, a third around once a week, and a fifth every month. A common reason for the abuse is elderly family members' economic dependence on their progeny.

According to sociologists, neglect of senior citizens – once revered and idolized in Indian society – (5) <u>is</u> largely attributable to the changing social landscape in Asia's third largest economy, currently home to over 100 million elderly people.

"Rapidly altering lifestyles and values, demanding jobs, rural-to-urban migration, a shift from joint to nuclear family structures and redefined priorities (6) <u>are</u> all leading to this undesirable situation," Veena Purohit, visiting professor of sociology at Jawaharlal Nehru University in New Delhi, tells IPS.

[…]

India is currently home to over 100 million elderly people.

Adapted from <www.ipsnews.net/2015/04/no-rest-for-the-elderly-in-india/>. Accessed on December 9, 2015.

4. Pick out the sentence that corresponds to what you can infer from the text.

a. The elderly in India depend economically on their families because they don't have any support from the government.

b. Indian society is changing and so is the way Indians treat their elderly.

c. Studies show that the majority of the elderly in India who live with their offspring suffer from negligence.

Units 1 & 2   **Further Practice 1**   39

Further Practice 1 – Units 1 & 2

5. Refer to the text on page 39 again. Why do sociologists blame the changing social landscape for elderly abuse?

6. Read the cartoon attentively. Then pick out the best option to complete the sentence.

The man and the woman are…

  a. bored.

  b. discouraged.

  c. indifferent.

7. In your opinion, which sentence best explains the objective of the cartoonist? Justify your answer orally.

  a. The cartoonist wanted to denounce the lack of jobs for people who are too young to retire, but too old to get a job.

  b. The cartoonist wanted to show how retirement laws are ironic because people have to work until they are 70, but there aren't enough opportunities for young workers.

  c. The cartoonist wanted to criticize the fact that only young people are accepted in the current job market.

8. Complete the movie review with the adjectives from the box.

> complete and utter   obvious and undeniable   prophetic
> unique fighting   young teenage

He Named Me Malala

2015-11-20 08:59
Marisa Crous

What it's about:

A documentary tracking the life of Malala Yousafzai, a schoolgirl shot by the Taliban on a school bus in 2012, who became an advocate for female education in the Swat Valley in Northwest Pakistan. The style of the film beautifully blends animation (to recreate moments from the past), which is intertwined with news coverage and interviews with Malala and her immediate family, now all living in the UK.

What we thought:

Afghan legend has it that Malalai of Maiwand (also known as Malala) was a teenage girl who died in battle whilst urging her comrades to fight back against the British in

Malala Yousafzai, accompanied by four other young women, spoke at a press conference at the United Nations, emphasizing the need to expand educational opportunities in Pakistan.

the 1880 Battle of Maiwan. Malala's father, school owner and educational activist Ziauddin Yousafzai named her after this brave soul. There's an ♦ link here. A ♦ "punished" for her beliefs in the most gruesome way. Malala Yousafzai survived her punishment, while Malalai of Maiwand was not so lucky.

The film shows Ziauddin Yousafzai's anguished face. He poignantly describes how he feels somewhat responsible for his daughter's fate. He named her, after all. Yet, the teenager remains adamant that her father didn't, in fact, choose her life for her. She became Malala all by herself.

The relationship between Malala and her father is incredible to watch. He describes it as being "one soul in two bodies". And although one could say that Malala seems to be a completely normal teenager in her interactions with her family (especially when teasing her younger siblings), you simply cannot deny this girl's ♦ spirit and incredible wisdom at such a young age.

Further Practice 1 – Units 1 & 2

What struck me most about Malala in this documentary is her ♦ disregard for the material and the superficial. When asked by a journalist who the man was who shot her, she answered that it was not a person, but an ideology. Still, she has never been angry. […]

It's a powerful film that should be seen by anyone who believes in the transformative power of education.

Extracted from <www.channel24.co.za/Movies/Reviews/he-named-me-malala-20151112>.
Accessed on December 9, 2015.

9. Write T (True) or F (False).

a. Malala's past is recreated by using old video footage and new interviews with her family.

b. Mr. Yousafzai chose her daughter's name because of a brave girl from the 19th century whose name was Malala.

c. The writer is surprised that Malala likes possessing lots of things.

d. The writer also says that Malala looks like any other girl, but it is clear that she shows great knowledge for her age and has a very combative soul.

e. The documentary is recommended for people who are convinced that society can be transformed by education.

10. Match the false sentences from the previous activity to the passages that correct them. There are extra passages.

a. "The film shows Ziauddin Yousafzai's anguished face. He poignantly describes how he feels somewhat responsible for his daughter's fate."

b. "The style of the film beautifully blends animation (to recreate moments from the past), which is intertwined with news coverage and interviews with Malala and her immediate family […]"

c. "It's a powerful film that should be seen by anyone who believes in the transformative power of education."

d. "What struck me most about Malala in this documentary is her complete and utter disregard for the material and the superficial."

11. *He Named Me Malala* is a documentary. Check the proper definition of this movie genre.

a. A movie or a television or radio program that provides a factual record or report.

b. Fiction based on imagined future scientific or technological advances and major social or environmental changes, frequently portraying space or time travel and life on other planets.

Extracted from <www.oxforddictionaries.com/us/>. Accessed on February 20, 2016.

12. After reading the review of *He Named Me Malala*, would you like to watch the movie? Why/Why not?

EXAM PRACTICE

Sixty is the new 40:
Healthy living means we now hit middle age later

19:00, 15 apr 2015
By Stephen Beech

A study found people across Europe were currently viewed as "old" when they hit 65 but predicted that by 2050 people in their 60s will be considered "middle-aged".

Sixty is the new 40, according to scientists who say longer, healthier lives mean people now hit middle-age later.

Doctor Sergei Scherbov, who led the study into ageing, said:

"What we think of as old has changed."

Age can be measured as time already lived or it can be adjusted taking into account time left to live.

What we think of as old has changed over time, and it will need to continue changing in the future as people live longer, healthier lives.

Someone who is 60 years old today, I would argue, is middle-aged – but 200 years ago, a 60-year-old would be a very old person."

[…]

Adapted from <www.mirror.co.uk/news/technology-science/science/sixty-new-40-healthy-living-5525916>.
Accessed on December 12, 2015.

Old fogeys: Or they were once considered so, anyway.

De acordo com o texto, podemos concluir que estão corretas as proposições:

I. O aumento da longevidade, a melhora na saúde e na qualidade de vida prolongam em algumas décadas a chegada da chamada meia-idade.

II. A velhice é apenas uma questão de ponto de vista.

III. O conceito de velhice está intimamente relacionado à forma como vive a população. Assim, estará em constante adaptação.

IV. Só se pode afirmar que uma pessoa entrou na terceira idade caso sua expectativa de vida não ultrapasse uma década.

a. Apenas a I.
b. I e III.
c. II e IV.
d. Apenas a II.
e. II e III.

UNIT 3

THE SILENCE OF DOMESTIC VIOLENCE

wavebreakmedia/Shutterstock.com

Nesta unidade você terá oportunidade de:

- discutir questões relacionadas à violência doméstica, bem como à eficiência da Lei Maria da Penha;
- reconhecer objetivos e algumas características das postagens de *blogs* e escrever uma;
- compreender um anúncio televisivo que apresenta uma situação real de violência doméstica;
- participar de uma interação oral sobre uma questão social relevante e posicionar-se criticamente em relação ao tema.

- Observe o rosto da menina. O que ela demonstra estar sentindo?
- Por que seu rosto é o elemento em evidência na imagem?

STARTING OUT

1. Look at the posters below and answer: what are they about?

Extracted from <www.thehideout.org.uk/wp-content/uploads/2015/07/Hideout_A4_Poster_-_Children.pdf>. Accessed on May 29, 2016.

Extracted from <www.thehideout.org.uk/wp-content/uploads/2015/07/Hideout_A4_Poster_-_Teenagers.pdf>. Accessed on May 29, 2016.

Extracted from <http://www.refuge.org.uk/files/Helpline-Poster_A2.pdf>. Accessed on June 1, 2016.

2. Now read the headings of the blog posts below and match them to their introductory lines.

   a. Oct 3, 2015
   Fraud

   b. Oct 3, 2015
   Using money for drugs

   c. Jul 19, 2015
   No Contact

   1. She would use the household income to buy drugs every day. I would have to struggle to pay bills such as rent, heating and food. […]

   2. You need to get you back, and no contact is the only way to do it. It ensures your sanity and your health. […]

   3. My husband gradually took control of our finances. […] He hid bank letters and any other mail relating to financial matters. […]

   Extracted from <www.hiddenhurt.co.uk/domestic-abuse-blog.html>. Accessed on February 19, 2016.

3. Why do you think the authors of the posts in activity 2 decided to write about their abusive experiences on a blog? Discuss your opinion with your classmates.

READING COMPREHENSION

Before Reading

1. Scan the blog post and look at the picture. Then answer these questions: which of the four items in bold best describes the picture? Why? Why do you think this picture was chosen to illustrate the text?

Reading

How do we prevent violence against women?

Friday, 11th December 2015

Last month, in a world first, Australia published a national framework based on the most up-to-date global research and data about the drivers of violence against women, and how this violence can be prevented.

What this new research tells us is this: while gender inequality sets the necessary social context that allows violence against women to flourish, there are four particular expressions of gender inequality that consistently predict higher rates of violence against women:

1. **Condoning of violence against women**. This can be anything from attitudes that blame the victim of violence to legal proceedings.

2. **Men's control of decision-making and limits to women's independence in public and private life**. This isn't just within individual relationships — think about laws, institutions and social norms that make this a daily reality for many Australian women.

3. **Rigid gender roles and stereotyped constructions of masculinity and femininity**. It's important to recognise that women and men, girls and boys aren't necessarily choosing these stereotyped roles for themselves, they're being taught by a society that these are their only choices… and if they step outside those gendered boundaries they'll be "punished" by not having friends, being turned down for a job, being teased or even experiencing violence.

4. **Male peer relations that emphasise aggression and disrespect towards women**. What this means is that in situations where men don't speak up against violence, or where violence, sexism and harassment of women is "funny" or a part of a bonding experience for men, then those cultures have a huge impact on creating a society where violence flourishes.

"This issue is complex and it's not as simple as 'cause and effect'. But what the research tells us – and has told us for many decades – is that where these four expressions of gender inequality are present, there is likely to be more violence against women."

Australia ranks 24th in the world on gender equality, according to the **Global Gender Gap Index**. If you think that doesn't sound too bad, look at the countries that rank higher than we do; most of the Scandinavian countries, Ireland, the Philippines, New Zealand, South Africa, Ecuador and the US. Australians often believe that we've achieved equality and it's time to move on, but the Global Gender Gap Index tells a different story.

The good news, however, is that it is possible to change things.

Look at the social justice movements that have changed the world and you'll see that they weren't led by governments or by any organisation. These movements are led by people. Sometimes, there was one individual who inspired others, who captured the public imagination — Rosie Batty is doing a fairly excellent job of that in Australia right now. But inspiring action is what Rosie wants to do — not just action from governments and funders, it's action from everyone in their daily lives that people like Rosie are calling for.

> *"Don't underestimate the part you can play. If everyone called out sexism and harassment, if everyone made an effort to educate themselves about the warning signs of violence, if everyone worked in their friendships and intimate relationships to enact gender equality, if everyone encouraged women's leadership and women's voices, we'd see a huge reduction in the prevalence of violence against women in Australia within a decade."*

At DVRCV, we have committed to focusing on the primary prevention of violence against women as one of our four strategic directions for the next three years. By working with others across Victoria to address the key drivers of violence against women, we can create a more equitable — and safe — society for everyone.

Add new comment

Your name

Subject

Comment

Adapted from <www.dvrcv.org.au/knowledge-centre/our-blog/how-do-we-prevent-violence-against-women>.
Accessed on February 21, 2016.

recognise (UK)
recognize (US)

emphasise (UK)
emphasize (US)

organisations (UK)
organizations (US)

2. What was DVRCV's main purpose in writing this post?

    a. To provide information about world ranking in gender equality.

    b. To disseminate the very good results Australia has had towards the prevention of violence against women.

    c. To expose expressions of gender inequality that often lead to more violence against women and to call society's attention to the need for immediate action against it.

3. *Global Gender Gap* is a measure that aims at examining four critical areas of inequality between men and women: economic participation and opportunity, education, political empowerment, and health and survival. If you click on *Global Gender Gap Index*, what kind of information do you think you'll find?

4. According to the post, there are four reasons why gender inequality leads to higher rates of violence against women in Australia. Go back to the text, read this part again, and discuss these questions in small groups: how does gender inequality in Brazil influence domestic violence? What are the similarities and differences between Australia's reality and ours? Justify your answers. Then share your views with the whole group.

5. In Brazil, the Maria da Penha Law was enacted to prevent domestic violence. Read the extract below and discuss in pairs: has Brazil succeeded in condoning violence against women since the law was enacted? Justify your answer.

O que diz a Lei Maria da Penha?

A Lei Maria da Penha (Lei nº 11.340/2006) é uma lei escrita por mulheres e para mulheres. Ela define que a violência doméstica contra a mulher é crime e aponta formas de evitar, enfrentar e punir a agressão. A lei indica a responsabilidade que cada órgão público tem de ajudar a mulher que é vítima de violência.

Com a Lei Maria da Penha, a justiça passou a ter poderes para conceder as chamadas medidas protetivas de urgência. Essas medidas se aplicam àquele que pratica a violência, determinando, por exemplo, seu afastamento do lar, a proibição de chegar perto da vítima ou a suspensão de porte de armas. Outras medidas dirigem-se à mulher vítima da violência e consistem, entre outras coisas, em seu encaminhamento para programa de proteção ou atendimento. [...]

Adaptado de: <www.spm.gov.br/central-de-conteudos/publicacoes/publicacoes/2015/livreto-maria-da-penha-2-web-1.pdf>. Acessado em: 22 de fevereiro de 2016.

6. Read the statements below and pick out the sentences that present some characteristics of blog posts.

a. Readers can leave comments.

b. Blog posts aim at promoting discussions among their readers.

c. Paragraphs are usually short and the information flows gradually through them.

d. They can't be updated frequently.

e. People publish blog posts to express their opinions and share experiences.

After Reading

- What is the proper thing to do when a man or a woman abuses his/her partner or any other family member?

- In your view, should the victim forgive his/her abuser? Why?

- Can social media and new technologies help mobilize people to stop or prevent domestic violence? Justify your answer.

- Is your community prepared to fight against domestic violence? Explain.

VOCABULARY STUDY

1. Refer to the text on pages 47 and 48 and find words that match the definitions below. Then use them to complete the passage that follows.

   a. ♦ : the state of being male or female (typically used with reference to social and cultural differences rather than biological ones).

   b. ♦ : aggressive pressure or intimidation.

   c. ♦ : prejudice, stereotyping, or discrimination, typically against women, on the basis of sex.

   d. ♦ : the action of stopping something from happening or arising.

   Extracted from <www.oxforddictionaries.com/us>. Accessed on February 22, 2016.

   > The Maria da Penha law
   > […]
   > The Maria da Penha law contains a comprehensive set of policies geared towards the eradication of the endemic problem of domestic violence against women in Brazil. It establishes special courts and stricter sentences for offenders, but also other instruments for ♦ and relief, such as police stations and shelters for women. […]

   Adapted from <www.wikigender.org/wiki/maria-da-penha-law/>. Accessed on February 22, 2016.

2. The wheel below portrays different types of domestic abuse. Use the section headings from the box to complete it. Write the answers in your notebook.

   Minimizing, Denying & Blaming   Using Children   Using Coercion & Threats   Using Economic Abuse
   Using Emotional Abuse   Using Intimidation   Using Isolation   Using Male Privilege

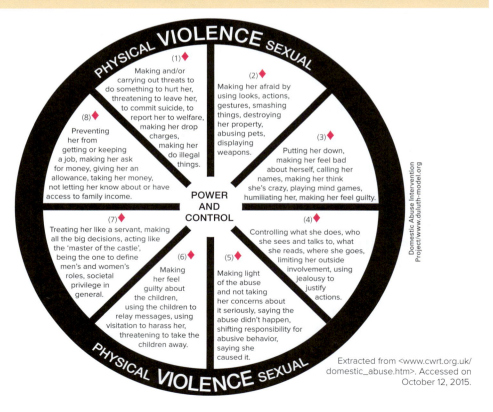

Extracted from <www.cwrt.org.uk/domestic_abuse.htm>. Accessed on October 12, 2015.

LANGUAGE IN CONTEXT

Conditionals

1. Read the extracts from the blog post on pages 47 and 48, pay attention to the sentences in bold, and answer: what do all of them indicate?

    a. "…and **if they step outside those gendered boundaries** they'll be 'punished' by not having friends, being turned down for a job, being teased or even experiencing violence."

    b. "**If you think that doesn't sound too bad**, look at the countries that rank higher than we do; most of the Scandinavian countries, Ireland, the Philippines, New Zealand, South Africa, Ecuador and the US."

    c. "**If everyone called out sexism and harassment, if everyone made an effort to educate themselves about the warning signs of violence, if everyone worked in their friendships and intimate relationships to enact gender equality, if everyone encouraged women's leadership and women's voices**, we'd see a huge reduction in the prevalence of violence against women in Australia within a decade."

2. Reread the extracts in activity 1 and identify the results of the parts in bold, which are conditions. Write them down in your notebook.

3. Choose the correct alternatives to complete the statements about the extracts above.

    a. Extract *a* refers to a ♦ possibility for a particular situation to happen in the ♦.
- real / future
- unreal / present

    b. Extract *b* contains a ♦ or a piece of advice.
- general truth
- recommendation

    c. Extract *c* refers to an ♦, ♦, or unlikely situation.
- real / possible
- unreal / impossible

4. Refer to the previous activities and match the columns.

a. We use conditionals when we	• are connected to the main clauses that refer to the results of those conditions.
b. The clauses that introduce conditions	
c. For conditions that refer to real possibilities in the future	• we use *if + simple past + would*.
	• we use *if + simple present + will*.
d. For conditions that refer to recommendations or pieces of advice	• want to express a conditional relation between situations or events.
e. For conditions that refer to unreal, impossible, or unlikely situations	• we use *if + simple present + imperative*.

For more information about Conditionals, go to Language Reference, pages 173 and 174.

The Silence of Domestic Violence   **Unit 3**   **51**

5. Read the poster and look for the passage which expresses a condition. Then compare that passage to the ones in activity 1 and talk to your classmate about what idea it conveys.

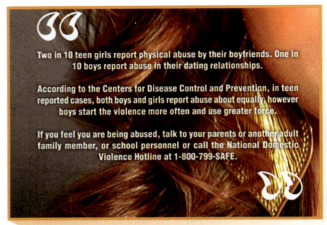
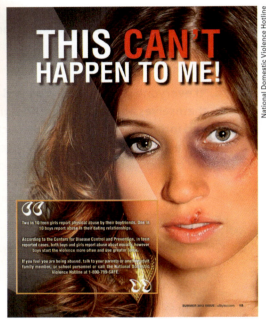

Extracted from <ww1.prweb.com/prfiles/2012/07/19/9719295/PRESSRELEASEDOMVIOLENCE.jpg>. Accessed on October 12, 2015.

6. Below are the headings of three different texts about domestic violence. Use the verb forms from the box to complete them.

're   were   would take

a. Domestic violence victims speak out:
'If I worked, he ♦ my money'

would take

Extracted from <www.theguardian.com/money/2014/oct/20/domestic-violence-victims-leave-work-partners-abuse-speak-out>. Accessed on February 23, 2016.

b. What would you do if you ♦ a victim of violence?

were

Extracted from <www.justiceoptions.ca/content/page/resource_12>. Accessed on February 23, 2016.

c. If You ♦ A Domestic Violence Survivor With Unexplained Symptoms, Read This

're

Extracted from <www.huffingtonpost.com/2015/06/05/domestic-violence-survivor_n_7514424.html>. Accessed on February 23, 2016.

52   Unit 3   The Silence of Domestic Violence

7. Unscramble the words in parentheses to form sentences to complete the article.

Why Are Some Relationships So Difficult?

Ever heard about how hard it is for someone to love you when you don't love yourself? It's a big relationship roadblock when one or both people struggle with self-esteem problems. Your girlfriend or boyfriend isn't there to make you feel good about yourself ♦ (your / own / can't / you / if / that / do / on). Focus on being happy with yourself, and don't take on the responsibility of worrying about someone else's happiness.

What if you feel that your girlfriend or boyfriend needs too much from you? ♦ (feels / or / a / a / if / like / relationship / burden / instead / joy / the / of / drag / a), it might be time to think about whether it's a healthy match for you. Someone who's not happy or secure may have trouble being a healthy relationship partner.

Also, intense relationships can be hard for some teenagers. Some are so focused on their own developing feelings and responsibilities that they don't have the emotional energy it takes to respond to someone else's feelings and needs in a close relationship. Don't worry ♦ (yet / if / not / you're / just / ready). You will be, and you can take all the time you need.

Ever noticed that some teen relationships don't last very long? It's no wonder — you're still growing and changing every day, and it can be tough to put two people together whose identities are both still in the process of forming. You two might seem perfect for each other at first, but that can change. If you try to hold on to the relationship anyway, ♦ (will / sour / there's / turn / chance / a / it / good). Better to part as friends than to stay in something that you've outgrown or that no longer feels right for one or both of you. […]

Adapted from <kidshealth.org/en/teens/healthy-relationship.html#>. Accessed on February 24, 2016.

8. Complete the conditionals in the poster below. Use the verbs *hear*, *see*, *need*, and *believe*.

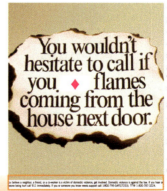

If you (1) ♦ a neighbor, a friend, or a co-worker is a victim of domestic violence, get involved. Domestic violence is against the law. If you (2) ♦ or see someone being hurt call 911 immediately. If you or someone you know (3) ♦ support call 1-800-799-SAFE(7233). TTY# 1-800-787-3224.

Extracted from <www.nrcdv.org/dvam/catalog/80>.
Accessed on February 23, 2016.

WRAPPING UP

Complete the sentences below in your notebook. Then report and justify your statements to the class.

a. If I got to know that a friend of mine was suffering some kind of abuse, ♦

b. If a child grows up in an environment of domestic violence, ♦

LISTENING COMPREHENSION

Before Listening

1. Look at the picture below. What do you think you will listen to?

Image captured from <www.youtube.com/watch?v=rTJT3fVv1vU>. Accessed on October 10, 2015.

Listening

2. Listen to the recording and check if your prediction was correct.

3. Listen to the recording again and answer these specific questions.

   a. Who does the woman call?

   b. What does she say at first?

   c. What does the operator tell her?

   d. What does the woman do when the operator tells her that she had called the emergency number?

   e. When does the operator realize the woman needs help?

   f. Can he help her? How?

   g. The operator asks her two more questions after saying that the police officer is going to her house. What are they?

After Listening

In pairs, read the last sentence of the announcement and exchange ideas on the message it conveys.

> "When it's hard to talk it's up to us to listen".

PRONUNCIATION PRACTICE

Listen to these questions extracted from the ad and write F for Falling Intonation or R for Rising Intonation. Then listen again and repeat.

a. "Where's the emergency?"

b. "What's going on there?"

c. "Do you know how long it'll be?"

d. "Do you have an emergency or not?"

e. "Is there someone in the room with you?"

f. "Are there any weapons in your house?"

g. "Can you stay on the phone with me?"

SPEAKING

In groups of three, discuss the questions below.
- ✓ Why was the announcement run during such an important sporting event?
- ✓ Did the ad get your attention? Why/Why not?
- ✓ Was it a clever way to ask for help without being noticed?
- ✓ Are we exposed to a lot of announcements like that? Should we be exposed to these more often? Justify your opinion.
- ✓ Do most women who are victims of domestic violence ask for help?
- ✓ Would you encourage a person who suffers from domestic violence to report the aggressor? Why/Why not?

Think of at least two actions that everybody can take to prevent domestic violence.

Choose a person from your group to present your ideas to the whole class.

If necessary, consult the Useful Language boxes in book 2.

WRITING

Planning your blog post

- Think of a few topics that interest you and that you would like to write about.

  Here are some suggestions:

  • health and fitness;

  • language learning;

  • bullying / cyberbullying;

  • vegan diet;

  • violence against women;

  • job market for teenagers.

- Be careful! Avoid choosing a topic you don't know too much about. Choose one that may be of interest to your audience.

- If necessary, search for information on the Internet and take notes.

Writing and rewriting your text

- Write a draft of your blog post in your notebook.

> ### REFLECTING AND EVALUATING
>
> Go back to your blog post and make sure you paid attention to the following questions:
>
> ✓ Did you choose an attractive title?
>
> ✓ Is there a clear introduction?
>
> ✓ Is the introduction of your text captivating?
>
> ✓ Is the content properly organized?
>
> ✓ Will people be interested in reading it?

- Ask a classmate to proofread your text. Consider his/her suggestions and make the necessary adjustments.

- After that, show it to your teacher.

After writing

- If your class has a blog, publish your blog post.

- Alternatively, stick your post to the wall of the classroom so that your classmates can read and comment on it.

SELF-ASSESSMENT

Chegamos ao fim da unidade 3. Convidamos você a refletir sobre seu desempenho até aqui e responder às questões propostas abaixo, escolhendo uma das seguintes opções:

Sim.

Preciso me preparar mais.

Questões

- Você tem conhecimento suficiente para expor sua opinião acerca do tema violência contra as mulheres, suas causas e consequências?
- Em suas ponderações sobre o tema, você está apto a refletir e comentar sobre a Lei Maria da Penha?
- Você se sente capaz de ler e compreender postagens de *blogs* em língua inglesa e reconhecer as características principais inerentes ao gênero? .
- Você reúne conhecimentos linguístico-discursivos suficientes para redigir uma postagem de *blog* em língua inglesa?
- Você está preparado para escutar um anúncio televisivo sobre violência doméstica, fazer inferências e discutir a respeito?
- Você se julga apto a discutir medidas preventivas contra a violência doméstica?

Refletindo sobre suas respostas

- Como você analisa a evolução do seu aprendizado em relação à unidade anterior?
- De que forma suas práticas de aprendizagem no decorrer desta unidade influenciaram suas respostas?
- O que você pode fazer para aprimorar ainda mais os conhecimentos adquiridos nesta unidade?

   a. Buscar por mais informações sobre a violência doméstica contra as mulheres no Brasil e no mundo.

   b. Ler e comentar postagens de *blogs* em língua materna e em língua inglesa sobre assuntos atuais e relevantes.

   c. Aprofundar meus conhecimentos de língua inglesa usando recursos diversos, de forma que minha participação nas atividades seja mais ativa.

   d. Outros.

UNIT 4

VOLUNTEERING

Nesta unidade você terá oportunidade de:

- discutir os benefícios do trabalho voluntário, bem como os tipos de trabalho voluntário que podem ser realizados em prol da sua comunidade;
- reconhecer objetivos e algumas características das entrevistas e fazer uma;
- compreender o relato de uma jovem sobre sua experiência com trabalho voluntário em um país estrangeiro;
- discutir a experiência de uma jovem com trabalho voluntário.

- Que ação está representada na imagem?
- Trata-se de uma ação que representa significativamente a cultura de nosso país?
- Há alguma característica na imagem que indica onde a foto foi tirada?

STARTING OUT

1. In pairs, discuss the quote below.

   "The best way to find yourself is to lose yourself in the service of others."
   (Mahatma Gandhi, Indian leader)

   Extracted from <www.brainyquote.com/quotes/quotes/m/mahatmagan150725.html>. Accessed on December 11, 2015.

2. Now compare the quote in activity 1 to part of the infographic entitled *Volunteering: Why Doing Good Is Good For You*. What do they have in common? Talk to a classmate, write down two sentences expressing your point of view in your notebook, and then share your opinions with the whole class.

Extracted from <www.happify.com/hd/volunteering-infographic/>. Accessed on April 23, 2016.

3. Volunteer work is very important for community institutions such as public schools and museums. Would you be interested in listening to, watching, or reading an interview with a volunteer on his long-time experience at a museum? Why/Why not? What aspects do you think would be dealt with in such an interview?

READING COMPREHENSION

Before Reading

1. Look attentively at the man in the picture below. Notice the position of his hands and the vest he is wearing. Then answer the questions orally: what does he do? How helpful can he be in the museum he works for?

Reading

Tuesday, May 5, 2015 - 8:10am
An Interview with Chris Hamming, Search Gallery Volunteer

For the last 14 years, Science World has been so fortunate to have Chris Hamming, former high school math and science teacher of 37 years, as a core volunteer in our Search: Sarah Stern Gallery. We caught up with Chris for this interview to thank him for his amazing presence in the gallery and to ask him about his experience as a long-time volunteer.

Why did you choose to volunteer with Science World and in the Search Gallery?

Chris: My background in high school and university education is in the math and science department. I was a math and science teacher for 37 years. Retirement was coming up. In Vancouver there was a conference about retirement. The simple message: keep busy, keep active. One day I was visiting Science World with my granddaughters and saw the sign: Volunteer Opportunities. I met Gloria (the volunteer coordinator at the time), had an interview and filled in some forms. After a while I heard that I could start volunteering. Since I was still teaching full time, I took shifts on Saturdays. Once my school teaching days were over, I switched over to Tuesday all day. Search Gallery was my gallery of choice because of my love of nature. I enjoy the great outdoors and spend a lot of time enjoying the natural world.

What do you like most about volunteering?

Chris: Volunteering at Science World is such a unique opportunity for me to meet people from all over the world and show them animals from Canada as well as other places. It is very rewarding for me to see very excited kids come into Search and look at and touch all the different animals or their skulls and pelts. They love petting the beaver, climbing in the Cedar tree, learning about bees, "oohing" and "awing" at the corn snakes and gazing with mouths wide open at the size of Stan, the T. Rex. It amazes them that the flower of the Titum Aran is big enough to be used as a baby bath, and that insects can look like sticks or dead leaves.

The time I spend in the KEVA Gallery is also very exciting. To me it is a gallery full of energy. There are great opportunities for young and old to show their creative abilities together with patience and persistence. They admire their creations with great feelings of satisfaction and accomplishment. The personalities, enthusiasm and insight of staff and fellow volunteers are making Science World such an exciting place to be part of.

Do you have a favourite story from your interactions with visitors in the Search Gallery?

Chris: The most rewarding thing that happens in Search is the times when little 5- or 6-year-olds grab me by the hand and lead me all over the gallery, looking at all the various items on display and asking me about them.

Our volunteers make a huge difference in the quality of science facilitation in our galleries. If you think you would like to join Science World's team of volunteers, keep an eye on our volunteer postings page for opportunities.

Extracted from <www.scienceworld.ca/blog/interview-chris-hamming-search-gallery-volunteer>.
Accessed on October 12, 2015.

1. Look for the only sentence that we cannot infer based on the interview.
   a. Chris Hamming was about to retire when he decided to look for a new job.
   b. He found the volunteer opportunity by chance.
   c. His granddaughters played a special role in his decision to volunteer at the Search Gallery.
   d. Gloria is his coordinator.

2. Copy the part that justifies your answer in the previous activity.

3. Pick out the best options to complete the sentences below.

   a. The purpose of this interview is...
      1 to publish the Search gallery programs.
      2 to promote Chris Hamming's financial donations to the gallery.
      3 to thank Hamming for his amazing presence in the gallery and encourage people to work as volunteers in Science World.

   b. The message from the conference in Vancouver was a turning point in Hamming's life because, after that,
      1 he decided to live an active life after retirement.
      2 he decided to volunteer.
      3 he decided to remain teaching.

   c. Hamming thinks that his experience as a volunteer at Science World is...
      1 pleasing and surprising.
      2 tiring, but enjoyable.
      3 unique and rewarding.

   d. The KEVA Gallery offers people opportunities to...
      1 develop their creativity.
      2 spend time and receive good energy.
      3 work and have fun simultaneously.

> *KEVA* são blocos para construção precisamente cortados e produzidos em pinheiro ou bordo. O museu *Science World* conta com um departamento denominado *KEVA Gallery*, no qual visitantes podem produzir diferentes construções utilizando tais blocos. Para saber mais sobre esse departamento, acesse: <www.scienceworld.ca/sites/default/files/KEVA.pdf>. Acessado em: 21 de fevereiro de 2016.

4. Read this extract of Chris Hamming's interview again and choose the quotation(s) that reflect(s) his point of view.

> "The most rewarding thing that happens in Search is the times when little 5- or 6-year-olds grab me by the hand and lead me all over the gallery, looking at all the various items on display and asking me about them."

   a. "Knowledge has to be improved, challenged, and increased constantly, or it vanishes." (Peter Drucker, Austrian educator and author)

   Extracted from <www.brainyquote.com/quotes/topics/topic_knowledge.html#RSI7dMYK6DqbASpg.9>. Accessed on February 10, 2016.

   b. "To acquire knowledge, one must study; but to acquire wisdom, one must observe." (Marilyn vos Savant, American writer)

   Extracted from <www.brainyquote.com/quotes/topics/topic_knowledge2.html#8PDKBSHlyFSLWtYu.99>. Accessed on February 10, 2016.

   c. "Perplexity is the beginning of knowledge." (Khalil Gibran, Lebanese poet)

   Extracted from <www.brainyquote.com/quotes/quotes/k/khalilgibr110137.html>. Accessed on February 10, 2016.

5. Answer the questions below.

  a. How long has Chris Hamming been working as a Search gallery volunteer?

  b. Why did he choose the Search Gallery?

  c. In your opinion, why did he mention his interaction with children as the most rewarding?

  d. Would you like to visit a museum with a trained volunteer like Mr. Hamming? Why/Why not?

  e. What's your opinion about Chris Hamming's option for life after retirement? Would you do the same? Justify your point of view.

6. In pairs, discuss the question below. Then share your view with the whole class.
Do you think that Hamming's point of view about volunteer work can influence people's opinion? Why/Why not?

7. Check some characteristics of interviews.

  a. Interviews are essentially oral. They can be transcribed to be published in printed and online newspapers, magazines, blogs, and websites.

  b. They are based on questions and answers. They can happen between one or more interviewers and one or more interviewees.

  c. Only journalists are able to conduct an interview.

  d. The interviewees express their opinions and the arguments which support their points of view.

  e. Open-ended questions are common in order to avoid yes/no answers.

  f. The short paragraph which usually introduces the interviewee aims at drawing the reader's attention by offering some previous information about him or her.

8. Now it's your turn. Write one more characteristic of interviews and one characteristic that belongs to another text genre. Challenge your classmate to guess which one belongs to interviews. Change roles.

After Reading

- Chris Hamming mentioned some benefits that come from the volunteer work he does. If you could volunteer, what benefits would that bring to you? What kind of work would you like to volunteer for? Why?

- Dr. Albert Schweitzer, a German physician (1875-1965), said, "Wherever a man turns he can find someone who needs him". Now think about your own community's needs and answer: What kind of volunteer jobs could help to fulfill them? Explain.

Volunteering **Unit 4** 63

VOCABULARY STUDY

1. Read the definitions below, go back to the interview on page 61, and find the phrasal verbs they refer to.

   a. ♦ : to talk to someone you have not seen for some time and find out what they have been doing

   b. ♦ : to be about to happen soon

   c. ♦ : to add information such as your name or address in the empty spaces on an official document

   d. ♦ : to stop doing one thing and start doing another

Extracted from <www.macmillandictionary.com>. Accessed on December 11, 2015.

2. Now read two extracts from the interview on page 61 and choose the alternative that best explains the expressions in bold. Then use one of the expressions to complete the headline that follows.

   a. "They love petting the beaver, climbing in the Cedar tree, learning about bees, **"oohing" and "awing"** at the corn snakes and gazing with mouths wide open at the size of Stan, the T. Rex."
- exclaiming in pain and suffering
- exclaiming in admiration or wonder

   b. "If you think you would like to join Science World's team of volunteers, **keep an eye on** our volunteer postings page for opportunities."
- observe carefully
- overlook

> **Coastguard Volunteers ♦ Close ♦ Lake Taupo**
> by YVONNE BALDOCK on 3 JUNE 2014
> in GOOD NEWS, ALL
>
> [...]

Extracted from <www.baytrust.org.nz/2014/06/coastguard-volunteers-keep-close-eye-on-lake-taupo/>. Accessed on December 11, 2015.

3. Look at the words in bold in the extracts below, infer when to use adjectives ending in *-ed* or *-ing*, and complete the rule.

> "It is very rewarding for me to see very **excited** kids come into Search and look at and touch all the different animals or their skulls and pelts."
> "The time I spend in the KEVA Gallery is also very **exciting**."

TIP

Ao encontrar palavras terminadas em *-ed* e *-ing* em um texto, identifique primeiramente sua função na oração para, depois, relacioná-las a seu sentido.

In English, we often use adjectives ending in ♦ to describe things and situations, while adjectives ending in ♦ are used to describe how people feel. In the extracts above, ♦ describes the kids' emotion and ♦ describes Chris Hamming's response to a situation: the time he spends in the KEVA Gallery.

Unit 4 Volunteering

LANGUAGE IN CONTEXT

Past Continuous

1. Read the extracts from the interview on page 61 and pay attention to the verb forms in bold. Then read the statements and choose the correct alternatives to complete them.

> "I was a math and science teacher for 37 years. Retirement **was coming up**."
>
> "Since I **was** still **teaching** full time, I took shifts on Saturdays."

a. The verb forms in bold indicate actions that *are in progress in the present / were in progress in the past*.

b. The verb forms in bold are formed by the Simple Past of the verb to be + *the main verb followed by -ing / the main verb in the Simple Past*.

c. Adverbs such as still *can be inserted / can't be inserted* between the verb to be and the main verb.

2. The verbs in bold in the extracts above are in the affirmative form of the Past Continuous tense. In pairs, read them again, reflect on how they're formed, and answer: How do we form their corresponding interrogative and negative forms?

For more information about the Past Continuous, go to Language Reference, pages 176 and 177.

3. Complete the story below with the Past Continuous of the verbs *call*, *wonder*, and *sit*.

> ### Looking Past Your Own Pain
>
> I met a dream-catcher in the most unusual way. I ♦ in my office in the basement of the Hospital, far away from patients, when I got this request. "Lisa, can you come up to Turner 4 to speak with a patient?" I went to the room they ♦ from and there sat a woman hooked up to her chemotherapy drip. She was so happy that I had taken time to come and speak with her. Through her battle with cancer she kept wondering how she could give back for all the kindness and caring she had received. This patient was also a professor at the local College, so she ♦ if she could bring her students into volunteering. We came up with a group project for her freshman class that needed to complete community service requirements. They planned and implemented a weekly activities session for our rehabilitation unit. […] She was a dreamer that didn't let her own problems stop her from reaching out and helping others.
>
> — Unknown. Submitted by Lisa Coble, Newport Hospital Manager of Volunteer Services, Newport RI

Adapted from <www.energizeinc.com/directory/q-others/stories>.
Accessed on December 11, 2015.

Volunteering **Unit 4** 65

Past Continuous and Simple Past

4. Read another extract from the interview on page 61 and identify both the action that was in progress and the action that was completed. After that, complete the statements.

"One day I was visiting Science World with my granddaughters and saw the sign: Volunteer Opportunities."

a. We use the ♦ for ongoing past actions and the ♦ for completed actions in the past.

b. The Past Continuous is often used with the Simple Past to indicate long and shorter actions, respectively. The ♦ actions are frequently interrupted by the ♦ ones.

5. Which alternative best completes the comic strip below?

Extracted from <www.grantland.net/volunteering.htm>. Accessed on December 11, 2015.

a. were asking / were saying / weren't telling

b. asked / said / didn't tell

6. Choose the correct verb forms to complete the text below.

Work with Children (James Aprelia, Germany)

I was a volunteer in a program created by VWI for a month in 2010. My work involved teaching street children different ways of how to stay healthy but I also worked there as a professor. I am half Indian and so my mother *was teaching / taught* me Hindi and this made it easier for me to get along with the children, and so I did not get to use the help of the translator that much. Before coming to Jaipur, I knew that the welfare level of the people is not high, but I have to say it was a bit of a shock when I saw with my own eyes how the people live there.

I never *was thinking / thought* that people could have it so bad anywhere in this world and still be so opened to foreigners. I was amazed to see how good the children reacted to my presence there. It is sad to say that children don't get any chance at a normal development, at a normal childhood, and basically at a normal life. Even now I remember their faces, the way they looked at me with their eyes, it was like they *were waiting / waited* for something, waiting for the bad to be over. […]

Adapted from <www.volunteeringwithindia.org/reviews/work-with-children-volunteer-stories#more-3700>. Accessed on December 11, 2015.

7. Complete the text with the correct forms of the verbs from the box.

> cause   come   pull out   pursue (negative)   wander

Androcles

A slave named Androcles once escaped from his master and fled to the forest. As he ♦ about there he came upon a Lion lying down moaning and groaning. At first he turned to flee, but finding that the Lion ♦ him, he turned back and went up to him. As he came near, the Lion put out his paw, which was all swollen and bleeding, and Androcles found that a huge thorn had got into it, and ♦ all the pain. He ♦ the thorn and bound up the paw of the Lion, who was soon able to rise and lick the hand of Androcles like a dog. Then the Lion took Androcles to his cave, and every day used to bring him meat from which to live. But shortly afterwards both Androcles and the Lion were captured, and the slave was sentenced to be thrown to the Lion, after the latter had been kept without food for several days. The Emperor and all his Court came to see the spectacle, and Androcles was led out into the middle of the arena. Soon the Lion was let loose from his den, and rushed bounding and roaring towards his victim. But as soon as he ♦ near to Androcles he recognised his friend, and fawned upon him, and licked his hands like a friendly dog. The Emperor, surprised at this, summoned Androcles to him, who told him the whole story. Whereupon the slave was pardoned and freed, and the Lion let loose to his native forest.

Gratitude is the sign of noble souls.

Extracted from <www.aesopfables.com/cgi/aesop1.cgi?1&Androcles>. Accessed on December 11, 2015.

8. In pairs, read the fable from activity 7 again. Then discuss the morals listed below and identify the one that best relates to Androcles'.

No one truly forgets injuries in the presence of him who caused the injury. (The Laborer and the Snake)
No act of kindness, no matter how small, is ever wasted. (The Lion and the Mouse)
Please all, and you will please none. (The Man, the Boy, and the Donkey)

Adapted from <www.aesopfables.com/aesop3.html>. Accessed on February 22, 2016.

▶ WRAPPING UP

Look at the pictures below and, in your notebook, write down three things that were happening and one that wasn't happening when the pictures were taken. Make sure to use the Past Continuous. Read your statements to a classmate and have him guess which one isn't true. Change roles.

3,000 volunteer workers plant young trees at the mouth of Mano River on October 6, 2013 in Minamisoma, Fukushima, Japan. 20,000 trees are planted to commemorate the victims with the hope that growing trees will protect people from future natural disasters.

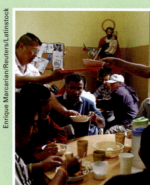

A volunteer gives food to a man at a community soup kitchen which is managed by the San Jose de Flores Roman Catholic parish church in a neighborhood of Buenos Aires on February 18, 2013.

Volunteering Unit 4 67

LISTENING COMPREHENSION

Before Listening

1. Look at the images below and answer: what do they all have in common?

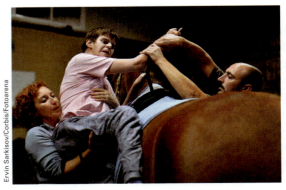

Ana Isabel from Blue Unicorn NGO provides a therapy session to a disabled patient in Yunquera de Henares (Guadalajara), Spain on September 21, 2013.

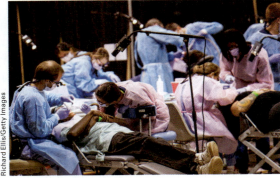

Volunteer dentists work on a tooth extraction during a free medical mission held by the SC Dental Association on August 23, 2013 in North Charleston, South Carolina. More than 1,000 people showed up to receive free dental and medical care.

Projeto Praia Sem Barreiras, in Candeias, Pernambuco, Brazil. The project ensures that disabled people or people with reduced mobility have access to leisure activities.

2. You are going to listen to Sarah Pitcher, an eighteen-year-old girl, talking about her experience in a volunteer program in Fiji. Her video was added to the Lattitude Global Volunteering blog. Lattitude Global Volunteering is an international youth development charity whose mission is to educate and develop young people worldwide by providing opportunities to volunteer abroad and to make a positive difference in the lives of others. What kind of information do you expect to hear from Sarah? Exchange ideas with your classmates.

> A República de Fiji, mais comumente conhecida como das Fiji, é um arquipélago de 322 ilhas na Oceania. Além do fijiano, o inglês e o hindi fijiano são os idiomas oficiais do país.
>
> Baseado em: <https://pt.wikipedia.org/wiki/Fiji#L.C3.ADnguas>. Acessado em: 18 de fevereiro de 2016.

Listening

3. Listen to the first part of Sarah's recording and answer the following questions. Use your own words.

   a. What kind of volunteer work did she do?

   b. What did she mention about her computer skills? Why?

68   Unit 4   Volunteering

4. Listen to the second part of the recording and find the inccrrect information in the sentences below. Then correct the statements orally. Finally, refer back to the transcript on page 196 and check your answers.

   a. All students at Navidula District School speak English well.
   b. On Fridays, Sarah goes to an environmental center in Korovou Town to teach English to the adults who work there.
   c. She lives in a hostel.
   d. She goes to school right after breakfast. After school she plays with her family members.
   e. She didn't feel comfortable with the place and the people as time went by.

After Listening

- Were your predictions in activity 2 correct? If not, why?
- From your point of view, was Sarah enthusiastic about her volunteer experience? Explain.

PRONUNCIATION PRACTICE

Pay attention to the pronunciation of these words.

/i/ each   cheeky
/ɪ/ will   still

Now listen to these words and identify to each colum they belong.

bit   in   need   river   seen
speak   teach   treat   which   with

/i/	/ɪ/
♦	♦
♦	♦
♦	♦
♦	♦
♦	♦

SPEAKING

In small groups, share your impressions about Sarah's experience. Discuss these questions:

✓ How did she react to the cultural differences she experienced? Explain.
✓ Would you react the same way? What would you do differently? Why?
✓ In what sense was it a good learning experience?
✓ Would you like to have a similar experience? Why/Why not?

Choose a person from your group to report your ideas to the whole class. Make comments or ask your classmates further questions if needed.

WRITING

In pairs, interview a person who volunteers. It can be one of your classmates, teachers, or someone from the school staff.

Planning your interview

- Talk to a classmate and choose a special person to interview. Ask yourself: has he/she done anything important for the community? Does he/she have an interesting life story or relevant facts to tell?
- Think of a short paragraph that introduces him/her.
- Take notes of everything you want to ask him/her and plan your questions. Don't forget that open questions avoid yes/no answers and consequently a poor interview.
- If possible, use a tape recorder to record the interview. You can use a cell phone, too.

Writing and rewriting your text

- Write a draft of your interview in your notebook.

> ### REFLECTING AND EVALUATING
>
> Go back to your interview and make sure you paid attention to the following topics.
>
> ✓ Did you write a meaningful short paragraph which introduces the interviewee?
>
> ✓ Are your questions written so that you can get interesting and relevant information?
>
> ✓ Are the questions fully answered by the interviewee?
>
> ✓ Is the interview transcribed and translated correctly?

- Ask a classmate to proofread your interview and give his/her opinion about it.
- Make all the necessary adjustments and write a clean copy.

After writing

- Exchange interviews and read your classmates'. Then arrange the desks in the classroom in a u-shape and comment on the best interview that you read.
- If possible, publish the best interviews on the school website or on the school blog.

SELF-ASSESSMENT

Chegamos ao fim da unidade 4. Convidamos você a refletir sobre seu desempenho até aqui e responder às questões propostas abaixo, escolhendo uma das seguintes opções:

Sim.

Preciso me preparar mais.

Questões

- Você reúne argumentos suficientes para abordar os benefícios que o trabalho voluntário pode trazer à comunidade e aos próprios voluntários?
- Você está apto a ler e compreender uma entrevista conduzida em língua inglesa e reconhecer as características principais inerentes ao gênero?
- Você reúne conhecimentos linguístico-discursivos para redigir uma entrevista em inglês?
- Você está preparado para ouvir relatos de voluntários, compreender informações detalhadas e discutir a respeito?
- Você reúne conhecimentos linguístico-discursivos para redigir uma entrevista em inglês?

Refletindo sobre suas respostas

- Como você analisa a evolução do seu aprendizado em relação à unidade anterior?
- De que forma suas práticas de aprendizagem no decorrer desta unidade influenciaram suas respostas?
- O que você pode fazer para aprimorar ainda mais os conhecimentos adquiridos nesta unidade?

  a. Buscar por mais informações sobre trabalho voluntário e seu impacto social.

  b. Ler entrevistas em língua inglesa para ter contato com diferentes pontos de vista e experiências de vida.

  c. Aprofundar meus conhecimentos em língua inglesa, usando recursos diversos, de forma que minha participação nas atividades seja mais ativa.

  d. Outros.

Volunteering **Unit 4** 71

Further Practice 2 – Units 3 & 4

1. Read the text and write the heading and subheadings from the box in the correct spaces.

> Domestic violence is a worldwide problem
> The worldwide violence against women and children
> Violence is never your fault – it's the abuser's

◆

[…]
Domestic violence is a pervasive, life-threatening crime that impacts on thousands of New Zealanders with serious physical, psychological, and economic effects.

Crime and injury statistics show how significant a problem with domestic violence is in our country. It is one of the leading causes of injury and death to women, and also leads to short and long-term health problems such as mental illness, and problems with sexual and reproductive health. […]

◆

The World Health Organization assessed the experience of violence in over 24,000 women across 10 countries. It found:
- Between 15% and 71% of women reported physical or sexual violence by a husband or partner.
- Many women said that their first sexual experience was not consensual (24% in rural Peru, 28% in Tanzania, 30% in rural Bangladesh, and 40% in South Africa).
- Between four and 12% of women reported being physically abused during pregnancy.
- Each year, about 5,000 women worldwide are murdered by their family members in the name of honour.
- Forced marriages and child marriages violate the human rights of women and girls, yet they are widely practiced in many countries in Asia, the Middle East and sub-Saharan Africa.
- Worldwide, up to one in five women and one in 10 men report experiencing sexual abuse as children. Children subjected to sexual abuse are much more likely to encounter other forms of abuse later in life.

◆

There are many common myths about domestic violence — such as "Why doesn't she just leave?" – but female and child victims don't "ask for it", and no one deserves to be abused. The responsibility for both the abuse and the personal changes needed to stop the behaviour lies firmly with the abuser.
[…]

Adapted from <womensrefuge.org.nz/domestic-violence/>. Accessed on February 21, 2016.

2. Check the best options to complete the sentences.

a. Domestic violence in New Zealand...

    1 is one of the major reasons why women get hurt or killed.

    2 is one of the major reasons why women have economic problems.

    3 is one of the major reasons why women present problems such as mental illness.

b. The text shows that...

    1 men and women are equally likely to suffer from domestic violence.

    2 forced marriages are also a form of domestic violence.

    3 pregnancy is the period when most women are physically attacked by their partners.

c. In domestic violence situations, it is always the abuser's fault because...

    1 women and children are not strong enough to defend themselves from their abusers.

    2 it is the abuser's behavior and violence towards the victims that creates the problem.

    3 victims can't leave their houses due to economic issues.

72   **Further Practice 2**   Units 3 & 4

3. Match the questions and the answers.

   a. What are some of the consequences of domestic violence on the victims?
   b. What different types of domestic violence are mentioned in the text?
   c. Why does the text refer to questions such as "Why doesn't she just leave?" as common myths?

   1 Most people believe that domestic violence victims want to be in that position, which is not true. They don't deserve to be abused, nor do they ask for it, but it's not that easy for them to change the situation.

   2 Marrying a person the victim doesn't want to marry is one type of domestic violence. Sexual or physical abuse from a spouse or boyfriend, minors being forced to engage in sexual activities, or people being forced to have their first sexual experience without their consent are mentioned as well.

   3 Victims may have mental and physical issues. They can also have problems related to their sexual and reproductive health in the future.

4. If you click on "Effects of abuse", you'll be able to see a list of effects of psychological and emotional abuse that domestic violence can have on its victims. Below you will find part of that list. Work in pairs to add more items.

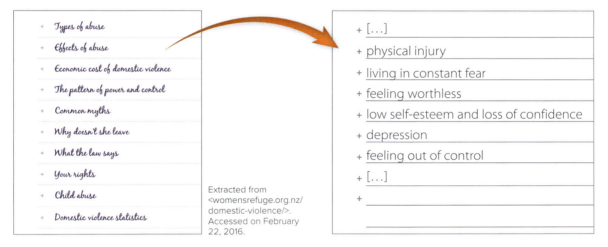

Extracted from <womensrefuge.org.nz/domestic-violence/>. Accessed on February 22, 2016.

5. Read the text below and discuss the question that follows with a classmate.

> **What is honour-based violence (HBV)?**
>
> Honour-based violence is a phenomenon where a person (most often a woman) is subjected to violence by her collective family or community in order to restore 'honour', presumed to have been lost by her behaviour, most often through expressions of sexual autonomy.
>
> **What is an honour killing?**
>
> An 'honour' killing is the most extreme form of HBV where the supposed offender against family 'honour' is killed to restore the 'honour' which has supposedly been lost through her behaviour. An 'honour' killing is the most extreme form of violence which may be expressed as a final resort; however, there are other lesser responses, such as forcing marriage or other forms of violence which may also be expressed.

Adapted from <hbv-awareness.com/faq/#eleven>. Accessed on April 22, 2016.

According to the text on page 72, about 5,000 women around the world die because of honor killings. What do you think governments could do to reduce this number? Explain your answer.

Units 3 & 4   **Further Practice 2**   73

Further Practice 2 – Units 3 & 4

6. The Domestic Violence Prevent Resource Centre Victoria (DVRCV) is an Australian non-profit organization whose mission is to prevent family violence. Read an extract of the infographic below and check the sentence that is not true.

Extracted from <www.dvrcv.org.au/sites/default/files/DVRCV%20Living%20in%20fear%20Infographic%20POSTER_1.pdf>. Accessed on April 22, 2016.

a. More than 3 in 10 women are victims of their partner abuse.

b. The most common reason of women murders in Australia is family violence.

c. Reports show that family violence is decreasing.

d. One third of children are exposed to domestic violence.

7. Look at the logo of DVRCV and read an extract of its mission. Then, in pairs, discuss the question that follows. How is the logo related to the mission of the organization?

DVRCV aims to prevent family violence and promote respectful relationships.
We aim to:
Lead debate and promote social change
Strengthen the community and service system response to violence against women and their children, from primary prevention to recovery
[…]

Extracted from <www.dvrcv.org.au/welcome-dvrcv>. Accessed on April 21, 2016.

8. Read about aboriginal people in Australia and, in small groups, discuss the question below.

> **Who Are Aborigines?**
> Aborigines are Australia's indigenous people. Recent government statistics counted approximately 400,000 aboriginal people, or about 2% of Australia's total population.
>
> Australian Aborigines migrated from somewhere in Asia at least 30,000 years ago. Though they comprise 500–600 distinct groups, aboriginal people possess some unifying links. Among these are strong spiritual beliefs that tie them to the land; a tribal culture of storytelling and art; and, like other indigenous populations, a difficult colonial history.

Extracted from <www.infoplease.com/spot/aboriginal1.html>. Accessed on April 22, 2016.

- In your opinion, why do aboriginal women are more exposed to family violence?

9. Choose the correct alternative to complete the news article below.

> ### How local voluntary efforts are making a positive change in the lives of HIV-positive children in Entebbe
>
> By Linda Givetash
> Posted Monday, December 7 2015 at 02:00
>
> While the effect of the support provided by New Dawn cannot be calculated, parents and children alike say the foundation has had a huge impact on their lives.
>
> Richard Musisi has brought his two sons, ages 8 and 10, to the foundation for the last two years following the death of his wife. It was his wife who initially ♦ the boys.
>
> "When they first ♦ here they ♦ good," he says through a translator.
>
> Providing for his family as a single father is a challenge.
>
> Being able to count on the monthly food package from New Dawn is a big relief. Musisi says he also grows vegetables at home – a skill learned through the foundation. "I know about the balanced diet that can help the children out," he says.
>
> The opportunity to see his boys healthy and having fun is a source of happiness for him, he explains.
>
> "When the children are playing with each other they are happy, and the care New Dawn is giving them is good enough for them to feel at home," Musisi says.
>
> And it is not just the children who have changed for the better.
>
> The community effort has inspired a culture of philanthropy and volunteering. The coordination of the monthly gathering relies entirely on volunteers.
>
> "I know where these people come from," says Nakanjako, who has volunteered with New Dawn from the beginning. "We ♦ kids who ♦ , and I have seen them grow up."

Between 60 and 90 children come to New Dawn Africa Foundation's monthly gathering to play, eat and take home a nutritious food package. Photo by Linda Givetash.

Further Practice 2 – Units 3 & 4

"This additional support, I know it is doing great work in their life," she added.

Even parents who struggle to feed their children have found ways to give back to the foundation. Segirinya recalls a mother, who arrived at the foundation barefoot, offering a sack of avocados to the group.

"I almost cried. She had nothing on her feet and here she is, bringing many avocados," Segirinya recalls.

These instances of people helping one another are encouraging to New Dawn's founders. Segirinya hopes that in the coming years the community will take over the leadership of New Dawn Foundation, allowing him to start up other projects.

"We should be our brother's keeper," Segirinya says. "When you see some of these positive things, you get motivated to do more."

Adapted from <www.monitor.co.ug/Magazines/Health---Living/Voluntary--efforts-HIV-positive-children-in-Entebbe/-/689846/2986124/-/sus1uiz/-/index.html>. Accessed on December 15, 2015.

a. was bringing – came – were not looking – found – died

b. brought – come – didn't look – found – died

c. brought – came – were not looking – found – were dying

10. Now answer the following questions.

a. How many children does the New Dawn Africa Foundation help?

b. What is Richard Musisi's story?

c. Besides providing Musisi's family with food packages, he learned something at the Foundation. What was that?

d. Do you know any Brazilian organization whose work is similar to that done at New Dawn Africa Foundation? If so, share the information. Then discuss: how important is this kind of organization to your community? Explain.

e. What does Segirinya mean when she says, "We should be our brother's keeper," and "When you see some of these positive things, you get motivated to do more."? Do you agree with her? Explain.

11. Copy the passage of the text which shows how people who have been assisted by the Foundation express their gratitude.

12. Complete the sentences based on the information in the text.

a. Musisi learned nutritional facts to ♦.

b. The Foundation relies 100 percent on ♦.

c. The New Dawn Africa Foundation has positively affected ♦.

d. Children go to the foundation not only for ♦.

e. New Dawn's founders ♦.

EXAM PRACTICE

Why volunteer?

Volunteering is a great way for people, regardless of their age, cultural background, location or circumstances, to get involved in the community.

But we are all different and may want to volunteer for different reasons. Some of us get involved for charitable reasons, some to meet new people or some to learn new skills.

Most of us don't know about the variety of volunteering opportunities or the many other benefits of volunteering.

Apart from the satisfaction of helping out your community, there can be heaps of reasons why you should volunteer. Here are just a few:

- Meet new people and make new friends.

- To give back to, or get involved in, my community.

- Experience new challenges.

- Raise awareness and support important community issues.

- Experience different cultures.

- Help people or contribute to social change.

- Develop professional networks.

- Find a pathway to getting a job or into a course or training.

- Learn new skills or gain experience in a variety of roles.

- Explore different career and job opportunities.

Research has also found a significant connection between volunteering and good health with reports showing that volunteers have:

- Longer lives

- Lower rates of depression

- Less incidence of heart disease

- Higher functional ability.

Adapted from <www.volunteer.vic.gov.au/information-for-volunteers/new-to-volunteering/why-volunteer>. Accessed on December 15, 2015.

O texto tem como propósito maior:

a. conscientizar o cidadão de que o trabalho voluntário é essencial para melhorar a qualidade de vida de quem o exerce.

b. relacionar os benefícios do trabalho voluntário à área profissional de quem o exerce.

c. enfatizar que a maior satisfação do voluntário é saber que pode ajudar a melhorar a vida de muitas pessoas.

d. estimular as pessoas a fazer trabalho voluntário, independentemente das razões e circunstâncias que as levem a tanto.

e. criticar o fato de que as pessoas desconhecem os benefícios do trabalho voluntário.

UNIT 5

AN EYE ON AFRICA

Nesta unidade você terá oportunidade de:

- refletir e discutir sobre a descendência de todos os seres humanos que vivem atualmente no planeta Terra, bem como sobre a influência da cultura africana em nosso país;

- reconhecer objetivos e algumas características de artigos de destaque e escrever um;

- compreender um diálogo entre um correspondente de um renomado jornal norte-americano e um paleantropologista acerca das origens do ser humano;

- discutir com os colegas o significado dos fósseis, o que eles dizem a nosso respeito e como são formados.

- O que podemos ver na imagem?
- A que momento histórico e social do Brasil podemos relacionar esta imagem? Justifique.

STARTING OUT Art History

1. How much do you know about African countries? Take the quiz and find out.

   1. This country is probably best known for its ancient history. Its main river, the Nile, was the lifeblood of one of the world's cradles of civilization. Its art and culture were a great influence on ancient Europe, and many of its most impressive monuments are still standing after thousands of years. What country is this?

      - Nigeria
      - Namibia
      - Egypt
      - Ethiopia

   2. The Cape of Good Hope juts from this country, a landmark that has shown captains for centuries that they were "turning the corner" in sailing around Africa. What country, so rich in gold and diamonds, is this?

      - South Africa
      - Sudan
      - Egypt
      - Mali

   3. This country is one of very few in Africa to have never been a colony, but it was occupied by Italy for a few years before and during World War II. What is this ancient nation, whose capital is Addis Ababa?

      - Ethiopia
      - Côte d'Ivoire
      - South Africa
      - Togo

   4. This country, whose capital is Nairobi, has been dominated by the Kikuyu people for much of its history, which has led to political tension. Historically, however, it has been one of the most stable nations in Africa, and has been a popular tourist and safari destination since its days as a British colony. What country, named for its tallest mountain, is this?

      - Egypt
      - South Africa
      - Libya
      - Kenya

   5. This country, which takes its name from one of Africa's great rivers, was first a personal colony of the cruel Belgian King Leopold II. Today, following several name changes, it is one of the largest nations in Africa. What country, whose capital is Kinshasa, is this?

      - South Africa
      - Democratic Republic of the Congo
      [...]
      - Rhodesia
      - Kenya

   Adapted from <www.funtrivia.com/playquiz/quiz28726520e3480.html>.
   Accessed on December 14, 2015.

2. Like educational quizzes, feature articles are good sources of information. In this unit, you are going to read part of a feature article about Africa published in a magazine. What particular aspect (such as culture, economics, sports, or tourism) do you expect to find in a feature article? Talk to your classmates.

READING COMPREHENSION

Before Reading

1. Skim the feature article and answer the questions: why was it published? Who wrote it?

Reading

BLACK HISTORY MONTH

History

The immense contributions that Africa made to civilisation in Europe have not been acknowledged by today's Europe, wich was steeped in the Dark Ages when the Africans were building marvellous cities and sumptuous palaces in Spain and Portugal, and bringing education and enlightenment to the whole of Europe. As we celebrate Black History Month, we take readers down memory lane, to the time when Africans commanded all they surveyed in Europe and brought civilisation to a continent groping in darkness. This lead piece is by **Baffour Ankomah**.

When Africa civilised Europe

'Looking at some unflattering pictures of half-naked Africans in glossy magazine advertisements, for example, Chief Obijol and his 'series of clicking sounds', racists would like to think that the African was inferior and slow to evolve. They would be terribly mistaken because the African, in his present sorry plight, is not a case of delayed evolution; he is a classic example of accelerated degeneration. There were black pharaohs in ancient Egypt, and before Europe was Europe, and while the Caesars were teaching the British Isles to read and write, the Ethiopian chancellor of the exchequer of Queen Candece was reading the Prophet Isaiah fluently."

This is how Prof. F.I.D. Konotey-Ahulu, the Ghanaian medical doctor, writer, and pan-Africanist, tries to dispel the notion that the African has had no part in civilising the word. In fact if you

believe the majority of Western historians and scholars, the African was in a frozen state until "discovered" by the European in the mid-15th century. What happened to the African before that, or what the African was doing or had done before the European "discovery", they have nothing to say about!

Which leads John G. Jackson, the African-American historian and author, to say that "the curious idea that a great white race has been responsible for all the great civilisations of the past is nothing more than a crude superstition propagated mainly by European-oriented racist historians." Because for 781 years, between 711 AD and 1492, Africans from ancient Northwest and West Africa, together with their Islamic fellows from Arabia, had put Southern Europe to the sword, conquered it, governed it, and brought civilization, education, and general enlightenment to Europe as a whole.

"This civilization brought by the African Moors," says Edward Scobie, the Dominican scholar, writer, and historian, "needs further and deeper examination, especially as Spain and Portugal were the first countries in Europe to benefit from the enlightenment which the African warrior-scholars carried with them from across the African mainland through the Mediterranean Sea to Iberia, and to other European countries further inland"."

Today, as Dr Ivan Van Sertima, another great African-American historian, lecturer and author, once said, "it would seem like racial chauvinism to suggest that Africans played a major role in the occupation and enlightenment of a critical part of Europe."

[…]

Extracted from *New African*, pages 72-73. October, 2015.

2. The objective of the article is to...

> **civilisation** (UK)
> **civilization** (US)

   a. refute the idea that Africa was discovered by Europeans.

   b. give readers a more in-depth view of Africa's contribution to the cultural development of Europe.

   c. denounce racism in the way historians see Africa nowadays.

3. Read the quotes from the article again and answer the questions.

> "the curious idea that a great white race has been responsible for all the great civilisations of the past is nothing more than a crude superstition propagated mainly by European-oriented racist historians."

> "This civilization brought by the African Moors," says Edward Scobie, the Dominican scholar, writer and historian, "needs further and deeper examination, especially as Spain and Portugal were the first countries in Europe to benefit from the enlightenment which the African warrior-scholars carried with them from across the African mainland through the Mediterranean Sea to Iberia, and to other European countries further inland"."

> "it would seem like racial chauvinism to suggest that Africans played a major role in the occupation and enlightenment of a critical part of Europe."

82   **Unit 5** An Eye on Africa

a. Why are the quotes mentioned in the article?

b. Do the three historians share the same views? Explain your answer.

4. Write T (True), F (False), or NM (Not Mentioned).

   a. Back then, Europeans were barely literate, whereas an African official could fluently read a religious text.

   b. According to European historians, there isn't much history in Africa prior to the arrival of the Europeans on the continent.

   c. The influence of African Moors in the cultural development of Europe has been deeply analyzed.

   d. There are many books about African history which portray a racist view of Africa's contribution to civilization in Europe.

   e. According to Dr. Ivan Van Sertima, not recognizing the importance of the African influence on the European enlightenment is a racist position.

5. The image shown in the article is the picture of Alhambra, a palace and fortress complex in Granada, Spain. It was built in the 13th century. Why was that image used? Does it help to make the text more meaningful? Explain.

6. Identify the only characteristic that doesn't belong to feature articles.

   a. Feature articles can be published in magazines and newspapers, as well as on websites.

   b. There are different kinds of feature articles: historical, seasonal, and profiles are some of them.

   c. Feature articles offer readers a more in-depth view of the topic.

   d. They are typically long because they provide a lot of details.

   e. They focus only on what happened, when, and to whom.

   f. They usually include attractive images to grab the attention of those who are scanning the pages.

After Reading

- Why is it so important to study Africa's history and influence? Explain your answer.
- What traits of African culture do you see in your country today? Give some examples.

VOCABULARY STUDY

1. Read the feature article on pages 81 and 82 again, look for synonyms for the words below, then compose and complete the diagram in your notebook.

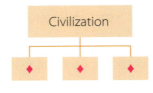

> SAT = Scholastic Aptitude Test
>
> SAT é um exame muito comum nos Estados Unidos, usado pelas universidades em processos de admissão para graduação.
>
> Baseado em: <www.estudarfora.org.br/conheca-o-sat/>. Acessado em: 4 de março de 2016.

2. Scan the text for the words or expressions below and infer their meanings. Then complete the passages below with them.

> plight   to dispel   mainland   chauvinism

[…] As a society, we can seek ♦ stereotypes through education and a social action. We can seek to give the world the full stories of Africans — how many children actually attend schools and sit for both the SATs and the Cambridge International Examinations, for example."

Extracted from <voicesofafrica.co.za/dispelling-stereotypes-about-africans/>. Accessed on December 15, 2015.

SA women battling ♦
06 March 2008 at 08:33am
South African crane operator Zoliswa Gila rises high above the pervasive chauvinistic view that her job should be reserved for members of the male sex. […]

Extracted from <www.iol.co.za/news/south-africa/sa-women-battling-chauvinism-1.392076#.Vm_mcEqDFHw>. Accessed on December 15, 2015.

[…] Many times people have wondered why I speak so passionately about the ♦ of Africa, many times people have asked why I burden myself with the plight of our continent. The answer is simple, it is because I am African, an African who is concerned about the staggering poverty and underdevelopment in the land and the inability of our governments, federal states and local authorities to function at the level they ought to, when you look at Africa today, whether you are looking at Ghana, Nigeria, Sierra Leon, or indeed any country in Africa, how is it that our gold, timber, oil, and other natural resources are taken away from us and given to those that have. […]

Adapted from <www.modernghana.com/news/630853/1/the-plight-of-africa.html>. Accessed on December 15, 2015.

[…] Tanzania was formed as a sovereign state in 1964 through the union of the theretofore separate states of Tanganyika and Zanzibar. Mainland Tanganyika covers more than 99 percent of the combined territories' total area. Mafia Island is administered from the mainland, while Zanzibar and Pemba islands have a separate government administration. Dodoma, since 1974 the designated official capital of Tanzania, is centrally located on the ♦. Dar es Salaam, however, remains the seat of most government administration, as well as being the largest city and port in the country. […]

Extracted from <www.britannica.com/place/Tanzania>. Accessed on December 15, 2015.

Unit 5   An Eye on Africa

LANGUAGE IN CONTEXT

Past Perfect

1. Look at these extracts from the feature article on pages 81 and 82 and then choose the correct words or expressions to complete the sentences.

> "What happened to the African before that, or what the African was doing or **had done** before the European "discovery", they have nothing to say about!"

> "Because for 781 years, between 711 AD and 1492, Africans from ancient Northwest and West Africa, together with their Islamic fellows from Arabia, **had put** Southern Europe to the sword, **conquered** it, **governed** it, and **brought** civilization, education, and general enlightenment to Europe as a whole."

a. The verb forms in bold indicate actions that happened *before/after* other actions in the *past/present*. They are in the Past Perfect tense.

b. To form the Past Perfect tense we use *had* + the main verb in the *Past Participle / Present Participle* form.

For more information about the Past Perfect tense, go to Language Reference, pages 180 and 181.

2. Complete the text with the Past Perfect form of the verbs *be up to*, *collect*, *learn*, and *steal*.

Picasso's African-Influenced Period - 1907 to 1909

[…]

Picasso's African Period lasted from 1907 to 1909. This period, which followed his Blue Period and Rose Period, was also called the Negro Period or Black Period.

As Henri Matisse exhibited his *Blue Nude* in 1907 and *The Dance* in 1909, Picasso countered with the work that has become one of the cornerstones of his fame, which we now know as *Les Demoiselles d'Avignon*. In this work, he began to incorporate African influences.

Before Picasso started his Black Period, he came into the possession of some ancient Iberian sculptures that he got from an acquaintance who ♦ them from the Louvre museum in Paris. In *Les Demoiselles d'Avignon,* the faces of the three women on the left are based on the Iberian sculptures. So as to avoid compositional monotony, Picasso based the faces of the two women on the right on the African totem art, that he ♦ also ♦ .

Throughout Picasso's career, periods would be concluded by a major artwork that contained all the new things he ♦. The painting *Life* concluded and summarized his Blue Period and *The Family of Saltimbanques* did the same for his Rose Period. Now it was up to the Demoiselles to show what he ♦ during his Black Period. […]

PICASSO, Pablo. *Les Demoiselles d'Avignon*, 1907. Oil on canvas, 243,9 × 233,7 cm. MoMA, New York.

Adapted from <www.pablopicasso.org/africanperiod.jsp>. Accessed on December 15, 2015.

3. Pick out the alternative that best completes the text below.

African Legends – The Curious Monkey

Once upon a time, in the deep of the jungle, a dog was comfortably asleep next to a fire. He was the first dog to ever be born into the world, and he was a happy dog. It's difficult to say whether he was good or bad, because all he ever did in the beginning was sleep. Until a monkey happened upon him.

The monkey was of course curious, as monkeys are, and scampered down from his tree to examine this strange creature he ♦ before. He looked at the dog from every possible angle, and when he was satisfied he ♦ the dog in its entirety, ran off to tell all the other monkeys about his strange encounter.

Soon word spread to all the animals of the jungle, and soon they were all involved in a debate as to what kind of creature it was. "It's not an elephant," said the elephant in all his wisdom. "Thank you for that profound observation," responded the monkey.

"It's not a giraffe," stated the shy giraffe. "Not an antelope either," cried the Kudu. Soon all the animals were asked by the monkey if they knew what it was, until only the tortoise ♦ . The wise old tortoise knew what the creature was, as she ♦ since the beginning of all creation. "That's a dog," said the tortoise, and on hearing his name, the dog suddenly awoke.

He sprang to his feet, looking bewildered at all of the animals around him. The dog was furious that he'd been waken, and charged furiously at the other animals, barking and scowling and snapping his jaws! The only animal that didn't run was the tortoise – she didn't have to. "You won't catch me, dog," she said as she withdrew into her shell, "But from this day on you're condemned to chase any creature you lay your eyes on."

That's how the saying came to be – "Better to let sleeping dogs lie."

[...]

Fiona Rogers/Corbis/Fotoarena

Adapted from <www.colours-of-the-rainbow.com/african-legends.html>.
Accessed on December 15, 2015.

- had never seen / had examined / hadn't responded / was

- had never seen / had examined / hadn't responded / had been around

- didn't see / had examined / didn't respond / were

4. Read the statements about the text in activity 3 and decide whether they are T (True) or F (False).

a. The monkey hadn't seen a dog before.

b. The tortoise had already expressed her opinion when all the other animals began to give theirs.

c. The dog was furious because the other animals had woken him up.

d. The tortoise had cursed the dog before the other animals ran away.

5. Complete the text with the verb forms from the box.

came up with	'd buried	had
had come up	had passed	was

The Lazy Townspeople

By Traditional

Once upon a time there was a town where all the people were exceedingly lazy. They didn't like to do any kind of work at all! […]

One day a hurricane blew through the town; after it ♦ the place looked even worse than before, but the worst thing was that an enormous tree had been blown over and thrown right across the main road leading to the market place. […] Nobody could be bothered to do anything about the obstruction. People were coming and going, looking at the tree and just walking around it. […] The Chief ♦ a plan to teach his townspeople a lesson. Very early the next day, before the sun ♦, he took some of his servants and got them to dig a hole under the tree. He hid some gold in the hole and got his servants to cover it up again. Then he made them swear to keep this affair a secret. Back at his palace, he instructed his town crier to go round and summon all the citizens to gather at the spot of the fallen tree that afternoon.

When they were all together, the Chief made a speech to his people suggesting that if all of them worked together, it would not take very long to remove the obstacle. One of the farmers said, "The hurricane put that tree there. Let's ask the hurricane to move it out of the way."

[…] The Chief was exasperated. He was just about to give up when a skinny young man stepped forward. He was just a poor farmer who ♦ no living relatives in the town: "I will have a go," he said, and started pulling and pushing to shift the heavy tree. The other townspeople just stood there and watched, some making fun of the young man. […] Once the tree had been moved to the side of the road, the Chief went up to the young farmer and took him to the spot where he ♦ the gold that morning. The Chief told him to dig there and promised him that he could keep whatever he found there. The young farmer started digging in the road, and very quickly uncovered the gold. He ♦ overjoyed.

The Chief said to him, "All this gold is yours to keep. You deserve it, and you can do with it as you please." And to the lazy townspeople he said, "Let this be a lesson to you all! Laziness doesn't get you anything. Rewards come to the person who is prepared to work hard."

Adapted from <fairytalesoftheworld.com/quick-reads/the-lazy-townspeople/>.
Accessed on December 16, 2015.

WRAPPING UP

In pairs, discuss the African proverbs below and rephrase them in your notebook using the Past Perfect tense. Then read your statements to the whole class and share your opinions about the proverbs.

"By the time the fool has learned the game, the players have dispersed."

"Because he lost his reputation, he lost a kingdom."

Adapted from <afritorial.com/the-best-72-african-wise-proverbs/>. Accessed on December 16, 2015.

An Eye on Africa **Unit 5** 87

LISTENING COMPREHENSION

Before Listening

1. In pairs, discuss the following questions:
   - Have you ever heard that all human beings are descendants from one African tribe? If so, what exactly have you heard?
   - What do you think of this theory? Share your views with your classmate.

Listening

 2. You are going to listen to Errol Barnett, an anchor and correspondent for CNN International, talk to the paleoanthropologist Ron Clarke about the origin of human beings. Listen to Errol's introduction and answer these questions.
   a. What are Errol's main questions? Use your own words and write what you have understood.
   b. What does he say he will do in order to understand where his ancestors link up in our human family tree?

 3. Listen to the second part of the recording and complete the transcript with the missing information.

> Paleoanthropologist Ron Clarke is among an elite few who've been unlocking these discoveries.
>
> "What do all of these findings mean?"
>
> "Well, you…you know, what makes us human is that we analyze our surroundings. We want to know how things work. How, why, where. And so, one of the big questions is how did we become human?"
>
> "How far back are we going in time?"
>
> "Here, we go back to around three million years ago."
>
> "Wow!"
>
> "And of course, in East Africa, ♦ go back much further, to beyond four million years. But we don't have those preserved at that age here."
>
> "Well, I want to, you know, take that time travel trip with you. We're at the location of your most famous discovery. So, can we head inside and take a look around?"
>
> "Sure."
>
> "Great."
>
> Professor Clarke leads me into the Sterkfontein Cave, which is currently owned by the University of the Witwatersrand, also known as Wits University. But more than a century ago, this was an active ♦. Unwittingly, miners blasted away rock containing some of the oldest fossils in the world. But it also allowed for Ron's predecessors to dig deeper into our past.
>
> "Now, my research tells me that there is no other cave in the world like this one. Why is that?"
>
> "That's true. We have a great number and variety of fossils relating to ♦ that date from about three million years ago up until a hundred thousand years ago."

88 Unit 5 An Eye on Africa

> "All right here."
>
> "All right here. And I'm going to show you one of the deepest and oldest."
>
> In the 1890s, miners handed over fossil remains to scientists, but it would take generations and many experts to make sense of what's here. In 1936, Professor Raymond Dart and his students realized a skull from this region, dubbed the Taung Child, was from a previously undiscovered ♦. A kind of half ape, half man called Australopithecus. It sent shock waves throughout the scientific world. A decade later, Dr. Robert Broom found a more complete Australopithecus skull in this cave, nicknamed "Mrs. Ples," adding to the excitement.

Transcribed from <www.youtube.com/watch?v=EnWTi8SrUOs>. Accessed on December 17 2015.

After Listening

Would you like to visit that cave, talk to Ron Clarke, and get to know more about our origins? Explain your thoughts and justify your reasons.

PRONUNCIATION PRACTICE

Listen again to some sentences from the recording that contain contractions and repeat them.

I**'ve** always wondered if we**'re** from Africa…
And **I'll** even have my own DNA tested…
But we **don't** have those preserved at that age here.

SPEAKING

In small groups, read this passage and discuss the following questions.

> "We have a great number and variety of fossils relating to our ancestors that date from about three million years ago up until a hundred thousand years ago."

- ✓ What do you know about fossils?
- ✓ What do fossils tell about us?
- ✓ How are they formed? Where can they be found?

Now choose a person from your group to share your knowledge with the whole class.

WRITING

In small groups, follow the steps below and write a historical feature article.

Planning your feature article

- Do some research on the magazines suggested by your teacher and decide where you would like to have your article published.

- Consider your intended audience and exchange ideas with your classmates on the topic you want to develop.

- Do some research on the topic. You can do it online, but you may also visit libraries and consult books. Remember: feature articles give readers a more in-depth view of the topic, so you need to gather as much information as possible. If possible, think about a unique point of view or interesting angle you'd like to present it from.

- Look for quotes or interviews from experts. Use them to lend authority to your article.

- Find relevant photos. They can help explain the story and grab readers' attention.

- Choose the format of your article. Feature articles do not have to follow a particular formula like some other text genres do. You can start the story with an ordinary moment and proceed to how it became unusual, or you can start with a dramatic moment and tell the history that led to that moment.

- Think of a thought-provoking title to grab readers' interest in reading your text.

Writing and rewriting your text

- Write a draft of your feature article in your notebook.

> **REFLECTING AND EVALUATING**
>
> Go back to your feature article and make sure you paid attention to the following topics.
>
> ✓ Is the topic of interest to the target audience?
>
> ✓ Does the article give readers a chance to understand more about the subject?
>
> ✓ Did you express your point of view clearly?
>
> ✓ Did you include quotes, interviews, and photos?
>
> ✓ Did you use the Simple Past and the Past Perfect correctly?

- Get feedback on your article. Ask another group to proofread your text and make comments. Did they give you helpful tips on improving your text?

- Make all the necessary adjustments, write a clean copy and show it to your teacher.

After writing

- Encourage students to exchange their articles and vote for the most interesting one.

SELF-ASSESSMENT

Chegamos ao fim da unidade 5. Convidamos você a refletir sobre seu desempenho até aqui e responder às questões propostas abaixo, escolhendo uma das seguintes opções:

Sim.

Preciso me preparar mais.

Questões

- Você adquiriu repertório suficiente para discutir a descendência da humanidade e a influência africana sobre o povo brasileiro e sua cultura?
- Você é capaz de compreender um artigo de destaque em língua inglesa sobre a origem dos povos, bem como reconhecer as características principais inerentes ao gênero?
- Você reúne conhecimentos linguístico-discursivos suficientes para produzir um artigo de destaque em inglês?
- Você se considera apto a escutar um paleantropologista falar sobre as origens do ser humano e compreender informações específicas?
- Você se julga apto a expor seus conhecimentos sobre a origem dos fósseis e as informações que eles nos trazem?

Refletindo sobre suas respostas

- Como você analisa a evolução do seu aprendizado em relação à unidade anterior?
- De que forma suas práticas de aprendizagem no decorrer desta unidade influenciaram suas respostas?
- O que você pode fazer para aprimorar ainda mais os conhecimentos adquiridos nesta unidade?
  - **a.** Buscar por mais informações acerca da origem do homem e da influência da cultura africana sobre o povo brasileiro.
  - **b.** Ler mais artigos de destaque em língua inglesa para desenvolver melhor minha capacidade de compreensão de informações mais detalhadas.
  - **c.** Aprofundar meus conhecimentos de língua inglesa, usando recursos diversos, de forma que minha participação nas atividades seja mais ativa.
  - **d.** Outros.

An Eye on Africa **Unit 5** 91

UNIT 6

SOCIAL MEDIA AND FALSE NEWS

Nesta unidade você terá oportunidade de:

- refletir e discutir a veiculação de informações falsas em redes sociais, bem como as consequências que isso acarreta;
- reconhecer objetivos e algumas características das notícias e escrever uma;
- compreender o relato de uma vítima de *cyberbullying* que teve sua vida amorosa exposta nas redes sociais;
- discutir com os colegas as possíveis soluções para o *cyberbullying*.

- O que podemos inferir da imagem?
- Que relação podemos estabelecer entre a imagem e o título da unidade?

93

STARTING OUT

1. Read the cartoons and answer: what current issue are they satirizing?

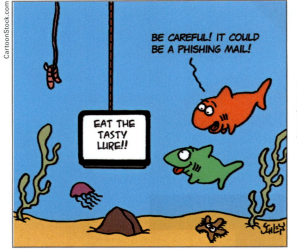

2. We often come across false information online. Where can we learn about online scams that trick people or rob them?

- In news reports.
- In movie reviews.
- In complaint e-mails.
- Others.

94 Unit 6 Social Media and False News

READING COMPREHENSION

Before Reading

1. Look at the logos in the photo and read the headline of the news report. Then answer orally: which social media platform providers do the logos represent? What do you expect to read about in the following news report?

Reading

Putrajaya wants social media to cull 'false news'

53 comments Published 17 Aug 2015, 9:49 am Updated 17 Aug 2015, 1:44 pm

The government is going on the offensive against alleged "false information" particularly on unnamed "news portals".

Communications and Multimedia Minister Salleh Said Keruak yesterday announced on his blog that his ministry will engage media platform providers to stem what it claims is "false information and rumours" on the Internet.

"The issue of false information has recently taken centre stage in the media, especially online news portals."

"In this respect, I have instructed the Malaysian Communications and Multimedia Commission (MCMC) to meet Facebook, Google and Twitter soon to seek their cooperation to stem the increasing tide of false information and rumours from spreading via their social media applications," wrote the newly minted minister.

"Although these three social media platform providers have been cooperating with various Malaysian authorities, the level of cooperation needs to be stepped up," he added.

Salleh said that although the government can restrict access to such social media, it was not practical as many are "using such applications positively and not for negative or reprehensive purposes".

"At this point of time, although it is possible for authorities to restrict access or block such applications, they will not do so to the majority of social media users," he said.

"However, this does not mean that the public can post unchecked information without respect or regard to the law."

"The online environment is not a lawless space and action can be taken against anyone found to have breached the law, including in the online space."

'Not doing enough'

Arguing "sensitive or unverified information might potentially spark an untoward situation likely to jeopardise public safety", the minister called on the three platforms to cooperate, as it is "vital in the public interest".

He urged the social media operators to do more to act upon complaints.

"For instance, in 2014, approximately 78 percent of MCMC's requests for removal of content were acted upon by social media providers, with *Facebook* acting upon approximately 81 percent of MCMC's requests.

"Latest figures at the end of July 2015 show that 49 percent have been acted upon, 33 percent by *YouTube*, 42 percent by *Facebook*."

Adapted from <www.malaysiakini.com/news/308808#ixzz3siRNzoVw>. Accessed on December 15, 2015.

jeopardise (UK) / **jeopardize** (US)
rumour (UK) / **rumor** (US)

Social Media and False News **Unit 6** 95

2. Identify the only sentence which is not true according to the news report on page 95.

a. The Malaysian government is on a campaign to restrain information that includes distorted or untrue facts from circulating on the Internet.

b. Unchecked data posted online could put people's safety in danger.

c. In Malaysia, people can post unchecked information without any regard to the law.

3. Read the questions and answer YES or NO. After that, match the questions to the parts of the news report that justify your choices.

a. According to the text, has Facebook, Google, and Twitter's cooperation with Malaysian authorities been enough to stop false information from circulating on the web?

b. According to Salleh Said Keruak, can people post anything on the cyberspace, even if it is a lie, without being punished for it?

c. Did the Malaysian government dismiss the idea of reducing access to social media because many people use it in a good way?

d. Are main social media providers reporting complaints about false information posted on their servers to the Malaysian Communications and Multimedia Commission?

1. "For instance, in 2014, approximately 78 percent of MCMC's requests for removal of content were acted upon by social media providers, with *Facebook* acting upon approximately 81 percent of MCMC's requests. Latest figures at the end of July 2015 show that 49 percent have been acted upon, 33 percent by *YouTube*, 42 percent by *Facebook*."

2. "However, this does not mean that the public can post information unchecked without respect or regard to the law. The online environment is not a lawless space and action can be taken against anyone found to have breached the law, including in the online space."

3. "Salleh said that although the government can restrict access to such social media, it was not practical as many are "using such applications positively and not for negative or reprehensive purposes""."

4. "Although these three social media platform providers have been cooperating with various Malaysian authorities, the level of cooperation needs to be stepped up, he added."

4. The news report on page 95 is from Malaysia. Read the text below about its political regime. Then discuss the questions that follow in small groups.

Political Regime

Malaysia is a federal state which consists of 13 states and 1 federal territory (Wilayah Persekutuan) with three components, city of Kuala Lumpur, Labuan, and Putrajaya. The chief of state is the King, who is chosen based on the principle of rotation among 9 sultans at the Sultans' Conference. The tenure is 5 years, and its position is ceremonial. The head of government is the Prime Minister, who must be a member of the Lower House.

The Government of Malaysia is closely modeled after the Westminster parliamentary system, a direct influence of the British colonization which ended in 1957. Malaysia has bicameral Parliament consisting of a nonelected Upper House and an elected Lower House. The Upper House has 70 seats, of which 44 are designated by the King and 26 appointed by the state parliaments. The Lower House has 222 seats, all of which are occupied by those who won by direct election. [...]

Adapted from <www.mitchellorenstein.com/wp-content/uploads/2012/07/Malaysia.pdf>. Accessed on March 4, 2016.

a. Malasya follows a political system of parliamentary federal monarchy. How do you relate the Malaysian political system to the content of the news report?
   b. Do authorities from democratic countries such as Brazil restrict access or block social media platform providers? Why/Why not?
   c. In your opinion, do Brazilian users of social media providers use them properly? Justify your answer.

5. Read the statements below and identify the ones that are true based on the news report on page 95.
   a. The report was published in an online newspaper.
   b. Readers can easily identify the name of the section where the report was published.
   c. The report tells readers about an event that happened locally.
   d. The headline catches the readers' attention and highlights the main fact reported.
   e. The exact time the report was published is not mentioned.
   f. Concrete details are not necessary in the report.
   g. Paragraphs are short. They give information in a clear and concise way.

6. In pairs, answer the question below. Report your answer to the whole class.
   What are the resources that online news reports offer to readers?

7. The news report on page 95 makes references to what people said. How can we identify these references?

8. Which verb tense is used in the report to refer to the event that has already taken place?

After Reading

- Do you spread news without checking whether it's true? If so, how? If not, why?
- There is an old saying that says, "Rumors travel faster than the speed of light." How does the Internet contribute to this?
- Do you know how to protect yourself against online rumors? Justify your answer.
- Read the definition below and answer the question that follows.

Extracted from <www.oxforddictionaries.com/us/definition/american_english/cyberbullying>.
Accessed on March 7, 2016.

- How do you think cyberbullying can be avoided? Explain.

VOCABULARY STUDY

1. Observe the words in bold in the extracts from the news report on page 95 and pick out their correct meanings.

> **TIP**
>
> Lembre-se de que uma mesma palavra pode ter significados diferentes; por isso, considere o contexto para descobrir seu significado adequado.

    a. "The government is going on the offensive against alleged "false information" particularly on unnamed "news **portals**""

- websites that function as entry points to the Internet

- iron or steel bents for bracing a framed structure, having curved braces between the vertical members and a horizontal member at the top

    b. "...his ministry will engage media platform providers **to stem** what it claims is "false information and rumours" on the Internet."

- to arise or originate
- to stop, check, or restrain

    c. "...to seek their cooperation to stem the increasing **tide** of false information and rumours..."

- the periodic rise and fall of the waters of the ocean and its inlets, produced by the attraction of the moon and sun, and occurring about every 12 hours

- current, tendency, or drift, as of events or ideas

Adapted from <www.oxforddictionaries.com/us>. Accessed on December 19, 2015.

2. Refer to page 95 and infer the meanings of the words and expressions in italics. Then choose the correct alternatives to complete the passage below.

> ## Internet hoaxes
>
> There are numerous chain letters, hoaxes, and other *false information / online news portals* floating around the Internet. These are not necessarily attempts to swindle you out of money, but they do waste everyone's time. Before passing along some anonymous *platform providers / rumor* or dire warning to a mailing list or to your friends, please take steps to confirm its authenticity. Often, simply googling for the subject heading will provide sufficient information. [...]

Adapted from <www.cs.cmu.edu/~help/security/hoaxes_scams.html>. Accessed on December 19, 2015.

3. Scan the text for the word *cooperate* and infer its meaning. What meaning does the prefix *co-* convey? Then compose and complete the chart in your notebook.

Prefixed Word	Meaning
costar	◆
cofound	◆
coproduce	◆
coexist	◆

LANGUAGE IN CONTEXT

Direct and Indirect Speech

1. Read the extracts from the news report on page 95 and identify the correct statements about them.

> "Although these three social media platform providers have been cooperating with various Malaysian authorities, the level of cooperation needs to be stepped up," he added.

> Salleh said that although the government can restrict access to such social media, it was not practical as many are "using such applications positively and not for negative or reprehensive purposes".

> "At this point of time, although it is possible for authorities to restrict access or block such applications, they will not do so to the majority of social media users," he said.

> He urged the social media operators to do more to act upon complaints.

- The first and second extracts refer to what Communications and Multimedia Minister Salleh Said Keruak actually said.
- The fourth extract reports Salleh Said's exact words.
- The third extract refers to Salleh's words rewritten by the editorial team of the newspaper.
- The second and fourth extracts feature Communications and Multimedia Minister Salleh Said Keruak's words reported by the author of the news report.
- Quotation marks are used to indicate Salleh's exact words in the first and third extracts.

2. Go back to the news report and look for all the verbs that indicate Salleh's words. Write them.

3. Match the columns.

a. In direct speech,
b. In indirect (or reported) speech,

- we report what the speaker says, but not using exactly the same words.
- we quote the speaker's exact words and use quotation marks.

For more information about Direct and Indirect Speech, go to Language Reference, pages 183 to 185.

4. Read the reported statements below and copy their corresponding quotes from the text on page 95 in your notebook. Pay attention to the changes and reporting verbs in bold.

a. Salleh **argued** that the issue of false information **had** recently **taken** centre stage in the media, especially online news portals.

b. Salleh **said** that at **that** point of time, although it **was** possible for authorities to restrict access or block such applications, they **would** not do so to the majority of social media users.

Social Media and False News **Unit 6** 99

c. He **added** that did not mean, however, that the public **could** post unchecked information without respect or regard to the law.

d. He **explained** that, for instance, in 2014, approximately 78 percent of MCMC's requests for removal of content **had been acted** upon by social media providers, with *Facebook* acting upon approximately 81 percent of MCMC's requests.

> Assim como em português, em inglês geralmente há mudanças de tempos verbais, pronomes e expressões de tempo e lugar quando passamos do discurso direto para o indireto.

5. Read the text and write DS for direct speech or IS for indirect speech.

Facebook blocks messages promoting terrorist propaganda

By IANS on Dec 18, 2015 at 4:57 PM

Facebook blocks a million messages every week that promote terrorism or radical ideologies, said executive director of UN Counter-Terrorism Committee Jean-Paul Laborde. "We must learn to move through social networks at the same speed or faster than terrorist organisations," Efe quoted Laborde as saying on Thursday. ♦

He said this while addressing a meeting on balance between protecting citizens and maintaining their online privacy, which according to Laborde is "a great challenge" for law enforcement, civil society and private companies.

"We must find the balance between ensuring freedom and privacy online, but at the same time it is necessary to protect the lives of all citizens of the world," said Laborde. ♦ "One area in which we must first defeat terrorist organisations such as Islamic State is the Internet and social networks," he added. ♦

To achieve these goals new relationships and connections must be forged between civil society, UN members and private enterprises like Facebook, Google, Microsoft and Twitter that control exchange of information online.

"Private companies do not want to look like the bad guy and are doing much to help," said Laborde ♦ and added YouTube cancelled at least 14 million videos of terrorist propaganda in the last two years. ♦

Adapted from <www.bgr.in/news/facebook-blocks-messages-promoting-terrorist-propaganda/>. Accessed on December 19, 2015.

EFE: Agência Espanhola de notícias (www.efe.com/efe/espana/1)
IANS: Indo-Asian News Service (www.ians.in)

organisations (UK)
organizations (US)

Unit 6 Social Media and False News

6. Change the verb forms to report the quotes.

a. "The Internet has been a boon and a curse for teenagers." (J. K. Rowling, English author)

Adapted from <www.brainyquote.com/quotes/quotes/j/jkrowlin462714.html>.
Accessed on December 19, 2015.

J. K. Rowling said that the Internet ♦ a boon and a curse for teenagers.

b. "I have one major problem with the Internet: It's full of liars." (John Lydon, English musician)

Extracted from <www.brainyquote.com/quotes/quotes/j/johnlydon526235.html#9MfIzRlo6jB3W8Rf.99>. Accessed on December 19, 2015.

John Lydon said that he ♦ one major problem with the Internet: It ♦ full of liars.

c. "Reclassifying the Internet as a telecommunications service will have dangerous repercussions for years to come." (Marsha Blackburn, American politician)

Extracted from <www.brainyquote.com/quotes/quotes/m/marshablac721336.html#WxprpHe3jmlsRuaf.99>. Accessed on December 19, 2015.

Marsha Blackburn said that reclassifying the Internet as a telecommunications service ♦ dangerous repercussions for years to come.

7. Complete the table as you read the passage below.

Jackie Chan slams death hoax; says 'I'm still alive'

By Indo-Asian News Service on May 18, 2015 at 7:00 PM

Hong Kong, May 18: International film star Jackie Chan, with roots in China, became a victim of an internet death hoax. But the martial arts expert has clarified he is very much alive. "I was shocked by two news reports when I got off the plane. First of all, don't worry! I'm still alive. Second, don't believe the scam on Weibo using my name about the Red Pockets," Chan said. "This is my official Facebook page and I only have 1 official Weibo page. Love you all," Chan, who attended the premiere of Bollywood superstar Aamir Khan's movie "PK" in China last week, tweeted on Saturday. [...]

Extracted from <www.india.com/showbiz/jackie-chan-slams-death-hoax-says-im-still-alive-388835/>.
Accessed on December 19, 2015.

Direct Speech	Indirect Speech
"First of all, don't worry! I'm still alive."	Jackie Chan told his fans ♦ because ♦.
"Second, don't believe the scam on Weibo using my name about the Red Pockets," Chan said.	Chan told his fans ♦.
"This is my official Facebook page and I only have 1 official Weibo page."	He tweeted that ♦.

WRAPPING UP

In your notebook, write down three questions about Internet rumors or scams to ask a classmate. Take notes on his/her answers and report them to the class. Don't forget to make all the necessary adjustments. Then change roles.

Social Media and False News **Unit 6** 101

LISTENING COMPREHENSION

Before Listening

1. Read this piece of news and discuss the questions as a group.

Fake news is a plague on social media

By Mark E Andersen
Sunday Sep 13, 2015. 4:15 PM HB

Fake news: It's all over the Internet. Sometimes it is easy to spot. Other times, it seems real, like when quotes from politicians fit our preconceived notions of what we think they would say in a given situation. If someone with good or nefarious intentions comes up with a meme or a well-written story, it can spread like wildfire on Facebook. This past week your social media feed may have been dotted with stories about **Led Zeppelin** getting back together to tour, the sons of **the Beatles** forming a band and going on tour, and **Scott Walker** really hating Labor Day.

Often these fake stories hide under the guise of satire. Satire is the use of humor, irony, exaggeration, ridicule, or all four to expose and criticize people's stupidity or vices, often within the context of politics and other topical issues. The stories about Led Zeppelin and the Beatles both are on websites that consider themselves satirical. Satire is hard to write. Many people, myself included, have tried and failed at it. That being said, it's easy to spot good satire when reading or watching it. *The Simpsons*, *Futurama*, and *South Park* all do — or in some cases, did — satire very well. George Orwell's *Animal Farm* is another example of satire. Fake news stories like the examples presented above are not satire. If the writers think they are, they've missed the mark.

A year ago Facebook started adding a **satire tag** to some of these hoax news stories. Unfortunately, this has not stopped the hoaxes from filling our news feeds.

[…]

Extracted from <www.dailykos.com/story/2015/9/13/1419950/-Fake-news-is-a-plague-on-social-media>.
Accessed on December 19, 2015.

- According to the author, is it always easy to identify fake news on the Internet? Why/Why not? Do you agree with him? Explain.
- What relation does Mark establish between fake stories and satire? What does he say about the writers who write stories like the ones mentioned about Led Zeppelin, the sons of the Beatles, and Scott Walker?
- What did Facebook decide to do to avoid filling the news feeds with hoax news stories? Did that help?

Listening

 2. You are going to listen to Monica Lewinsky, a former White House intern, talk about her experience as a cyberbullying victim after her affair with then-President Bill Clinton was exposed. Listen to the first part of the recording and complete the sentences below with the missing information.

a. Monica said she had an affair with her boss ♦.
b. She was ♦ old at that time.
c. Their affair lasted ♦.

 3. Now listen to the whole recording and find out if the sentences below are T (True) or F (False). Then rewrite the false ones with the correct information. Refer to the transcript on page 197 and check your answers.

a. Monica said she was already a public figure – but not as public as Bill Clinton – when they started having an affair.
b. She was the first person to have her reputation completely destroyed worldwide via the Internet.
c. She felt overjoyed when her affair was exposed the way it was.
d. Surviving was hard, but now she wants to help victims of "The Shame Game" to survive as well.

4. What do you understand from the passage below? Read it and write about it in your notebook. Use your own words. If necessary, use a dictionary to help you.

> "When I ask myself how best to describe how the last 16 years has felt, I always come back to that word: shame. That's what happened to me in 1998 when public Monica, that Monica, that woman, was born — the creature from the media lagoon. I lost my reputation. I was publicly identified as someone I didn't recognize. And I lost my sense of self, lost it, or had it stolen because in a way it was a form of identity theft."

After Listening

In pairs, read the passage below again, reflect, and talk about what Monica meant.

> "I was publicly identified as someone I didn't recognize."

SPEAKING

In groups of three, discuss the following questions.
- ✓ Why do people cyberbully?
- ✓ What are some solutions for victims of cyberbullying?
- ✓ What are the most common effects of cyberbullying?
- ✓ Is it possible to prevent cyberbullying? How?
- ✓ Do people in your school suffer from cyberbullying very often? What can you and your schoolmates do to help avoid this?

WRITING

In pairs, write an online news report.

Planning your online news report

- Decide on the topic of your news report.
- You can write about a fact that has recently happened
  - in your school;
  - in your community;
  - in your neighborhood;
  - in the city etc.
- Do some research about the fact itself and interview people who can give further information about it.
- Always aim for credible sources.
- Take notes of all relevant pieces of information.
- Organize the information in order to write a coherent news report.
- Create a captivating headline.
- Find relevant photos. They enhance the credibility of your report.

Writing and rewriting your text

- Write a draft of your online news report in your notebook.

> ### REFLECTING AND EVALUATING
>
> Go back to your online news report and make sure you have considered the questions below.
>
> ✓ Does the headline highlight one of the facts reported?
> ✓ Does the topic draw your audience's attention?
> ✓ Does the text contain detailed information about the story?
> ✓ Are there images, interviews, or quotations?
> ✓ Did you write an impartial report?
> ✓ Is your news report concise?
> ✓ Did you check punctuation and spelling?

- Reread your text before asking the teacher for correction.
- Write a clean copy making all the necessary adjustments.

After writing

- Publish your online news report on the school website or on the classroom blog.

SELF-ASSESSMENT

Chegamos ao fim da unidade 6. Convidamos você a refletir sobre seu desempenho até aqui e a responder às questões propostas abaixo, escolhendo uma das seguintes opções:

Sim.

Preciso me preparar mais.

Questões

- Você é capaz de posicionar-se criticamente em relação à veiculação de informações falsas na internet?
- Você é capaz de ler e compreender uma notícia em língua inglesa sobre a veiculação de informações falsas na internet, bem como reconhecer as características principais inerentes ao gênero?
- Você reúne conhecimentos linguístico-discursivos suficientes para produzir uma notícia em inglês, a ser veiculada eletronicamente?
- Você está preparado para escutar relatos, em língua inglesa, de vítimas de *cyberbullying*, compreender e discutir informações específicas?
- Você se julga apto a expor e fundamentar algumas sugestões que ajudem a minimizar as ocorrências desse ato na sua escola?

Refletindo sobre suas respostas

- Como você analisa a evolução do seu aprendizado em relação à unidade anterior?
- De que forma suas práticas de aprendizagem no decorrer desta unidade influenciaram suas respostas?
- O que você pode fazer para aprimorar ainda mais os conhecimentos adquiridos nesta unidade?
  - **a.** Buscar por mais informações sobre as causas do *cyberbullying* e suas consequências para as vítimas em diferentes fontes de informação.
  - **b.** Ler mais notícias em língua inglesa, a fim de aprimorar meu conhecimento sobre o assunto, bem como minha capacidade de análise crítica.
  - **c.** Aprofundar meus conhecimentos de língua inglesa, usando recursos diversos, de forma que minha participação nas atividades seja mais ativa.
  - **d.** Outros.

Social Media and False News **Unit 6** 105

Further Practice 3 – Units 5 & 6

1. Read the text and then find the paragraphs where the following information is given.

> ## Mapungubwe: SA's lost city of gold
>
> (1) One thousand years ago, Mapungubwe in Limpopo province was the centre of the largest kingdom in the subcontinent, where a highly sophisticated people traded gold and ivory with China, India and Egypt.
>
> (2) The Iron Age site, discovered in 1932 but hidden from public attention until only recently, was declared a World Heritage site by the United Nations Educational, Scientific and Cultural Organisation (Unesco) in July 2003.
>
> (3) Mapungubwe is an area of open savannah at the confluence of the Limpopo and Shashe Rivers and abutting the northern border of South Africa and the borders of Zimbabwe and Botswana. It thrived as a sophisticated trading centre from around 1220 to 1300.
>
> (4) In its statement on the listing, Unesco describes Mapungubwe as the centre of the largest kingdom in the subcontinent before it was abandoned in the 14th century.
>
> (5) "What survives are the almost untouched remains of the palace sites and also the entire settlement area dependent upon them, as well as two earlier capital sites, the whole presenting an unrivalled picture of the development of social and political structures over some 400 years," Unesco said.
>
> (6) Mapungubwe was home to an advanced culture of people for the time — the ancestors of the Shona people of Zimbabwe. They traded with China and India, had a flourishing agricultural industry, and grew to a population of around 5,000.
>
> (7) Mapungubwe is probably the earliest known site in southern Africa where evidence of a class-based society existed (Mapungubwe's leaders were separated from the rest of the inhabitants).
>
> [...]

centre (UK)
center (US)

Adapted from <www.southafrica.info/about/history/mapungubwe.htm#.VnAThhp97v0#ixzz3uWXpmoGA>.
Accessed on December 24, 2015.

a. Mapungubwe's geographic characteristics

b. The year the Iron Age site was discovered

c. Population of the old Mapungubwe civilization

d. The century Mapungubwe was abandoned

2. Identify the only sentence we can't infer from the text.

a. The people who lived in Mapungubwe were traders.

b. There are enough remains to teach us about its social development and its political structures.

c. The Iron Age site was hidden because authorities were afraid of damage caused by tourism.

d. The decline of this civilization started in the 14th century.

3. Answer the questions below.
a. In your opinion, why would a place like Mapungubwe be listed as a World Heritage site?
b. What is the purpose of Unesco in declaring a place as World Heritage?
c. There are many places in Brazil and around the world which are listed as World Heritage sites. Exchange ideas with a classmate and list some examples that come to your mind.

4. Read the poster below and write T (True), F (False), or NM (Not Mentioned).

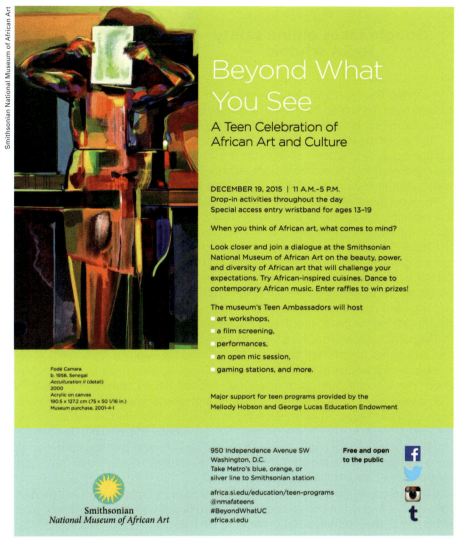

Extracted from <africa.si.edu/>. Accessed on December 24, 2015.

a. People who attend this event will be able to try African-inspired food.

b. The museum offers a special ticket price for teens between 13 and 19 years old.

c. The Smithsonian National Museum of African Art wants to defy people's previous ideas about African art.

d. The museum will offer the opportunity to dance traditional African music.

e. African artists will present their artwork to the audience.

5. Discuss the questions below with a classmate. Then share your views with the whole class.

a. What comes to your mind when you think of African art? Explain your answer.

b. Do you know any museums dedicated exclusively to the African influence on Brazilian culture? If so, which ones? If not, would you like to visit one? In your opinion, why is it important to have such institutions in our country?

Further Practice 3 – Units 5 & 6

6. Read the following news report and check the sentence that best expresses its message.

Google takes online safety to SA schools

Phindile Chauke

Yesterday Google South Africa began offering Internet safety workshops to children in public schools as part of its Online Child Safety campaign.

The first of the workshops aimed at eradicating child pornography and other risks on the Internet were conducted with pupils from Jules, Anchor Comprehensive, Vuwani, Diepdale and Emshukantambo secondary schools in Gauteng yesterday.

The workshops were kick-started at Jules Secondary School in Jeppestown, east of Johannesburg, where several pupils filmed the alleged rape of a 8th-grade girl by two other boys on the school grounds using cellphones and distributed the footage four years ago.

Google SA Public Policy Manager Fortune Mgwili-Sibanda said: "While the emphasis is on the great benefits of the Internet, the workshops promote digital literacy. They are interactive. We get the children to create things, like an app (application), what to do when they encounter problems online and how to deal with issues of safety."

"They also debate about anonymity online; whether it is good or bad. It is basically to improve their online experience," said Mgwili-Sibanda.

The public schools' workshops were organised in partnership with the Films and Publications Board and several government departments, including the Gauteng department of education.

Google, the world's biggest Internet search engine, also joined forces with Mxit, a social network for school children with cellphones, and the Nelson Mandela Children's Fund.

The workshops were extended to parents and teachers, who are expected to monitor the children's activities. "It is not enough for parents to buy Internet enabled cellphones – they must have access to the devices and monitor them," Mgwili-Sibanda said.

"There is a need for digital literacy in public schools, and with the education department having distributed some tablets in schools, this is the right time to make the children aware of the power of the Internet."

Gauteng department of education MEC (Member of Executive Council) Barbara Creecy said: "We are happy the private sector has joined hands with the government to ensure children enjoy the Internet, while minimising the risks."

Georges Gobet/AFP Photo

minimising (UK)
minimizing (US)

Adapted from <citizen.co.za/126160/google-takes-online-safety-to-sa-schools/>.
Accessed on December 25, 2015.

a. Google South Africa and local government departments are doing their best to eradicate child pornography and other risks on the Internet.

b. Google South Africa is doing its best efforts to eradicate child pornography and other risks on the Internet, but local government departments declared they could not help.

c. Google South Africa is developing children's literacy in private schools.

7. Answer the questions that follow.

a. Are the workshops that Google South Africa is offering helpful? Why/Why not?

b. Would they be effective in your community? Justify your answer.

c. Have you ever participated in a workshop like the ones mentioned in the news report? If so, which one? If not, would you like to? Why/Why not?

8. Read the passage extracted from the news report and answer the *wh-questions*.

> "Yesterday Google South Africa began offering Internet safety workshops to children in public schools as part of its Online Child Safety campaign."

Who?   When?   What?   Where?

9. Go back to the news report in the previous page, read the passages in quotation marks again and answer: what do they represent?

10. Read Barbara Creecy's quote again and choose the alternative which correctly reports what she says.

> "We are happy the private sector has joined hands with the government to ensure children enjoy the Internet, while minimising the risks."

a. Barbara Creecy says that they were happy the private sector has joined hands with the government to ensure children enjoy the Internet, while minimising the risks.

b. Barbara Creecy said that they were happy the private sector joined hands with the government to ensure children enjoy the Internet, while minimising the risks.

c. Barbara Creecy said that they were happy the private sector had joined hands with the government to ensure children enjoyed the Internet, while minimising the risks.

11. Which text best corresponds to the cartoon below?

a. Do you swear to tell the truth based on your beliefs that everything you read on the Internet is true?

b. If you lie in court, I will sue you.

c. Is everything that you have said here true?

12. Read the definitions of troll. Then read the cartoon and answer the questions that follow.

- an imaginary, either very large or very small creature in traditional Scandinavian stories, that has magical powers and lives in mountains or caves
- someone who leaves an intentionally annoying message on the internet, in order to get attention or cause trouble

Extracted from <dictionary.cambridge.org/dictionary/english/troll>
Accessed on February 11, 2016.

Further Practice 3 – Units 5 & 6

"Why do I always get un-friended? I'm a nice troll."

a. What is the relationship between the definitions and the cartoon? Justify your answer.

b. Is the character really a nice troll? Why?

13. Read part of an editorial about the app YIK Yak and then answer the questions.

> **Editorial: Anonymous platforms for cyberbullies hurt our kids**
> By Dylan Thorne
> 10:01 AM Saturday May 23, 2015
>
> YIK Yak. It sounds benign, if a little childish. But this smartphone app is causing concern across the world.
>
> The app works on a geographic basis, like a giant message board. It allows students to post comments anonymously, and only those within a 16km radius can see what's happening.
>
> They can then "up vote" or "down vote" comments. If a comment, or "yak", gets many up votes, it gets a high score, rewarding the user with "yakarma". Messages can also be commented on, starting a thread of conversation.
>
> It promises a place where you can "share your thoughts and keep your privacy" – via a social media network.
>
> It doesn't take a rocket scientist, or a programmer for that matter, to figure out that "sharing thoughts" and "anonymous" are a bad combination. […]

Adapted from <www.nzherald.co.nz/bay-of-plenty-times/news/article.cfm?c_id=1503343&objectid=11453564>.
Accessed on December 16, 2015.

a. What kind of app is YIK Yak?

b. Why is the app causing concern across the world? Is there a real reason for such a concern? Explain your views.

14. Read the following extract from the Indian newspaper *The Telegraph* and discuss the following questions with a classmate.

> "[…] harassment on social networking sites is emerging as one of the biggest problems in the online world. Six out of 10 people aren't aware of what constitutes a cybercrime. As a result they aren't reported. Neither the victims nor the abusers know what an offence is."

offence (UK)
offense (US)

Adapted from <www.telegraphindia.com/1120104/jsp/opinion/story_14959931.jsp#.VnwevZN97v0>.
Accessed on December 25, 2016.

a. Do you agree that most bullies don't know that they commit a crime when they offend someone? Justify your answer.

b. Why aren't cybercrimes reported most of the time? Would you report the crime if you were a victim?

EXAM PRACTICE

People Consume Facebook Conspiracy Theories as Real News

By Phi Tran

Aug 14, 2014 – 02:35 PM

Differentiating between real and fake stories on social media can be a challenge for the uninitiated, especially when conspiracy theories and lies can spread farther than news from traditional sources.

The World Economic Forum listed massive digital misinformation as one of the main risks for modern society because, even if the lifetime of false information is short and it is generally unlikely to result in severe real-world consequences, it is conceivable that a false rumor spreading virally through social networks might impact the public opinion before being effectively corrected.

In a recent study from Cornell University, 270,000 Facebook posts from 73 different Facebook pages were analyzed and showed just how easy conspiracy stories spread. Of the 270,000 posts, only 60,000 came from mainstream scientific sources while 200,000 came from alternative conspiracy news. Moreover, the conspiracy news also received much more "likes" than their counterpart. Alternative stories got 6.5 million likes while science sources received 2.5 million likes.

[…]

Extracted from: <www.adweek.com/socialtimes/facebook-real-news-vs-conspiracy-theories/202992>.
Accessed on December 15, 2015.

Considere as seguintes afirmações sobre o texto e responda se as afirmativas são verdadeiras ou falsas.

I. Os usuários de mídias sociais não se esforçam para diferenciar uma notícia falsa de uma verdadeira.

II. Embora a vida útil de uma notícia falsa seja curta, a desinformação é um dos maiores problemas da sociedade moderna.

III. Redes sociais são terrenos férteis para a disseminação de boatos.

   a. F, V, V

   b. F, F, V

   c. F, F, V

   d. F, V, F

   e. V, V, V

UNIT 7

MANAGING YOUR MONEY

Nesta unidade você terá oportunidade de:

- refletir e discutir a importância de administrar recursos e planejar as finanças de maneira racional, bem como da inserção de aulas de educação financeira no currículo escolar;

- reconhecer os objetivos e algumas características das fábulas e escrever uma;

- compreender o áudio de um vídeo sobre um programa australiano de educação financeira;

- entrevistar os colegas de sala sobre hábitos relacionados ao uso do dinheiro no cotidiano.

- O que podemos ver na imagem?

- Estabelecendo uma relação entre a imagem e o título da unidade, de que forma você acredita que a unidade poderá contribuir no seu cotidiano?

STARTING OUT

 Geography
Math

1. Work in pairs. Read the map extracted from the infographic *Cost of Living Around the World* and answer the questions in your notebook.

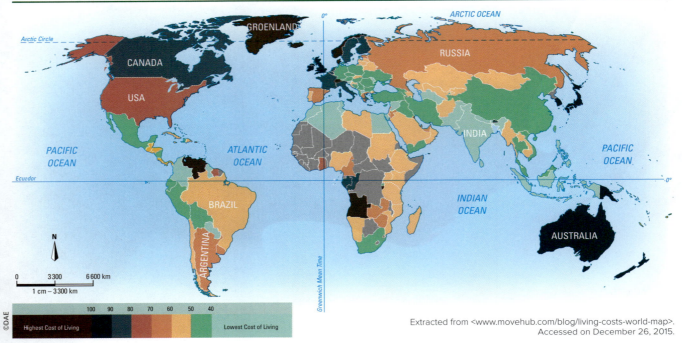

Extracted from <www.movehub.com/blog/living-costs-world-map>.
Accessed on December 26, 2015.

   a. Which are the countries with the highest cost of living?

   b. Which are the cheapest countries to live?

   c. What is the cost of living like in Brazil according to the map?

   d. What is the relation between the cost of living and a person's quality of life? Why/Why not?

   e. Would you like to live in a country with a higher cost of living? Why/Why not?

   f. What are the advantages and disadvantages of living in a place with a very low cost of living?

   g. How does your family usually plan how it spends money?

   h. Some people say that "money makes the world go round." Do you agree with this old saying? Why/Why not?

2. Relate the old saying below to your answers in activity 1.

   > "An investment in knowledge pays the best interest."
   > (Benjamin Franklin, American statesman and diplomat)

   Extracted from <www.forbes.com/sites/robertberger/2014/04/30/top-100-money-quotes-of-all-time/#5614b0e0675e>. Accessed on June 5, 2016.

3. Learning how to use money wisely has been a challenge since early times and many stories from antiquity till now teach lessons on personal finances. Think about the usefulness of those stories, talk to a classmate, and share your opinions with the whole class.

READING COMPREHENSION

Before Reading

1. Skim the following narrative and pay attention to the characters in the story. Then answer orally: what do the characters have in common?

Reading

The Money-Box

In a nursery where a number of toys lay scattered about, a money-box stood on the top of a very high wardrobe. It was made of clay in the shape of a pig, and had been bought from a potter. In the back of the pig was a slit, and this slit had been enlarged with a knife, so that dollars, or crown pieces, might slip through; and, indeed there were two in the box, besides a number of pence. The money-pig was stuffed so full that it could no longer rattle, which is the highest state of perfection to which a money-pig can attain. There he stood upon the cupboard, high and lofty, looking down upon everything else in the room. He knew very well that he had enough inside him to buy up all the other toys, and this gave him a very good opinion of his own value. The rest thought of this fact also, although they did not express it, for there were so many other things to talk about. A large doll, still handsome, though rather old for her neck had been mended, lay inside one of the drawers which was partly open. She called out to the others, "Let us have a game at being men and women, which is something worth playing."

Upon this there was a great uproar; even the engravings, which hung in frames on the wall, turned round in their excitement, and showed that they had a wrong side to them, although they did not have the least intention of exposing themselves in this way, or objecting to the game. It was late at night, but as the moon shone through the windows, they had light at a cheap rate. And as the game was now to begin, all were invited to take part in it, even the children's wagon, which certainly belonged to the coarser playthings. "Each has its own value," said the wagon. "We cannot all be noblemen; there must be some to do the work."

The money-pig was the only one who received a written invitation. He stood so high that they were afraid he would not accept a verbal message. But in his reply, he said, if he had to take a part, he must enjoy the sport from his own home. They were to arrange for him to do so; and so they did. The little toy theatre was therefore put up in such a way that the money-pig could look directly into it. Some wanted to begin with a comedy, and afterwards to have a tea party and a discussion for mental improvement, but they commenced with the latter first. The rocking-horse spoke of training and races; the wagon of railways and steam power, for these subjects belonged to each of their professions, and it was right they should talk of them. The clock talked politics – "Tick, tick;" he professed to know what was the time of day, but there was a whisper that he did not go correctly. The bamboo cane stood by, looking stiff and proud: he was vain of his brass ferrule and silver top, and on the sofa lay two worked cushions, pretty but stupid. When the play at the little theatre began, the rest sat and looked on; they were requested to applaud and stamp, or crack, when they felt gratified with what they saw. But the riding-whip said he never cracked for old people, only for the young who were not yet married. "I crack for everybody," said the cracker.

"Yes, and a fine noise you make," thought the audience, as the play went on.

It was not worth much, but it was very well played, and all the characters turned their painted sides to the audience, for they were made only to be seen on one side. The acting was wonderful, excepting that sometimes they came out beyond the lamps, because the wires were a little too long. The doll, whose neck had been darned, was so excited that the place in her neck burst, and the money-pig declared he must do something for one of the players, as they had all pleased him so much. So he made up his mind to remember one of them in his will, as the one to be buried with him in the family vault, whenever that event should happen. They all enjoyed the comedy so much that they gave up all thoughts of the tea party, and only carried out their idea of intellectual amusement, which they called playing at men and women; and there was nothing wrong about it, for it was only play. All the while, each one thought most of himself, or of what the money-pig could be thinking. His thoughts were on, as he supposed, a very distant time — of making his will, and of his burial, and of when it might all come to pass. Certainly sooner than he expected — for all at once down he came from the top of the press, fell on the ground, and was broken to pieces. Then the pennies hopped and danced about in the most amusing manner. The little ones twirled round like tops, and the large ones rolled away as far as they could, especially the one great silver crown piece who often had to go out into the world, and now he had his wish as well as all the rest of the money. The pieces of the money-pig were thrown into the dust-bin, and the next day there stood a new money-pig on the cupboard, but it did not have a farthing in its inside yet, and therefore, like the old one, it could not rattle. This was the beginning with him, and we will make it the end of our story.

Adapted from <www.aesopfables.com/cgi/aesop1.cgi?hca&a58>. Accessed on December 21, 2015.

2. Which is the only sentence we can't infer from the text?

   a. The money-pig is aware of his privileged position.

   b. The toys show the money-pig some respect.

   c. All the toys and objects are as arrogant as the money-pig.

   d. The acting wasn't perfect, but the play was great.

   e. The narrator of this story is not one of its characters.

3. Read the passages below and complete the sentences.

   > "[…] he stood upon the cupboard, high and lofty, looking down upon everything else in the room."
   >
   > "[…] he said, if he had to take a part, he must enjoy the sport from his own home. […]"
   >
   > "[…] he made up his mind to remember one of them in his will, as the one to be buried with him in the family vault, […]"

   a. The character these passages refer to is the ♦.

   b. The passages are examples of ♦.

4. Based on the fable, answer the questions that follow.

   a. The money-pig couldn't rattle because he was full of coins. The new money-pig couldn't rattle either, but for a different reason. What is that reason?

   b. Fables usually teach a life lesson. Which lesson did you learn from this fable?

5. Read the definition below and answer the question that follows.

> **Anthropomorphism** is the attribution of human characteristics and qualities to non-human beings, objects, natural or supernatural phenomena. [...]

Extracted from <www.newworldencyclopedia.org/entry/Anthropomorphism>. Accessed on December 24, 2015.

Which passages from the text present anthropomorphism?

a. "The rest thought of this fact also, although they did not express it, [...]".

b. "A large doll, still handsome, though rather old, for her neck had been mended, lay inside one of the drawers which was partly open."

c. "[...] even the engravings, which hung in frames on the wall, turned round in their excitement, [...]".

d. "The acting was wonderful, [...]".

6. Go back to the text once again, find more examples of anthropomorphism, and write them in your notebook.

7. Talk to a classmate and answer the questions.

a. Do you think fables are interesting and meaningful to readers of all ages? Justify your answer.

b. In ancient times, fables were only transmitted orally. Cordel literature, myths, folktales, legends, proverbs, and chants are examples of Brazilian oral literature. How important are these kinds of literature to the culture of a country?

8. Identify some characteristics of fables.

a. The characters can be animated or inanimate. They present human traits.

b. The characters have fully developed personalities.

c. The plot is very complex and the events aren't in chronological structure.

d. The moral is implied or stated for social or personal benefit.

e. Fables are fictional narratives in the sense that they did not really happen.

f. Readers are led to consider how the moral might apply to their lives.

g. The setting is usually uncertain.

After Reading

- As we have noticed in the fable *The Money-Box*, not everyone knows how to deal with money. Do you know how to deal with money wisely? Would you like to improve your financial education? Explain your answer.

- How important is setting a goal for saving money to achieve something you really want for the future?

- According to the *SCPC (Serviço Central de Proteção ao Crédito)*, about 6.3 million young Brazilians between 18 and 24 years old are in debt. What can you do to avoid being included in this statistic?

Managing Your Money **Unit 7**   117

VOCABULARY STUDY

1. Read the extracts from the fable on pages 115 and 116 and find out the correct meanings of the phrasal verbs in bold.

   a. "There he stood upon the cupboard, high and lofty, **looking down upon** everything else in the room."
   - admiring and respecting
   - regarding with disdain

   b. "The little toy theatre was therefore **put up** in such a way that the money-pig could look directly into it."
   - extinguished
   - arranged

   c. "They all enjoyed the comedy so much that they **gave up** all thoughts of the tea party, and only **carried out** their idea of intellectual amusement, which they called playing at men and women; and there was nothing wrong about it, for it was only play."
   - desisted from / put into practice
   - investigated / banned

2. According to the *Oxford Advanced Learner's Dictionary*, an idiom is "a group of words whose meaning is different from the meanings of the individual words". Refer back to the fable on pages 115 and 116 and look for the idiom whose meaning is *came to a decision*.

   > **TIP**
   >
   > Aprender expressões idiomáticas (*idioms*) é importante porque tais expressões tornam a língua falada mais informal e natural. Mas lembre-se de que não devemos traduzi-las ao pé da letra, pois seus significados nunca são literais.

3. The idioms listed in the chart are all related to money. Use an English-English dictionary to look for their meanings and write them in your notebook. Then use two of them to complete the cartoons, making any necessary adjustments.

Idioms	Definitions
bring home the bacon	♦
chicken feed	♦
cost an arm and a leg	♦
go Dutch	♦
nest egg	♦

a.

"Yes, it is a nice ship but it ♦ me ♦."

Extracted from <www.cartoonstock.com/directory/e/expensive_ship.asp>. Accessed on December 26, 2015.

b.

"When I was a girl my father ♦. Now we both work just to afford eggs."

Extracted from <www.jantoo.com/cartoons/keywords/bringing-home-the-bacon>. Accessed on December 26, 2015.

LANGUAGE IN CONTEXT

Reflexive Pronouns

1. Read the extracts from the fable on pages 115 and 116 and find out what the words in bold refer to. Then choose the correct words or expressions in parentheses to complete the sentences.

> "Upon this there was a great uproar; even the engravings, which hung in frames on the wall, turned round in their excitement, and showed that they had a wrong side to them, although they did not have the least intention of exposing **themselves** in this way, or objecting to the game."

> "All the while, each one thought most of **himself**, or of what the money-pig could be thinking."

a. When the object is ♦ (the same as / different from) the subject, we use reflexive pronouns such as *themselves* and *himself* in the extracts above.

b. Singular reflexive pronouns end in ♦ (-selves / -self) and plural reflexive pronouns end in ♦ (-selves / -self).

For more information about Reflexive Pronouns, go to Language Reference, pages 187 and 188.

2. Read the passages below and look for reflexive pronouns. After that, write them in your notebook.

a.

8 Tips for Dealing with Debt Collectors
March 7th, 2016

Sure, we all want to be able to manage our finances properly. But when things get out of control, you may have to prepare yourself for dealing with debt collectors.
So today I have 8 important tips for what to do when you're in collection.
[…]

Extracted from <blog.101financial.com/8-tips-for-dealing-with-debt-collectors/>. Accessed on March 10, 2016.

b.

Success Story of the Week – Krystle Silva
February 22nd, 2016

[…]
When the economy crashed in 2010, our life shifted with loss of income. We started to drown in our bills. We couldn't pay our mortgage for 10 months and our car got repossessed. After consulting with those who have experience in chapter 7 bankruptcy, we decided to file. It was hoped this would give us a fresh start and pull ourselves up from the bottom.
In 2015, I told myself, "with every New Year comes a New Year resolution", so I was ready to make another change. A friend of mine told me about a program called 101 Financial. The presentation piqued my interest, and I was referred to an instructor from the program. I was in awe with how the program could save my life. I was eager to get started and learn more about it.
[…]

Adapted from <blog.101financial.com/success-story-of-the-week-krystle-silva/>. Accessed on March 10, 2016.

3. Use reflexive pronouns to complete these fables. Then find the words the reflexive pronouns refer to.

a.

The Miser

An old man sells all of his goods for a large lump of gold, which he then proceeds to bury in a hole just outside his property. Every day he visits the spot, uncovering the gold, looking at it for a bit, then covering it back up.

One of the man's employees notices this odd behavior and follows the old man. He sees the buried gold, and when the old man returns home, the employee removes the gold and runs away with it.

The next day the old man finds that his gold is missing and cries out in agony. A neighbor hears the old man's story and suggests that he place a rock in the hole and cover it back up. "It makes no difference, does it? You didn't do anything with the gold anyway."

The lesson: Working hard is great. Making money is great. Saving money is fine. But money ♦ is nothing more than pieces of paper or lumps of minerals. Don't forget that money's true purpose is in service of a happy, healthy life. The size of the lump doesn't make much difference if you don't know how to use it to feel fulfilled.

Adapted from <www.moneymanagement.org/Community/Blogs/Blogging-for-Change/2014/July/Important-money-lessons-from-classic-fables. aspx>. Accessed on December 26, 2015.

b.

The One-Eyed Doe

There was once a doe who had lost an eye. She grazed near the sea, with her good eye towards the land, and her missing eye towards the shore. She did this to protect ♦, feeling that she could see danger coming sooner if she kept her good eye pointed towards the fields and the forest. One day, however, a pair of boatmen was floating nearby and saw the doe grazing. They steered their little boat closer and closer until they were close enough to use a bow and arrow and shoot the doe, who never saw them coming because she was so focused on the fields and forest.

The lesson: Don't overcompensate. That's probably not the lesson you took from this fable initially, but I think the doe's downfall has a lot to do with her becoming so focused on her own shortcomings. She could only see out of one eye and she became so hung-up on that limitation that she overcompensated, thinking she could only be safe if she kept her good eye to the fields, forgetting that danger comes from all sides and not trusting in her own ability to keep ♦ safe. If you've made mistakes with money, do ♦ a favor – don't get hung up on what's gone wrong before. Don't become so focused on what you think you can't do well that everything else suffers as a result. Because just like the doe, you're more capable than you think you are.

Adapted from <www.moneymanagement.org/Community/Blogs/Blogging-for-Change/2014/July/Important-money-lessons-from-classic-fables. aspx>. Accessed on December 26, 2015.

Passive Voice III

4. Read another extract from *The Money-Box* and write AV for Active Voice or PV for Passive Voice.

"The doll, whose neck **had been darned** ♦, was so excited that the place in her neck burst, and the money-pig declared he must do something for one of the players, as they **had** all **pleased** ♦ him so much."

> Lembre-se de que a voz passiva é formada pelo verbo *to be* no mesmo tempo verbal do verbo principal da frase correspondente na voz ativa, seguido pelo particípio passado desse mesmo verbo.

For more information about the Passive Voice, go to Language Reference, page 189.

120 **Unit 7** Managing Your Money

5. Change part of the extract from activity 4 into the Passive Voice.

> The doll, whose neck had been darned, was so excited that the place in her neck burst, and the money-pig declared he must do something for one of the players, as ◆ so much by them all.

6. Identify three other Past Perfect Passive Voice statements in the text on pages 115 and 116 and copy them in your notebook.

7. Complete the following fable with the verb forms from the box.

> had been played   killed   was going to throw

The Goose with the Golden Eggs

One day a countryman going to the nest of his Goose found there an egg all yellow and glittering. When he took it up it was as heavy as lead and he ◆ it away, because he thought a trick ◆ upon him. But he took it home on second thoughts, and soon found to his delight that it was an egg of pure gold. Every morning the same thing occurred, and he soon became rich by selling his eggs. As he grew rich he grew greedy; and thinking to get at once all the gold the Goose could give, he ◆ it and opened it only to find nothing.

Greed oft o'er reaches itself.

Extracted from <www.aesopfables.com/cgi/aesop1.cgi?sel&TheGooseWiththeGoldenEggs>.
Accessed on December 27, 2015.

8. Read the joke below and rewrite the sentence in bold in the Passive Voice.

Money Line

Pulling into my service station 45 minutes late one morning, I shouted to the customers, "I'll turn the pumps on right away!" What I didn't know was that **the night crew had left them on all night**. By the time I got to the office, most of the cars had filled up and driven off. Only one customer stayed to pay. My heart sank. Then the customer pulled a wad of cash from his pocket and handed it to me.

"We kept passing the money to the last guy," he said. "We figured you'd get here sooner or later."

Extracted from <www.rd.com/joke/money-line-joke/>. Accessed on December 27, 2015.

WRAPPING UP

In pairs, think about the situation below and answer the question. Then report and justify your answer to your classmates and listen to their answers as well.

Suppose you **had been given** a large amount of money at the end of last year. Would you have spent it on **yourself** or would you have saved it for future use?

Managing Your Money **Unit 7** 121

LISTENING COMPREHENSION

Before Listening

1. Read the text below and discuss the questions that follow with the class.

   realised (UK)
   realized (US)

   > Financial literacy education (FLE) has become a global priority. In Australia, FLE has been added to the primary and secondary school curriculum. Teachers now have the added responsibility of educating students after receiving some form of professional development. Of concern is how teachers are being financially educated and supported to teach FLE critically and effectively. We find that more is needed to guide, educate and support educators in this area with clearer policy objectives, improved professional development and program evaluation required. Without a more robust and evidenced based approach we fear the policy intentions of FLE in schools may not be realised.
   > […]

   Extracted from <www98.griffith.edu.au/dspace/bitstream/handle/10072/64067/97677_1.pdf?sequence=1>. Accessed on December 26, 2015.

   - Together with some other countries around the world, Australia has added financial literacy education to the school curriculum. What exactly do you think these schools will teach their students? Does a financial literacy class really help young learners with the skills they need to manage their money? Explain.
   - Are Brazilian schools doing the same? What have you heard about it?
   - Do you have FLE classes at your school? If so, how do they help you and your classmates? If not, would you like to have them? Why/ Why not? Justify your answers.
   - Do you think these lessons should be taught to primary, secondary or high school students? Why? How would each of them benefit from FLE lessons?

Listening

2. MoneySmart is a website run by the Australian Securities and Investments Commission (ASIC) that helps people make the most of their money. It has a program called MoneySmart Teaching, which is the only Australian Government consumer and financial literacy program for primary and secondary students and teachers. This program teaches young people five basic financial principles: planning, saving, spending, investing, and donating. Listen to the video recording *Why should schools be MoneySmart?* and answer: In what situations do kids interact with money at school? Check your answers with a classmate.

3. Listen to the video recording again and answer these questions.
   a. According to one of the speakers, how old are children when they start learning about money?
   b. What happens if we talk to children about money and good money management?
   c. Do kids enjoy learning about financial literacy?
   d. Does the whole school community benefit when kids are finally literate or are the children the only ones who take advantage of this?

After Listening

Do all the speakers have the same views on financial literacy as part of the school curriculum? How would you sum up their views? Refer to the transcript on page 198 and check your answers. Then think: is there anything you left out when summarizing the speakers' views? What?

> **PRONUNCIATION PRACTICE**
>
> Pay attention to the pronunciation of /m/ and /n/ at the end of these words.
>
>   from   curriculum   children   even
>
> Now listen and repeat these words.
>
>   from   curriculum   them   program   team
>   children   even   then   canteen   learn

SPEAKING

Below you will find an extract of the news article *High school students' money skills tested*, published in September 2015 on *Newshub*, the New Zealand television, Internet and radio news service of TV3. Read this extract, do some research with your classmates about the issues mentioned in the article, and share the results with the whole group.

> [...]
> **Using money**
> The research found that nearly 90 percent of students have a bank account and 60 percent have EFTPOS cards.
> About half of the students use Internet banking, and about 20 percent have used telephone banking.
> Cash is still the most common way of making a purchase.
> About a third of students frequently or sometimes use a credit card.
>
> **Ways of earning money**
> The most common way of earning money is doing jobs at home, or working at a part-time job. Pocket money and gifts of money are common.
> About 60 percent of students have sold possessions for money at some time. Seven percent say they do this regularly.
>
> **Saving money**
> Fifty-one percent of students regularly save, and another 37 percent sometimes save. The main way to save is through a bank account (71 percent), but 57 percent say they keep their money in a safe place.
> Borrowing is common – 67 percent have borrowed money and 79 percent have loaned money. The researchers say it is likely that these are "small, short-term transactions with family or peers".
> Eighty-eight percent of students agree it is okay to borrow money if they can pay it back and 79 percent believe it is important to get advice about borrowing money.
>
> Adapted from <www.newshub.co.nz/business/high-school-students-money-skills-tested-2015090307#axzz3vW925J1x>.
> Accessed on March 8, 2016.

EFTPOS

(*electronic funds transfer at point of sale*) significa transferência eletrônica de fundos no ponto de venda, ou seja, são as conhecidas maquininhas de cartão.

WRITING

In pairs, write a fable on money issues. Follow the steps below.

Planning your fable

- Think of the problem of your fable.

- Decide on the steps of the plot.

- Choose the moral of your fable.

- Discuss characters, setting, and the events.

- Don't aim for complex chararacters.

- Think of the ending. You can decide if the problem gets solved or not.

- Finally, choose a title for your fable.

- Take notes of all the decisions you and your classmate have made.

REFLECTING AND EVALUATING

Go back to your fable and make sure you paid attention to the following topics:

✓ Did you choose a life lesson as the moral?

✓ Are the characters animals, elements of nature, or objects?

✓ Do the characters have human qualities?

✓ Is the teaching of your fable clear enough?

✓ Did you choose appropriate setting?

Writing and rewriting your text

- Write a draft of your text in your notebook.
- Read your fable once again and ask the teacher for correction.
- Write a clean copy making all the necessary adjustments.

After writing

- Along with your classmates, plan a dramatic reading of the fables to present to the school students.
- Alternatively, exchange the fables among classmates, read them, and vote for the most interesting, meaningful, and creative ones.
- You can publish your fable on the school website or post it on the school blog.

SELF-ASSESSMENT

Chegamos ao fim da unidade 7. Convidamos você a refletir sobre seu desempenho até aqui e a responder às questões propostas abaixo, escolhendo uma das seguintes opções:

> Sim.

> Preciso me preparar mais.

Questões

- Você é capaz de discutir a importância de administrar o dinheiro e de fazer um planejamento financeiro para alcançar seus objetivos?
- Você se sente capaz de ler e compreender uma fábula em língua inglesa e reconhecer as características principais inerentes ao gênero?
- Você reúne conhecimentos linguístico-discursivos suficientes para redigir uma fábula?
- Você se considera apto a escutar um programa de educação financeira e discutir sua relevância no contexto escolar?

Refletindo sobre suas respostas

- Como você analisa a evolução do seu aprendizado em relação à unidade anterior?
- De que forma suas práticas de aprendizagem no decorrer desta unidade influenciaram suas respostas?
- O que você pode fazer para aprimorar ainda mais os conhecimentos adquiridos nesta unidade?
  - **a.** Procurar por mais informações acerca de como alcançar e manter a saúde financeira.
  - **b.** Ler mais fábulas em língua inglesa para aprimorar minha compreensão sobre seus ensinamentos.
  - **c.** Aprofundar meus conhecimentos de língua inglesa, usando recursos diversos, de forma que minha participação nas atividades seja mais ativa.
  - **d.** Outros.

UNIT 8

HIGH SCHOOL IS OVER... NOW WHAT?

Nesta unidade você terá oportunidade de:

- refletir e discutir sobre os desafios, responsabilidades e obrigações que virão após a conclusão do Ensino Médio;
- reconhecer objetivos e algumas características dos discursos de formatura e escrever um;
- compreender um discurso de formatura;
- conversar com os colegas sobre os prós e contras das cerimônias de formatura.

- Que ação está representada na imagem?
- Trata-se de uma ação que representa significativamente a cultura de nosso país?
- Há alguma característica na foto que indica onde ela foi tirada?

STARTING OUT History Sociology

1. Read the texts below and answer the questions: where do you think they were extracted from? How did you figure that out? Then share your answers with the class.

   a.
   > **'We are ready ... to face what comes next'**
   > Joshua Ogden
   > Everett High School
   > Class speaker, 2011
   > When I was asked by the students of my graduating class to speak at graduation, I knew that I should probably give a typical, boring speech about how we are going to be the best class that ever graduated. Just kidding, that is what everyone asked me not to do. I would rather reflect on what has made the past four years of our lives memorable, and why we as a class are finally ready to take the next steps in our lives.
   > [...]

   Extracted from <www.heraldnet.com/section/gradspeeches?SchoolSearch=Everett%20High%20School&FirstNameSearch=Joshua&LastNameSearch=Ogden>. Accessed on December 28, 2015.

   b.
   > **'Life is about discovery'**
   > Ternessa Cao, Lakewood High School
   > Valedictorian, 2011
   > *"What lies behind us and what lies before us are tiny matters compared to what lies within us."* – Ralph Waldo Emerson.
   > From our past, we have had so many memorable moments: Ones that have made us laugh to the point where our stomachs ached, and ones that have inspired us to be who we are. I want you to remember all of your experiences at Lakewood. They are one of a kind.
   > [...]

   Extracted from <www.heraldnet.com/section/gradspeeches?SchoolSearch=Lakewood%20High%20School&FirstNameSearch=Ternessa&LastNameSearch=Cao>. Accessed on December 28, 2015.

   c.
   > **'Find that happy memory and hold onto it forever'**
   > Srishti Mathur, Bothell High School, 2015
   > Good afternoon, my fellow students of the Bothell High School class of 2015. Congratulations – we've officially made it to graduation day, the day that most of us have been dreaming of for a long, long time. To all the families here today, know that we appreciate everything that you do to support us. From roaming the halls on the first day of sophomore year to walking here today at graduation, we have each grown individually and as a community of students. The Bothell motto of "build, belong, become" has guided us all. Through our high school experience, we have learned to build our skills as students, we have found friends and communities where we feel like we belong, and we have become adults who are ready to take on the world.
   > [...]

   Extracted from <www.heraldnet.com/section/iFrame_cce_GradSpeeches?SchoolYearSearch=&SchoolSearch=Bothell%20High%20School&FirstNameSearch=Srishti&LastNameSearch=Mathur>. Accessed on December 28, 2015.

2. Read the graduation speeches again and check possible functions of these texts:

   • informative   • argumentative   • entertaining   • persuasive   • motivational

Unit 8   High School is Over... Now What?

READING COMPREHENSION

Before Reading

1. The figure of speech known as a "simile" is a stated comparison between two different things that have certain qualities in common. It is usually expressed through the use of words such as "like" or "as". Skim Megan Lee Qi Jun's graduation speech and find the simile she used to express how she felt about the transformation she went through at Pathlight School.

Reading

2. Read the graduation speech below and check the best alternatives to answer the questions.

Graduation speech

By Megan Lee Qi Jun
2013 GCE 'O' Level Graduate
Pathlight School

Good evening, everyone. I am Megan Lee, a Pathlight alumna. I graduated from Pathlight School last year, and am now waiting to enter polytechnic, where I will be pursuing a Diploma in Visual Communication and Media Design. Tonight, I will be sharing with you my experience in Pathlight School.

Before I came to Pathlight, I was in a mainstream primary school, and did not cope well in there. At that time, I could not express myself as effectively and confidently as I do now.

I was one of the quiet ones who kept mostly to themselves. Furthermore, I did not understand how to communicate with others appropriately. Therefore, I did whatever I felt like doing without considering their feelings. As a result, I faced all kinds of problems: bullying, teasing, teachers who didn't understand my condition, and even being personally targeted by some of my classmates, becoming unpopular amongst them.

The frustration of not being understood was what eventually transformed me into a blazing rebel. Rebellion was my form of protesting against the way I was treated. I hated it. I hated my school. Only a handful of teachers actually understood my condition and told the class I was 'special', and tried to help me in their own ways.

Being rebellious, I resisted their attempts to help me, so they gave up on me and went down without a fight. In Primary 4, things escalated and after numerous incidents and being sent to the Principal's office, I was expelled.

Even my own parents didn't understand my condition back then. They thought I was just a spoilt brat. When the Child Guidance Clinic recommended my parents to send me to Pathlight School, my father claimed that I was being sent there because of my bad behaviour, urging me to change so that I could get out quickly.

This misconception stayed on for a few years. I didn't understand myself, or the school that I was going to. All I knew was that my days were full of misunderstanding, frustration and misery.

When I first entered Pathlight, I felt the difference on my first day of school. My very first form teacher introduced herself to me and to the class. I made my first friends on the same day. The small classroom setting helped me to get to know my classmates personally and befriend them more easily. Furthermore, there was no more bullying or ostracism.

The flames of my rebelliousness were quelled and over the years, I settled into becoming a gentle and composed lady. It was a process of metamorphosis. I felt like I was freed from an oppressive cocoon where I had

> **TIP**
> Conhecer e identificar as figuras de linguagem presentes nos textos nos permitem interpretá-los de forma mais abrangente, atribuindo novos sentidos às palavras e expressões.

High School is Over... Now What? **Unit 8** 129

been trapped for years, to finally emerge and unfurl my wings to realise my potential. Indeed, Pathlight is a place where lives are transformed.

Pathlight teachers put in their entire heart when helping me. They took time to understand me. They believed in me. They were persistent and never gave up on me. Of course, I haven't forgotten the therapists, either. They too, played an important part in my life in counselling and guiding me.

Finally, as I prepared myself for my 'O' Levels last year, I saw that all the teachers had put in their greatest effort to secure our best for the final challenge. They helped to explain the concepts we still failed to understand and guided us when we were perplexed. On top of that, they took time to have personal consultation with us. I felt strangely calm throughout the year, unlike most 'O'-Level students. And at last, when I received my results this year, my joy was unparalleled. I had scored exceptionally well for nearly all of subjects, beyond what I could ever imagine.

As I traverse life's uncertain path, when my foot slipped into the mire, there were people who pulled me out. This imagery depicts my deepest appreciation and gratitude for those who have helped me and walked with me in my journey.

Although we have finally arrived at the crossroads, and it is time to part ways, I will never forget any of you. I will never forget those who believed in me. I will never forget those who served and made me the person I am today.

These lessons and experiences I shall carry with me as I enter polytechnic. I strive to show the world my capability and continue to be the mature and refined student that Pathlight has groomed me to be. These I shall manifest through both my studies and my character. I have bright hopes for my immediate future!

Thank you for listening to my speech. I hope that my words have inspired you and convinced you of the reality of transformation brought about by faith and patience. I am a living testimony of this.

Thank you, everyone.

Adapted from <www.pathlight.org.sg/events/2014/megan-lee-s-graduation-speech-2014>.
Accessed on December 27, 2015.

a. What was the main point of Megan Lee's speech?

- Her parents' efforts to help her overcome her problems.

- The problems she overcame and her gratitude for Pathlight School.

- The intellectual maturity she developed at Pathlight School.

b. How does Megan Lee classify herself before Pathlight School?

- An inattentive student.

- A rebellious student.

- A dynamic student.

c. Which passage best summarizes what Megan thinks about Pathlight?

- "When I first entered Pathlight, I felt the difference on my first day of school."

- "Pathlight teachers put in their entire heart when helping me."

- "[...] Pathlight is a place where lives are transformed."

3. Megan Lee says that she acted without considering people's feelings. She explains her behavior and the consequences she suffered then. What were they?

4. The sentences below express some real facts or some hypotheses related to Megan's life story. Write F (Fact) or H (Hypothesis).

  a. The teachers at her old school tried to help and understand her, but they soon gave up.

  b. Before looking for help for their daughter at the Child Guidance Clinic, Megan's parents talked to many people about her problems.

  c. Teachers from Pathlight School never gave up on Megan and taught her much more than what was in the books.

5. Refer to Megan's speech and write down one sentence that can be classified as either a fact or a hypothesis. Read it to a classmate so that he/she can classify it correctly. Change roles.

6. Answer the questions in your notebook.

  a. What happened on Megan's first day at Pathlight School? How did she feel? Do you remember your first day at school? How did you feel?

  b. Megan said that she went through a process of metamorphosis over the years at Pathlight School. How did that happen?

7. Learning is a lifetime activity. We learn new things throughout our school years that will be helpful for the rest of our lives. What are the life lessons that will remain from your student time, after you finished high school? How important are they to you?

8. Check the only sentence that does not represent a characteristic of graduation speeches.

  a. They usually present a catchy introduction in order to grab the audience's attention.

  b. They can present pieces of the author's personal experiences during school years.

  c. They provide detailed information about the speaker's plans for the future.

  d. They may present some figures of speech such as similes.

  e. The language can be formal or informal and the tone is usually friendly.

  f. Besides students, other people can deliver graduation speeches, including teachers, student's family members, or others.

9. In pairs, add one more characteristic of graduation speeches to the ones listed in the previous activity.

After Reading

- Is there anything you wish you had done differently during your school years? What exactly?

- What do you feel when you look at life beyond high school? Explain your answer.

- Considering that you are moving from one phase of your life to another in which obligations and responsibilities increase, do you think you are ready to face adulthood and what comes with it? Why?

- What are your plans for the near future?

VOCABULARY STUDY

1. Refer to the text on pages 129 and 130 and look for words to complete the explanations below. Then use two of them to complete the quotes that follow.

    a. If people are ♦, they are hard to control and do not behave in the way we expect them to.

    b. When a person is ♦, he or she is disliked by most people.

    c. To make someone leave a school or an organization is to have them ♦.

    d. If people are drawn into the ♦, they are in such a difficult situation that it is hard to escape.

    e. When people ♦ to do something, they try really hard to do that thing or to make that thing happen.

    > a. "When I first went to school, I was fighting all the time. The soldier mentality was still in me. I kept getting ♦. I found it hard to take instructions from anyone who wasn't a military commander." (Emmanuel Jal, Sudanese musician)
    >
    > Extracted from <www.brainyquote.com/quotes/quotes/e/emmanuelja554641.html?src=t_expelled >. Accessed on December 28, 2015.

    > b. "My education in the public schools of New York City between 1932 and 1944 was an excellent preparation for a life in science. Because of the Depression, these schools were able to attract a remarkably talented and dedicated collection of teachers who encouraged their students to ♦ for the highest levels of accomplishment." (Robert Fogel, American historian)
    >
    > Extracted from <www.brainyquote.com/quotes/quotes/r/robertfoge566612.html>. Accessed on April 24, 2016.

2. In "I am Megan Lee, a Pathlight alumna", the word *alumna* comes from Latin (the feminine of *alumnus*). That process of adopting words from another language into our language is called *borrowing*. Find another example of a borrowed word in the text and write it in your notebook.

    TIP
    Reconhecer os processos de formação das palavras é um passo importante para a compreensão de novos vocábulos.

3. The words listed in the table below are from Chinese, French, German, Italian, Japanese, and Spanish. Read them and write the origin in the correct space.

♦	♦	♦	♦	♦	♦
catalogue	camarilla	karaoke	feng shui	strudel	a cappella
gourmet	coyote	kimono	ketchup	kindergarten	graffiti
massage	dengue	origami	tofu	pretzel	opera
perfume	mosquito	sashimi	zen	rottweiler	novel

Unit 8 High School is Over... Now What?

LANGUAGE IN CONTEXT

Verb Tense Review

1. Read the extracts from the graduation speech on pages 129 and 130, pay attention to the verb forms in bold, and match them to what they describe.

a. "I **strive** to show the world my capability and **continue** to be the mature and refined student that Pathlight has groomed me to be."

I. Finished actions in the past

b. "I graduated from Pathlight School last year, and **am** now **waiting** to enter polytechnic,"

II. Routine actions

c. "Although we **have** finally **arrived** at the crossroads,"

III. An action that happened at an indefinite time in the past

d. "I **will** never **forget** any of you."

IV. An action that happened before the other, in the past

e. "As a result, I **faced** all kinds of problems: bullying, teasing, teachers who **didn't understand** my condition,"

V. An action in progress at the moment

f. "I **had scored** exceptionally well for nearly all of subjects, beyond what I could ever imagine."

VI. A prediction for the future

2. In the following text, look for the actions that refer to present time and the ones that refer to past time and write them in your notebook.

Australian exchange students say Chinese peers 'driven by competition'

Updated 4 Dec 2013, 9:50am

Exchange students in China and Australia say it is easy to see why China's secondary students have recently been rated among the world's smartest.

A recent OECD report found students from the Chinese city of Shanghai ranked as the world's best in maths, reading and science.

Australian teens placed equal 17th in maths, equal 10th in reading and equal 8th in science.

Year 10 student Ella Clarke, who is currently studying in central China, says students there work longer, harder and face more pressure than in Australia.

maths (UK) / math (US)

"The head teacher told the class that high school is about three things: eating, sleeping and learning," she said.

"I think that pretty much sums up the lives of these kids over here."

[...]

Extracted from <www.abc.net.au/news/2013-12-04/chinese-and-australian-education-systems-compared/5135440>. Accessed on December 29, 2015.

High School is Over... Now What? **Unit 8**   133

3. Read the beginning of Aarushi Chaturvedi's graduation speech and copy, in your notebook, the parts that provide the information requested.

Aarushi Chaturvedi

I remember the day when I first stepped through those large crimson painted gates of The Indian School, a little girl clinging to her mother's fingers as tightly as she could. There in front of her stood the Principal; her loving smile encouraged the little girl to venture into the place where she had to spend the next 14 years of her life. That little girl was none other than me.

From that day to this day I never had a cause for concern or fear about schooling. I knew I was in great hands. I feel very proud of all my achievements; I dedicate them all to my teachers and parents who have been beacons of light, guiding me to success.

As we gather here today we stand on the threshold of a new journey. We will go our separate ways, that is true, but we will forever be bound by the memories we have created together in these 14 years at The Indian School.

[…]

Adapted from <theindianschool.in/graduation-speeches/>. Accessed on December 29, 2015.

a. Two actions that started at indefinite times in the past and continue up to the present.

b. Two predictions for the future.

4. Choose the best options to complete the text below.

Exam stress: A ticking time bomb for students

Muaz Shabandri & Olivia Olarte-ulherr
Filed on March 8, 2014

[…]

Two Indian students ◆ already ◆ (did…commit / have…committed) suicide in less than a month, possibly due to exam-related stress, calling attention to the failure of school counsellors to address depression and suicidal tendencies.

[…]

Students in Indian curriculum schools ◆ (have / had) to take examinations in Grade 10 and 12 at the end of the year. These exams are seen as a stepping stone for selecting a career of choice. Parents over-emphasise performance in these board exams and in some households, cut off television connections, minimise cell-phone usage, ◆ (reduce / reduced) play time and even seclude children from social gatherings. The increased pressure and social seclusion negatively impact students.

School authorities deny their role in creating exam-related stress and believe the recent reforms in examination system ◆ (had helped / have helped) students.

[…]

While the reforms in examination system ◆ (helped / have helped) many students perform better in recent years, psychiatrists ◆ (believe / will believe) more needs to be done to help students cope with depression.

According to Dr Veena Luthra, consultant psychiatrist at the American Centre for Psychiatry and Neurology in the Capital, depression among teenagers and sometimes even in very young children is quite common but often "not picked-up or diagnosed". "I've seen a lot of severe depression cases with some at risk of suicide. Depression is the most common reason for suicide," she ◆ (is saying / said).

A major sign of depression is when a student ◆ (shows / has shown) a marked change in regular behaviour. It can include the child keeping to himself, becoming less social, losing interest in things or developing a lack of concentration resulting in lower grades at school.

> **emphasise** (UK) / **emphasize** (US)
> **minimise** (UK) / **minimize** (US)

[…]

Extracted from <www.khaleejtimes.com/nation/education/exam-stress-a-ticking-time-bomb-for-students>. Accessed on December 29, 2015.

5. Complete the text with affirmative or negative forms of the verbs from the box in the correct tenses.

be	do	know	think
define	end	there to be	want

Five things I wish I♦ when I finished high school

By Jo Messer

[…]

1. Most people don't know what they want to do when they finish school – it's normal!

Like many students, I didn't actually know what course I wanted to do after Year 12, despite getting good marks. At the time I ♦ I was the only one in the world going through this dilemma! However, the fact is that most students don't know what they want to do when they finish school, and those that do are in the minority. If you're not sure, that's ok. […]

2. Your marks ♦ your course or career choice

Don't let your choice of further study be solely determined by your HSC results. Consider your motivations and interests and do not let your marks sway you from what you really want to do. […]

3. There is more than one road to the same destination

Students may be disappointed when they get their results. There is a whole range of reasons why people might not achieve their best results at high school and this does not mean they ♦ successful. […]

4. You need to be aware of what your influences are

When I look back on finishing Year 12, I now realise I was scared stiff of leaving the security of high school. I had had a positive experience and good friends, and ♦ to face the big wide world on my own. My choices were influenced by who I knew and which university they were going to, and other factors such as my parents and erroneous preconceptions about courses and occupations.

[…]

5. If you take a year off, use it wisely

I deferred my first year of study because I didn't know what I wanted to do. During that time I ♦ work experience, volunteered and got a casual job. The year flew past, and at the end of it I knew a little bit more about the world of work, my skill set and what I didn't want to do. […]

Your learning never ♦.

Your learning does not conclude at the end of high school, nor at the end of a degree or even when you get your first job. In fact, that's only the start! The road ahead will be full of twists and turns, and sometimes the destination will be clear while at other times it might feel like you're going in circles. ♦many opportunities for gaining new knowledge and skills, for changing direction and ultimately for personal growth. This is what a career – and life – is all about!

Extracted from <www.careerfaqs.com.au/news/news-and-views/five-things-i-wish-id-known-when-i-finished-high-school/>.
Accessed on December 29, 2015.

WRAPPING UP

In pairs, exchange ideas about the tips given by Jo Messer and, in your notebook, write two other tips about the reality at your school. Make sure to use mixed verb tenses in your text. When you're finished, read them to your classmates.

LISTENING COMPREHENSION

Before Listening

1. Your graduation cerimony is a time to reflect on memories, celebrate academic acomplishments, and appraise the past. It's also a time to consider the future. Now that you are about to finish high school and start a new journey, read the following inspirational quotations. Then talk about them with your classmates.

   a. *"Your education is a dress rehearsal for a life that is yours to lead."*
   (Nora Ephron, American playwright and director)

   b. *"It is impossible to live without failing at something, unless you live so cautiously that you might as well not have lived at all — in which case, you fail by default."* (J.K. Rowling, British novelist)

   c. *"The important thing is not to stop questioning."*
   (Albert Einstein, German physicist)

2. You are going to listen to Gwen Stacy's graduation speech in the movie *The Amazing Spider-Man 2*. In her speech she says, "And even if we fail, what better way is there to live?" Which quotation from the previous activity is this sentence related to? How are they related? Do you agree with the message they convey? Explain.

Listening

3. Listen to the graduation speech once and find the sentences that correspond to the statements below. Write them down in your notebook.

   a. Gwen's fellow graduates' families are listening to her speech.

   b. Life is valued because it doesn't last forever.

   c. We should make our lives worth living.

   d. It's easy to feel optimistic on nice days such as the graduation day, but difficult days will come as well.

   e. Students move apart on the graduation day, but that does not mean they will forget each other.

4. Listen to the graduation speech again and answer the following questions.

  a. What does Gwen say to express she is happy to be the Valedictorian?

  b. What sentence does she use to compare the four years of high school to life?

  c. What piece of advice does she give her fellow graduates?

  d. What does she say to end her speech?

After Listening

What does Gwen Stacy's speech have in common with Megan Lee Qi Jun's speech? Justify your answer.

> **PRONUNCIATION PRACTICE**
>
> Listen and pay attention to how words are connected.
>
> four **years of** high school
>
> **makes it** precious
>
> **say it** today
>
> Now connect the words that end in a consonant sound to the words that start with a vowel sound. Then listen and repeat.
>
> an honor to be   it's easy to
>
> each other into everything   more than ever
>
> even if we   remind us that
>
> hold on to hope   we look around

SPEAKING

What do you think of graduation ceremonies? In your view, does everybody appreciate this kind of event? In your notebook, make a chart similar to the one below and complete it with arguments for and against graduation ceremonies.

For	Against
It's a time when parents, grandparents, and whole extended families celebrate the passage from youth to adulthood.	Families spend an amount of money they sometimes don't have.

Share your ideas in small groups.

After you have listened to all participants' arguments, choose one person to report to the whole group whether most people are for or against graduation ceremonies and explain the reasons.

High School is Over... Now What? **Unit 8**   137

WRITING

Write a short graduation speech to be delivered to teachers, classmates, friends, and family.

Planning your graduation speech

- Consider your experiences in high school years. Think about the people you have met, especially teachers, classmates, and school staff. Remember what you have learned and everything you have experienced with them over the years. Ask yourself how important these people have been to you.

- You can develop your text based on life lessons, maturity, friendship, or moral values such as gratitude.

- Think of the beginning, the body, and the end of your speech so that the parts make sense.

- Take notes in your notebook.

> ### REFLECTING AND EVALUATING
>
> Go back to your speech and make sure you paid attention to the following topics:
>
> ✓ Did you include greetings?
>
> ✓ Did you thank the audience?
>
> ✓ Did you start your speech with a catchy introduction in order to hook people in?
>
> ✓ Did you present some of your personal experience?
>
> ✓ Did you choose an appropriate tone according to the audience?

Writing and rewriting your text

- Write a draft of your graduation speech.

- Ask a classmate to proofread your speech and give his/her opinion.

- If necessary, make adjustments and write a clean copy.

After writing

- Read your graduation speech to the whole class and vote for the most beautiful or most meaningful one.

- Alternatively, you and your classmates can display all graduation speeches on a school wall so that everyone can read and vote for the best one.

SELF-ASSESSMENT

Chegamos ao fim da unidade 8. Convidamos você a refletir sobre seu desempenho até aqui e a responder às questões propostas abaixo, escolhendo uma das seguintes opções:

Sim.

Preciso me preparar mais.

Questões

- Você é capaz de expor suas reflexões sobre seus anos escolares e de discutir acerca das possibilidades de caminhos a serem trilhados após a conclusão do Ensino Médio?
- Você é capaz de ler e compreender um discurso de formatura de Ensino Médio em inglês e reconhecer as características principais inerentes ao gênero?
- Você reúne conhecimentos linguístico-discursivos suficientes para redigir um discurso de formatura em língua inglesa?
- Você está preparado para escutar um discurso de formatura e compreender informações específicas?
- Você se julga apto a discutir os prós e contras das cerimônias de formatura?

Refletindo sobre suas respostas

- Como você analisa a evolução do seu aprendizado em relação à unidade anterior?
- De que forma suas práticas de aprendizagem no decorrer desta unidade influenciaram suas respostas?
- O que você pode fazer para aprimorar ainda mais os conhecimentos adquiridos nesta unidade?
  a. Buscar por mais informações acerca das responsabilidades que virão após a conclusão do Ensino Médio.
  b. Ler diferentes discursos de formatura em língua inglesa para desenvolver melhor minha capacidade de compreensão de informações mais detalhadas.
  c. Aprofundar meus conhecimentos de língua inglesa, usando recursos diversos, de forma que minha participação nas atividades seja mais ativa.
  d. Outros.

High School is Over... Now what? **Unit 8** 139

Further Practice 4 – Units 7 & 8

1. Look at the picture and answer the questions.

Extracted from <www.contextolivre.com.br/2014/09/a-cigarra-e-formiga.html>. Accesed on December 26, 2015.

   a. The picture illustrates a scene from a famous fable. Do you know which fable it is? Tell your classmates what you know about the fable.

   b. What kind of contrast can you see in the picture?

2. Read the fable *The Ant and the Grasshopper* by Jean de La Fontaine. Then check the best alternatives to answer the questions.

The Ant and the Grasshopper

In a summer's day a Grasshopper was hopping about, chirping and singing to its heart's content. An Ant passed by, bearing along with great toil an ear of corn he was taking to the nest. "Why not come and chat with me," said the Grasshopper "instead of toiling and moiling in that way?" "I am helping to lay up food for the winter," said the Ant, "and recommend you to do the same." "Why bother about winter?" said the Grasshopper; we have got plenty of food at present." But the Ant went on its way and continued its toil. When the winter came the Grasshopper had no food and found itself dying of hunger, while it saw the ants distributing every day corn and grain from the stores they had collected in the summer. Then the Grasshopper knew: It is best to prepare for the days of necessity.

[…]

Adapted from <www.savingadvice.com/articles/2012/01/24/109007_money-lessons-from-aesops-fables.html>. Accessed on December 26, 2015.

   a. Which human traits do the characters represent?
      1 Laziness and hard work.
      2 Apathy and selfishness.
      3 Happiness and ignorance.

   b. Fables usually teach a lesson. Which lesson does the fable *The Ant and the Grasshopper* teach?
      1 It is fine to have some fun, but always remember that difficult times may come and for that you must be prepared.
      2 Don't forget to take care of your health because it is the most valuable thing you have.
      3 The ones who attain top positions are the ones who help others achieve their goals.

   c. Which quote sums up the lesson taught in the fable?
      1 "Find your own style. Don't spend your savings trying to be someone else. You're not more important, smarter, or prettier because you wear a designer dress." (Salma Hayek, Mexican actress)
      2 "Experiences are savings which a miser puts aside. Wisdom is an inheritance which a wastrel cannot exhaust." (Karl Kraus, Austrian writer and journalist)
      3 "Nothing ever comes to one, that is worth having, except as a result of hard work." (Booker T. Washington, American educator)

Extracted from <www.brainyquote.com>. Accessed on December 25, 2015.

3. Read a version of the fable *The Ant and the Grasshopper* by Brazilian writer Monteiro Lobato and complete the sentences.

A cigarra e a formiga boa – fábula de Monteiro Lobato

Houve uma jovem cigarra que tinha o costume de chiar ao pé dum formigueiro. Só parava quando cansadinha; e seu divertimento então era observar as formigas na eterna faina de abastecer as tulhas. Mas o bom tempo afinal passou e vieram as chuvas. Os animais todos, arrepiados, passavam o dia cochilando nas tocas. A pobre cigarra, sem abrigo em seu galhinho seco e metida em grandes apuros, deliberou socorrer-se de alguém.

Manquitolando, com uma asa a arrastar, lá se dirigiu para o formigueiro. Bateu – tique, tique, tique...

Aparece uma formiga, friorenta, embrulhada num xalinho de paina.

— Que quer? – perguntou, examinando a triste mendiga suja de lama e a tossir.

— Venho em busca de um agasalho. O mau tempo não cessa e eu...

A formiga olhou-a de alto a baixo.

— E o que fez durante o bom tempo, que não construiu sua casa?

A pobre cigarra, toda tremendo, respondeu depois de um acesso de tosse:

— Eu cantava, bem sabe...

— Ah!... exclamou a formiga recordando-se. Era você então quem cantava nessa árvore enquanto nós labutávamos para encher as tulhas?

— Isso mesmo, era eu...

— Pois entre, amiguinha! Nunca poderemos esquecer as boas horas que sua cantoria nos proporcionou. Aquele chiado nos distraía e aliviava o trabalho. Dizíamos sempre: que felicidade ter como vizinha tão gentil cantora! Entre, amiga, que aqui terá cama e mesa durante todo o mau tempo.

A cigarra entrou, sarou da tosse e voltou a ser a alegre cantora dos dias de sol.

Extraído de: A cigarra e a formiga boa, de Monteiro Lobato © Monteiro Lobato - Todos os direitos reservados.

a. The ant examined the grasshopper from top to bottom because ♦

b. The ant decided to offer shelter to the grasshopper because ♦

4. Answer the questions below.

a. The characters in both fables are the same, but in Lobato's version the ant acts differently. How different does it act?

b. What is the moral of Lobato's version?

c. In your opinion, which version teaches the most relevant lesson? Explain your answer.

5. Read the definition of *parody* and answer the question below.

> **Parody**
>
> writing, music, art, speech, etc. that intentionally copies the style of someone famous or copies a particular situation, making the features or qualities of the original more noticeable in a way that is humorous

Extracted from <dictionary.cambridge.org/dictionary/english/parody>. Accessed on February 10, 2016.

• Which fable is a parody, Monteiro Lobato's or La Fontaine's? Justify your answer.

Further Practice 4 – Units 7 & 8

6. Read the poll (a collection of opinions on a subject) and answer the questions.

If money gets tight, the first thing I will do is:

Earn more – get another job or work more hours	250	
Donate less – give less to charity	56	
Spend a little less – don't buy as much	479	
Stop spending – only buy stuff I need	721	
	Total Votes: **1 506**	

Adapted from <www.themint.org/polls/index.php?id=19>. Accessed on December 25, 2015.

If you spot a great item at the mall that you can't afford right now, what will you do?

Borrow! I'll ask my family/friends to loan me the money on the condition I pay it back	94	
Charge it! I'll figure out a way to pay off the credit card bill in stages	81	
Forget it! I can't afford it and don't want to owe money that I don't have	276	
Save for it! I'll put money aside each month until I have the full amount to buy it	469	
	Total Votes: **920**	

Adapted from <www.themint.org/polls/index.php?id=18>. Accessed on December 25, 2015.

If someone gives me $1,000 and tells me to "invest it wisely," I will:

Put it in the stock market	415	
Put it in a savings account	1033	
Give it to a friend to invest for me	25	
Ask my parent or another person for advice	231	
Buy a collectible that would grow in value, like baseball cards, or comic books etc.	94	
	Total Votes: **1 798**	

Adapted from <www.themint.org/polls/index.php?id=16>. Accessed on December 25, 2015.

a. What would your answers to these situations be? Justify them.

b. Why did you dismiss the other options?

7. Some of the sentences below are wrong. Find and correct them in your notebook.

a. Most of the people who answered this poll prefer to dismiss the idea of purchasing an item they couldn't afford.

b. More than half of the people who answered this poll prefer putting their money in the bank.

c. Less than ten percent of the people who answered this poll said that they would reduce the amount of money they spent on charity.

d. Just a few people would spent less while going through a difficult financial period.

8. Identify the sentences you can infer about the answers to the poll.

   a. When money is tight, the majority of people prefer cutting down on expenses to working more hours.

   b. Most people prefer buying something that really want to worrying about credit card bills.

   c. Just a small percentage of people would trust $1,000 to someone else to invest.

9. Number the statements according to the corresponding comic strip.

1.

Extracted from <www.thecomicstrips.com/store/add.php?iid=111818>.

2.

Extracted from <www.thecomicstrips.com/store/add.php?iid=111816>.

   a. The mother doesn't feel much better with her husband's comforting words.

   b. The mother and daughter are both emotional about the daughter's graduation.

   c. The father reminds the wife of what's going to happen in the next school year.

10. Answer the questions about the comic strips.

    a. What do they have in common?

    b. Both parents are proud of their daughter. What does a person's graduation mean to his/her loved ones? Explain your answer.

    c. Is there any special celebration when students graduate at your school? If so, what do you like most about it? If not, do you intend to celebrate your graduation somehow? How?

Units 7 & 8   Further Practice 4   143

Further Practice 4 – Units 7 & 8

11. Choose the correct options to complete the graduation speech below.

Graduating from high school: Tears, fears and peers

Amy Ma, about to graduate from high school, (a)♦ the excitement,
fear and apprehension that she's feeling.

Like the very many people before me, my high school years (b)♦ to an end; in fact next week, I (c)♦ my last few lessons, clear out my locker one last time, say my final goodbyes to classmates and teachers and eventually graduate with all my peers. [...]

Jumbled reactions

When I think about graduating from high school, I get a knot at the pit of my stomach. It's difficult to describe a jumble of fear, a pang of regret, and sprinkles of nervousness with a side of excitement. There's a lot of uncertainty and expectation in the air, and I suppose that's what makes it so exciting, but equally as frightening. Am I moving off to university? Should I just start working and get experience? How will I do in my HSC? A fear develops because we're afraid we might not find the answers to these questions, or even worse when we do find them, we may not like the answers at all. The only things we can control are our ability to work our hardest and do our best to look after our health during this gruelling and stressful time. Just give everything your best effort and it will all work itself out in the end when your hard work (d)♦.

Parting ways with the profs

The next hardest thing about graduating from high school is parting with the teachers you (e)♦ so close to over the years. There are teachers who put so much effort into their classes, inspiring and empowering their students to learn and to succeed. These are the teachers who are the hardest to say goodbye to. But the truth is they (f)♦ for you to leave all along. They want you to go out into the world armed with as much information as possible to tackle all the big issues. It's hard to repay a person who (g)♦ such an impact on your life, but a small gift or all your thoughts and thanks written in the form of a letter or card certainly helps make parting ways easier.

Farewell to my friends

The most difficult part for me is by far saying farewell to my classmates. My six years in high school were spent building close and memorable connections with friends. Seeing everyone moving off to fulfill their respective dreams and ambitions certainly makes me wonder if we'll ever cross paths again. [...]

Adapted from <au.reachout.com/graduating-from-high-school-tears-fears-and-peers>. Accessed on December 28, 2015.

a. • discussed
• discusses

c. • 'll have
• have

e. • have grown
• grew

g. • made
• has made

b. • are coming
• came

d. • is paying off
• pays off

f. • were preparing
• prepared

12. Reflect on the questions that follow and answer them. Share your views with your classmates.

Are you afraid of not seeing your classmates again? What can you do to keep in touch with them and not lose contact?

EXAM PRACTICE

"A body goes through changes during the teen years. When you started dating, my hair turned gray. When you started driving, I got heart palpitations..."

Considere as proposições abaixo.

   I. A adolescência dos filhos é um período conturbado para a família.

   II. A filha não é uma motorista responsável.

   III. A comicidade do cartum reside no fato de o pai referir-se às transformações de seu próprio corpo, e não àquelas pelas quais passa o corpo da filha.

   IV. O cartum reflete o conflito de gerações, aqui representado por pai e filha.

   Estão corretas as proposições

a. I e III.

b. Apenas III.

c. II e IV.

d. Apenas I.

e. II e III.

Career Planning

Unit 1

What does a senior caregiver do?

A senior caregiver is a person who assists <u>senior citizens</u>, when necessary, in the performance of the <u>activities of daily living</u>. It is not a medically skilled position, as the job consists primarily of what are considered custodial duties. Skilled medical jobs, such as the administration of medications and other medical services are usually performed by those trained in such duties. In some cases, however, it may be deemed medically appropriate that a senior caregiver have more advanced medical training in order to be able to respond properly in case of an emergency. In these cases, it may be determined to have a certified <u>nursing assistant</u> or even a full-fledged nurse perform the caregiving duties, although this is not common.

There are six activities of daily living (ADLs) that are considered essential for all people: *eating, bathing, toileting* and *dressing* are self-explanatory; *transferring* refers to the senior's ability to move from bed to chair and vice-versa, and *continence* is the ability to control one's urinary and fecal discharge. Some authorities recognize a seventh ADL; *mobility,* or the ability to move about freely. "Assistance" with ADLs may be hands-on or it may be stand-by; that is, a senior caregiver may be required only to be available to render assistance in the event the patient is unable to carry it out, or it may be the case that the senior is absolutely incapable of performing the ADL alone and must be assisted.

A senior caregiver's duties are not very complex, then, but some training is required, as well as a temperament that's amenable to routinely carrying out chores that many would consider demeaning, such as helping another adult dress, or assisting an adult who is incontinent. In addition, because the loss of the ability to perform ADLs is often associated with the onset of <u>dementia</u>, senior caregivers must also be capable of dealing with the sometimes unreasonable nature of the demands of those afflicted by this condition. [...]

Adapted from <www.wisegeek.com/what-does-a-senior-caregiver-do.htm>.
Accessed on March 12, 2016.

1. How can caregivers help older adults? Explain.

2. What factors should you take into consideration when deciding to be a caregiver? Justify your answer.

Unit 2

What is a filmmaker?

Also known as: moviemaker, independent filmmaker.

A filmmaker, or film director, is someone who is in charge of making, leading, and developing movie productions. It is a career that allows an individual to use their leadership as well as creative thinking skills to lead and direct major motion pictures or made-for-television films.

A filmmaker spends very long hours making sure the film is being shot in a way that will provide entertainment for the audience and will highlight the actors and actresses' strengths. They will see each film through, from where the film is shot, to how the script will be played out, to what actors and actresses best fit the roles of the characters. The filmmaker also manages the financial end of the production.

[…]

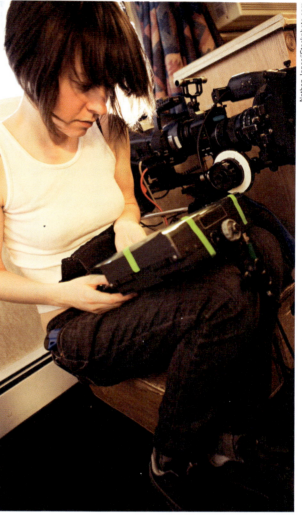

How can I become a filmmaker?

Aspiring filmmakers should begin by independently watching movies, reading film history books, reading websites and blogs on the film industry and top filmmakers, attending film festivals, etc. Even at the high school level, courses in drama, English and photography would be helpful.

Many filmmakers start out as actors themselves, in order to understand various directing techniques and styles from the receiving end. Someone who has a background in acting would be prime for attending a filmmaking program. […]

There are many film or multimedia programs offered at colleges and universities. Narrative techniques, sound, lighting, cinematography, editing and computer-generated imaging is learned. As well, reading and writing scripts while enrolled in screenwriting classes, teaches the aspiring filmmaker about movie pacing and formatting. Different movie genres such as science fiction, horror, and fantasy are studied. Valuable contacts in the industry and opportunities for internships can be made while enrolled in school.

Qualities that filmmakers should have are a passion for film, leadership, decisiveness, confidence, and organization.

Adapted from <www.sokanu.com/careers/filmmaker/>. Accessed on March 12, 2016.

1. Besides the qualities mentioned in the text, what other qualities should a filmmaker have? Why? Do you have any of these qualities? Which one(s)?

2. If you were a filmmaker, what kind of movie would you like to make? Justify your answer.

Career Planning

Unit 3

What is a psychologist?

A psychologist is someone who studies mental processes and human behaviour by observing, interpreting, and recording how people relate to one another and the environment. Some psychologists work independently, doing research or working only with patients or clients. Others work as part of a healthcare team, collaborating with physicians, social workers, and others to treat illness and promote overall wellness.

What do psychologists do?

Psychologists will typically do the following:

- Conduct scientific studies to study behaviour and brain function (neuropsychologist)
- Collect information through observations, interviews, surveys, tests, and other methods
- Find patterns that will help them understand and predict behaviour
- Use their knowledge to increase understanding among individuals and groups
- Develop programs that improve schools and workplaces by addressing psychological issues
- Work with individuals, couples, and families to help them make desired changes to behaviours
- Identify and diagnose mental, behavioural, or emotional disorders
- Develop and carry out treatment plans
- Collaborate with physicians or social workers to help treat patients

Psychologists seek to understand and explain thoughts, emotions, feelings, and behaviour. Depending on the topic of study, psychologists use techniques such as observation, assessment, and experimentation to develop theories about the beliefs and feelings that influence a person's actions.

[…]

They also may administer personality, performance, aptitude, or intelligence tests. They look for patterns of behaviour or cause-and-effect relationships between events, and use this information when testing theories in their research or treating patients.

[…]

Adapted from <www.sokanu.com/careers/psychologist/>. Accessed on December 25, 2015.

1. Psychologists help a wide range of people of all ages with all sorts of problems. In what ways can they help people?

2. Would you like to be a psychologist? Why/Why not?

Unit 4

HR professionals manage a valuable resource: people

Curious as to what you'll do in an HR career? Here are breakdowns by human resources role.

Each company has its own unique culture.

It encompasses the values, visions, ideals, norms, working language, systems and habits of a group who work together. A good human resources employee develops and manages their company's culture. They recruit new hires, maintain benefits and payroll, mediate conflict and engage in training and development. Their role is at the core of a company's success.

[…]

What does a human resources worker do?

Human resources specialists are responsible for recruiting, screening, interviewing and placing workers. They may also handle employee relations, payroll and benefits, and training. Human resources managers plan, direct, and coordinate the administrative functions of an organization. They oversee specialists in their duties; consult with executives on strategic planning; and link a company's management with its employees.

HR specialists tend to focus on a single area, such as recruiting or training. HR generalists handle a number of areas and tasks simultaneously. Small companies will typically have one or two HR generalists on staff, while larger ones may have many devoted to particular areas and services.

Some typical daily tasks for an HR worker include:
- Consult with employers to identify needs and preferred qualifications
- Interview applicants about their experience, education and skills
- Contact references and perform background checks
- Inform applicants about job details such as benefits and conditions
- Hire or refer qualified candidates
- Conduct new employee orientations
- Process paperwork

[…]

Adapted from <www.allbusinessschools.com/business-careers/human-resources/job-description/>. Accessed on March 15, 2016.

1. Among all the responsibilities of a human resources worker, which one is the most challenging? Why do you think so?

2. Based on the information in the text, would you like to be a HR professional? Justify your answer.

Career Planning

Unit 5

What is an editor?

An editor is someone who is a critical reader, and a lover of words. He or she will prepare a client's manuscript for publication by polishing, refining and enhancing it. An editor is seen as a gatekeeper between the writer and the audience, which is why editors have to take a dual sided point of view in order to keep both parties happy.

Authors know their stories inside and out and have had a strong relationship with their manuscript for months or sometimes years. Audiences, on the other hand, have no emotional attachment to books that they have not read yet and are quick to judge any novel that they pick up to read.

An editor needs to edit a manuscript from both points of view. Changes that are to be made must feel like the author's authentic voice to keep him or her happy with the new and improved manuscript. The manuscript may also need changes that will keep the audience pulled in and interested for the length of the novel. One of an editor's many challenges is to find a balance between the two.

[…]

What is the workplace of an editor like?

An editor's hours are generally determined by the production schedule, and by the type of editorial position he or she has.

Advances in electronic communications have changed the work environment for writers and editors alike. Editors are able to do a lot of their editing from their homes, but most salaried editors work in-house, dealing with production deadlines and the pressures of trying to produce accurate work. This is advantageous because they get to learn how the production works from the inside. With experience, editors will know what they can handle and what projects might be too much.

Schedules and budgets are tight in a publishing house so a lot of employers don't want to risk new freelancing editors. They may be less likely to hire someone with no in-house experience.

[…]

Adapted from <www.sokanu.com/careers/editor/>. Accessed on December 23, 2015.

1. Editors plan, coordinate, and revise material for publication, not just in the case of novels, but also of school books, newspapers, magazines, and websites. Do you think you like to be an editor? Why/Why not?

2. If you were an editor, what kind of manuscript would you like to work on? What would the subject be? Would you consider editing school books? Why/Why not?

Unit 6

Psychoanalyst

Psychoanalysts and psychoanalytic, psychotherapists work with people who suffer from a range of emotional problems including depression, phobias, anxiety, trauma and obsessions. Together with their patients, they explore how unconscious factors affect their behaviour as well as past and current relationships.

[…]

Psychoanalysis is based on the idea that we are often unaware of many of the factors that influence our emotions and behaviour. In other words, our lives are shaped not only by conscious but also unconscious processes. Painful experiences from the past can be re-enacted in the present and cause emotional and mental distress, sometimes in the form of symptoms, difficulties in sustaining healthy relationships, depression or low self-esteem. As long as processes remain unconscious, it is very hard to free oneself of these difficulties, despite advice from friends and family or the strongest willpower.

Psychoanalysts provide a reliable and safe setting to help patients to become aware of their unconscious conflicts. The analyst and the patient (or analysand) develops a unique relationship where no judgments are made and whatever is said in a session is held in the strictest confidence. Analysts don't give advice but encourage patients to talk freely and make sense of their experiences, dreams, fantasies, anxieties, feelings and memories. As patients speak about what concerns them, they can begin to work with their suffering rather than against it. As a result, emotional and physical symptoms are alleviated and patients can discover meaningful ways of conducting their lives and relationships.

Psychoanalysis can help with:
- Trauma, anxiety, panic attacks
- Depression, feelings of loss and emptiness
- Problems with sexuality
- Difficulties in making or sustaining relationships at home or work
- Addiction
- Self-harm
- Lack of confidence
- Difficulty in coming to terms with a life change such as bereavement, divorce or job loss
- Emotional issues expressed through physical symptoms

Psychoanalysis usually involves intensive work and requires an important commitment from patients in terms of time and energy. Patients can attend 50-minute sessions 2 to 5 times a week. The length of time a person may be in analysis is very variable and is determined by the individual's needs. […]

Adapted from <myjobsearch.com/careers/psychoanalyst.html>. Accessed on December 28, 2015.

1. Psychoanalysts help people get to know themselves deeply, using different methods and techniques. How would knowing yourself better help you deal with your problems?

2. Besides excellent listening and observing, what other skills should a psychoanalyst have? Why? Do you have these skills? Would you like to be a psychoanalyst?

Career Planning

Unit 7

What is a financial analyst?

[…]

A financial analyst is someone who manages various aspects of other people's money. Some analysts work as investment advisors, either on their own or with a brokerage firm. Depending on the wealth and size of their clients, they may manage portfolios worth millions of dollars. Other financial analysts work for banks or insurance companies, ensuring that even when a loan defaults or a claim is paid, the company maintains a positive cash flow. Still others specialize in mergers and acquisitions, determining the profitability of two companies combining their forces in a merger or one company buying another company in an acquisition.

What does a financial analyst do?

Financial analysts evaluate the financial situation in their area of expertise and generate appropriate reports, both written and oral, regarding their recommendations. They monitor and interpret available data such as industry and economic trends, forecast the current trends into probable future profitability, determine a fair market value for the sale of company stock, and recommend action to their company or investors.

Some financial analysts support the growing "green" industries. These analysts may evaluate a vacant building for the feasibility of retrofitting it, or he or she may analyze the costs and benefits of including green technologies in new construction. The financial analyst may also be involved in generating venture capital for green startup companies. They may monitor and interpret climate change data or clean water data in order to calculate supply and demand, or whether or not to invest in water rights, energy futures, and other tradable commodities within the green industry.

Successful financial analysts are excellent critical thinkers; they can logically determine the best course of action regarding any potential investment. They should be lifelong and active learners in order to remain current regarding market conditions and new technologies, and to be able to predict the long-term results of their investment decisions.

An analyst identifies potential problems within his or her investment options and either seeks a solution to the problem or opts out of the opportunity. Excellent communication skills, combined with the ability to distill large quantities of complex data into clear, concise presentations, allow an analyst to convey his or her investment opportunities in a manner that encourages clients to sign on.

[…]

Adapted from <www.sokanu.com/careers/financial-analyst/>. Accessed on December 28, 2015.

1. When you start working you will have to deal with your personal finance so as to control your expenses, savings, and investments. How could a financial analyst help you do this?

2. Taking into account the way you usually deal with your money, would you consider that you have what it takes to be a good financial analyst? Explain.

3. How could a financial analyst help people in your community?

Unit 8

What does a guidance counselor do?

A guidance counselor works in a school setting to help students better prepare for continuing education, or to help facilitate decisions made about future careers. The requirements for becoming a guidance counselor vary among schools. These professionals tend to have at least a Bachelor of Arts (B.A.) in psychology, but may also have a B.A. in career counseling. Some places require high school counselors to have a master's degree as well, and many schools require the counselor to be licensed. In the college setting, counselors may not have a B.A., but may be experts in their teaching area. Sometimes the counselor at the college level is called an academic advisor.

In the elementary setting, guidance counselors are frequently catchall counselors who help to facilitate testing for learning disabilities and may also manage Individualized Education Plans (IEPs) for students in need of them. They tend not to offer psychological assistance, but may participate in observation of students in classroom settings or in psychological or intelligence testing. Children in need of significant counseling for psychological issues usually meet with a school psychologist, although in some schools, funding issues can mean that access to a psychologist may be significantly limited.

Usually, a guidance counselor in an elementary school is simply called a counselor. Regardless of title, these employees can be an excellent resource for children and parents. If a parent is concerned about a child's learning abilities, contacting the elementary counselor is a good first step. The counselor may be particularly helpful if the administration of the school does not take the parent's concerns seriously.

In the middle school setting, the guidance counselor may still participate in some educational testing for students deemed "at academic risk". He or she usually also helps students make decisions regarding choices in electives and whether they are challenged enough or too much by their present classes. When courses are too hard or too easy, he or she may be able to help the student change his or her schedule.

[…]

Adapted from <www.wisegeek.com/what-does-a-guidance-counselor-do.htm>. Accessed on December 23, 2015.

1. Have you ever talked to a guidance counselor? If so, share the experience. If not, how do you think you would benefit from a conversation with him or her?

2. What are the main skills a guidance counselor should have so as to help students effectively?

Learning from Experience 1

The Story of Movies

Objectives

- use experience as the primary foundation for learning;
- learn about the story of the movies from the silent era up to the 2010s;
- produce a short documentary about the story of movies;
- reflect on the cultural, historical and artistic significance of movies to our society and community in particular;
- think about the activity as a whole, considering the process and the final results.

Stage 1: Warming Up

Discuss the quote below with your classmates.

> "Cinema is a matter of what's in the frame and what's out."
> (Martin Scorsese, American director)

Extracted from <www.brainyquote.com/quotes/quotes/m/martinscor164712.html?src=t_movies >. Accessed on January 2, 2016.

Stage 2: Expanding Your Knowledge

In small groups, read the article and talk about how it relates to the quote in stage 1. Then address the whole class to report your opinions.

World Cinema History

The history of world movies goes back to the end of the 1800's. It is now more than 200 years that the world of cinema has had the chance to develop through many experiments and innovations. Technology has been one of the major contributing factors to the development of world cinema. From the very start of world cinema the hearts of millions have been captured by its magic.

The world cinema journey began in silence. Movies were created without sound as the technology of sound was not available at the beginning. A device did not exist that could synchronise sound with the picture. Cinema remained silent for the first thirty years until sound technology was developed late in the 1920's.

The world of cinema was quite unorganised in the first ten years of its life although gradually over a short time the industry established itself. Movies that contained one shot and produced by just one person began to be taken over by movies that were a few minutes long, had various scenes and were produced by larger companies with professional methods.

Probably the most successful movie making company was in the USA. They had the largest production group until 1900. This company produced a lot of peep show kind of movies which were done with the help of a machine called Mutoscope. France was the next country to show its calibre in the world cinema field. France was home to one of the first companies to shoot scenes for a movie outside the studio and they also sent cameramen to shoot films all over the world. The biggest producer in France was Georges Méliès, who started to use trick effects in 1898.

The first cameras used in movies were tied or fixed to a tripod. All the early movie cameras were completely fixed whilst taking film shots. Camera movements were done by mounting the movie camera onto a moving vehicle.

The history of world cinema has undergone a long course of research, creation and application of new techniques. Numerous methods have been tested and applied to give film making a place in the finest of performing arts across the globe.

Adapted from <www.cypruscinema.com/article_world-cinema-history >. Accessed on January 2, 2016.

synchronise (UK) / **synchronize** (US)
unorganised (UK) / **unorganized** (US)
calibre (UK) / **caliber** (US)

Stage 3: Getting Down to Action

- Work in groups of 6 to 8. Some of you will be involved in a study group to read and discuss the texts suggested by the teacher, as well as to watch some videos, while others will search for information on how to prepare short documentaries; some will be in charge of the production and exhibition of the documentary, while others will work on the backstage.
- Plan in advance how you will document the project preparation steps and the shooting of the final product, the documentary. The backstage documentation will be very useful while editing the final version of the documentary and in the evaluation process as well.
- Write a script and create a title for the documentary.
- If possible, create a storyboard to help you plan your documentary shot by shot.
- Have your teacher comment on the script and suggest adjustments.
- Before the exhibition of the documentary, make posters to promote it inside the school.

Stage 4: Analyzing and Sharing the Results

- Analyze the project's records. Prepare and carry out a class presentation, in English, on the preparation steps in the making of the documentary. Remember to have the final product (the documentary itself) available for analysis as well.

Stage 5: Reflecting and Evaluating

- Has the event engaged members of the school staff and students in promoting meaningful learning?
- What were the difficulties you encountered since the beginning of the project? How did you overcome them?
- What have you learned from this experience? How can you improve the project so that it yields better results next time?

EXTRA RESOURCES

- <sesc-se.com.br/cinema/historia+do+cinema+mundial.pdf>
- <www.wikihow.com/Make-a-Short-Documentary-Film>
- <www.desktop-documentaries.com/making-documentaries.html>
- <www.infoplease.com/ipea/A0150210.html>
- <resources.goanimate.com/marketing/what-is-a-storyboard-and-why-do-you-need-one>

Accessed on January 2, 2016.

Learning from Experience 2

Volunteering Fair

Objectives

- use experience as the primary foundation for learning;
- learn more about volunteering and discuss its impacts on our community;
- organize and conduct a Volunteering Fair;
- get to know the work of various volunteering institutions through their presence at stands in the Volunteering Fair;
- attract volunteers to the projects that are available in the neighborhood;
- make an online call for participation to invite volunteering institutions and the school community;
- reflect on the event considering the process and the results.

Stage 1: Warming Up

In pairs, explore the mind map and come up with two new words to complete it.

Extracted from <http://tayloritex.com/the-people/volunteers/>. Accessed on January 2, 2016.

Stage 2: Expanding Your Knowledge

Read the poem below. Then answer the questions that follow.

Everyday heroes

Here's to the everyday heroes,
The volunteers who do what they can,
To ease the suffering of others,
And be of service to their fellow man.

May they know the true satisfaction
That comes from helping others
Less fortunate than themselves,
But no less their sisters and brothers.

May they feel the gratitude in our hearts
For all of the good that they've done.
The appreciation that we all feel for them
Is truly second to none.

Extracted from <charity.lovetoknow.com/Volunteer_Appreciation_Poem>. Accessed on January 2, 2016.

1. What is your definition of volunteering?

2. List some reasons why people volunteer.

3. What types of volunteer work would fit your community needs?

Stage 3: Getting Down to Action

- Work in groups of 4. Some of you will be involved with the participants, others with the volunteering institutions, some will make the online call for participation and others will be in charge of the posters to promote the event. Some students may also act as ambassadors to welcome participants from the school community and neighborhood.
- Design a logo for the fair.
- Make an online call for participation addressing volunteering institutions so they can submit their proposals of interaction boards or exposition stands. If possible, invite people from the community who take part in any kind of volunteer work to participate in the event as well. They can talk about their own experiences in one of the stands.
- After organizing the fair, make posters to promote it inside and outside the school.
- Plan in advance how you will document the event. Try to use different formats such as pictures and video recordings.
- Organize at least one meeting with the volunteering institutions and other participants to explain their roles and your expectations for their contribution to the fair.

Stage 4: Analyzing and Sharing the Results

- Analyze the records. Prepare and carry out a class presentation, in English, on the contents of the event.
- If possible, share the results with the institutions that worked in partnership with the school in this project.
- Don't forget to analyze your own performances as well.

Stage 5: Reflecting and Evaluating

- Has the fair engaged members of the community, school staff, and students in general in knowing more about volunteering, especially concerning opportunities that are feasible for you and your classmates?
- What were the difficulties you encountered since the beginning of the project? How did you overcome them?
- What have you learned from this experience? How can you proceed the next time you engage in a similar task so as to improve the outcome?

EXTRA RESOURCES

- <diadovoluntario.weebly.com/feira-de-voluntariado.html>
- <nacoesunidas.org/acao/voluntariado/>
- <www.empregopelomundo.com.br/noticias/onu-convoca-voluntarios-para-trabalho-online/>

Accessed on January 2, 2016.

Learning from Experience 3

My Cultural Heritage

Objectives
- use experience as the primary foundation for learning;
- learn about cultural heritage and research on the cultural heritage of your community;
- analyze, present, and discuss the research findings;
- organize and conduct an exposition entitled My Cultural Heritage;
- reflect on the task considering the process and the results.

Stage 1: Warming Up

Read the chart and decide whether or not you agree with it. Then share your opinion with the class.

HERITAGE CYCLE

- By Understanding comes a thirst to understand
- By Valueing they will value it
- By Caring they will want to care for it
- From Enjoying it will help people enjoy it

The Heritage Cycle Image from cultureindevelopment.nl

Extracted from <www.cultivatingculture.com/2013/04/05/the-importance-of-cultural-heritage/>. Accessed on January 2, 2016.

Stage 2: Expanding Your Knowledge

Read the text and look for the passages that show how you feel about your cultural heritage.

The Importance of Cultural Heritage

Not everyone feels a connection with their cultural heritage, but many people do. What is it about cultural heritage that draws these people to it? Some may think traditions are archaic and no longer relevant, and that they are unnecessary during these modern times. Perhaps for some, they aren't; but for others, exploring cultural heritage offers a robust variety of benefits.

Culture can give people a connection to certain social values, beliefs, religions and customs. It allows them to identify with others of similar mindsets and backgrounds. Cultural heritage can provide an automatic sense of unity and belonging within a group and allows us to better understand previous generations and the history of where we come from.

In large cities especially, it can be easy to feel lost and lonely among so many other cultures and backgrounds. New York City, for example, is a huge melting pot of people from all over the country and the world. There are large communities based around certain cultural heritages, including Irish, Italian, Asian, and others.

Another benefit that comes from preserving cultural heritage as a whole is the communal support. Those that identify strongly with a certain heritage are often more likely to help out others in that same community. […]

Cultural heritage is made up of many large and small things. We can see it in the buildings, townscapes, and even in archaeological remains. Culture can be perceived through natural sources as well: the agriculture and landscapes associated with it. It is preserved through books, artifacts, objects, pictures, photographs, art, and oral tradition. Cultural heritage is in the food we eat, the clothes we wear, the religions we follow, and the skills we learn. Sometimes we can touch and see what makes up a culture; other times it is intangible.

[…]

Adapted from <www.cultivatingculture.com/2013/04/05/the-importance-of-cultural-heritage/>. Accessed on January 2, 2016.

Stage 3: Getting Down to Action

- Work in small groups. Do some research on 3 items belonging to the cultural heritage of your community. Those can be tangible or intangible assets that you consider part of the cultural heritage of your community.

- Don't forget to document your research. Remember to gather not only pieces of written information, but also photos that illustrate what is being talked about. You can also interview people who are willing to talk about that specific aspect of cultural heritage you are researching about.

- Gather all the data the group has found and bring them to the classroom.

- After listing the most interesting pieces of information collected, discuss them with your group, and prepare the exposition following the teacher's instructions.

- Write one text to present each cultural heritage item researched. Be careful to find a balance between written texts and illustrations.

- Have your teacher correct them and then prepare the exposition.

- Remember to document the final product (the exposition itself) and make it available for analysis later.

Stage 4: Analyzing and Sharing the Results

- Analyze the project's documents. Prepare a class presentation about the exposition using the material collected throughout the project.

- Consider preparing an online exposition on the school website and encourage the school staff and students to make comments and participate actively with further ideas concerning the community's cultural heritage.

Stage 5: Reflecting and Evaluating

- Has the event engaged members of the school staff and students in promoting meaningful learning?

- What were the difficulties you encountered since the beginning of the project? How did you overcome them?

- What have you learned from this experience? How can you expand this type of work to effectively promote knowledge and reflection about cultural heritage in your community?

EXTRA RESOURCES

- <www.khanacademy.org/humanities/art-history-basics/beginners-art-history/a/what-is-cultural-heritage>

- <en.unesco.org/themes/intangible-cultural-heritage>

- <www.unesco.org/new/pt/brasilia/culture/world-heritage/cultural-heritage/>

Accessed on January 2, 2016.

Learning from Experience 3

Learning From Experience 4

A Flash Mob

Objectives
- use experience as the primary foundation for learning;
- learn about flash mobs and discuss ideas to prepare one;
- debate over the cause you want to support and disseminate;
- present a class flash mob to surprise, touch, and unite the school community for a cause;
- reflect on the task considering the process and the results.

Stage 1: Warming Up

Read the definition below and, in your notebook, write your own definition of flash mobs.

> A large public gathering at which people perform an unusual or seemingly random act and then disperse, typically organized by means of the Internet or social media. [...]

Extracted from <www.oxforddictionaries.com/us/definition/american_english/flash-mob?q=flash+mob>.
Accessed on January 3, 2016.

Stage 2: Expanding Your Knowledge

In pairs, read the text and talk about the flash mobs listed.

Five Flash Mob Videos That Will Brighten Your Day

Sometimes all you need is a little spontaneous song and dance to make you smile. So here it is: The best flash mobs of all time, from around the world, appearing in the most unexpected places.

On the Train
Passengers boarding the Copenhagen subway on a run-of-the-mill weekday are greeted with the sweet sounds of a flute, shortly joined by a fully-fledged symphony orchestra. Look at the passengers' faces as they listen to the music during this unforgettable train ride.

In the Airport
An *a cappella* group takes over the arrivals gate at London's Heathrow Airport for a massive welcome home.

In the Middle of a Test
To help relieve the stress during an exam for the incoming first-year engineering students at the University of Toronto, a professor teams up with upperclassmen to perform a spoof of *Les miserables*' "One Day More."

In the Hospital
A classical music flash mob swarms the lobby at Hadassah Medical Center in Jerusalem. Composed of students from the Jerusalem Academy of Music and Dance, the group of 40 musicians plays Tchaikovsky's "Waltz of the Flowers" from the *Nutcracker* while a ballet dancer performs for delighted patients, family, and staff.

On a Lunch Break

Unsuspecting shoppers get a big surprise while enjoying their lunch when over 100 participants descend on this mall food court.

Adapted from <www.rd.com/culture/5-flash-mob-videos-that-will-brighten-your-day/>. Accessed on January 3, 2016.

Stage 3: Getting Down to Action

- Work in small groups and come up with ideas for the cause your flash mob is going to support and disseminate.
- Share ideas with the whole class and make decisions about the cause, the target audience, the participants, and where and when the flash mob is going to be performed.
- Debate over the way the cause is going to be disseminated, whether through music, dance, theater sketches, posters, speeches, gestures etc.
- Write down a script and show it to your teacher so he/she can help with any necessary adjustments.
- Don't forget to plan how to mobilize the audience on the day of the event and how the flash mob is going to be recorded as well.
- During the presentation, have someone observe the audience's reactions to evaluate if they responded to the message as you expected them to.
- After the presentation, talk to the audience to explain the meaning and the objectives of the project. Listen to their opinion about what they have seen and thank them for their co-participation.

Stage 4: Analyzing and Sharing the Results

- Carry out a class discussion regarding your impressions about the task performed. Share what you have heard from the audience and listen to your classmates' opinions.
- Analyze the project's records. Prepare and conduct a class presentation, in English, on the preparation steps in the making of the flash mob. Present your conclusions on the effectiveness of the project.
- Remember to have the final product (the flash mob recording) available for analysis as well.

Stage 5: Reflecting and Evaluating

- How were the people involved in the flash mob inspired by your cause? Have they understood the meaning of the performance? Has the flash mob aroused any discussions? Explain your answers.
- Has the event engaged members of the school staff and students in promoting meaningful learning?
- What have you learned from this experience? What could you have done differently so as to have better results?

EXTRA RESOURCES

- <www.natcom.org/CommCurrentsArticle.aspx?id=3846>
- <noticias.terra.com.br/educacao/professores-surpreendem-com-flash-mob-e-parodia-de-les-miserables,73b64d6f31a580b03548176fc9a365088d3eRCRD.html>
- <youtu.be/91S_Kwtz7g8>
- <youtu.be/lyt16efRrBo>

Accessed on January 3, 2016.

Learning from Experience 4   161

Studying for Enem

Enem 2010

THE WEATHER MAN

They say that the British love talking about the weather. For other nationalities this can be a banal and boring subject of conversation, something that people talk about when they have nothing else to say to each other. And yet the weather is a very important part of our lives. That at least is the opinion of Barry Gromett, press officer for the MET Office. This is located in Exeter, a pretty cathedral city in the southwest of England. Here employees – and computers – supply weather forecasts for much of the world.

Speak Up. Ano XXIII, nº 275.

Ao conversar sobre a previsão do tempo, o texto mostra

a. o aborrecimento do cidadão britânico ao falar sobre banalidades.

b. a falta de ter o que falar em situações de avaliação de línguas.

c. a importância de se entender sobre meteorologia para falar inglês.

d. as diferenças e as particularidades culturais no uso de uma língua.

e. o conflito entre diferentes ideias e opiniões ao se comunicar em inglês

Enem 2011

Going to university seems to reduce the risk of dying from coronary heart disease. An American study that involved 10 000 patients from around the world has found that people who leave school before the age of 16 are five times more likely to suffer a heart attack and die than university graduates.

World Report News. **Magazine Speak Up**. Ano XIV, nº 170. Editora Camelot, 2001.

Em relação às pesquisas, a utilização da expressão *university graduates* evidencia a intenção de informar que

a. as doenças do coração atacam dez mil pacientes.

b. as doenças do coração ocorrem na faixa dos dezesseis anos.

c. as pesquisas sobre doenças são divulgadas no meio acadêmico.

d. jovens americanos são alertados dos riscos de doenças do coração.

e. maior nível de estudo reduz riscos de ataques do coração.

GLASBERGEN, R. **Today's cartoon**. Disponível em: http://www.glasbergen.com. Acesso em: 23 jul. 2010.

Na fase escolar, é prática comum que os professores passem atividades extraclasse e marquem uma data para que as mesmas sejam entregues para correção. No caso da cena da charge, a professora ouve uma estudante apresentando argumentos para

a. discutir sobre o conteúdo do seu trabalho já entregue.

b. elogiar o tema proposto para o relatório solicitado.

c. sugerir temas para novas pesquisas e relatórios.

d. reclamar do curto prazo para entrega do trabalho.

e. convencer de que fez o relatório solicitado.

War

Until the philosophy which holds one race superior

And another inferior

Is finallty and permanently discredited and
abandoned,

Everywhere is war – Me say war.

That until there is no longer

First class and second class citizens of any nation,

Until the color of a man's skin

Is of no more significance than the color of his eyes –

Me say war.

[…]

And until the ignoble and unhappy regimes

that hold our brothers in Angola, in Mozambique,

South Africa, sub-human bondage have been
toppled,

Utterly destroyed –

Well, everywhere is war – Me say war.

War in the east, war in the west,

War up north, war down south –

War – war – Rumors of war.

And until that day, the African continent will not
know peace.

We, Africans, will fight – we find it necessary –

And we know we shall win

As we are confident in the victory.

[…]

> MARLEY, B. Disponível em: http://www.sing365.com.
> Acesso em: 30 jun. 2011 (fragmento).

Bob Marley foi um artista popular e atraiu muitos fãs com suas canções. Ciente de sua influência social, na música *War*, o cantor se utiliza de sua arte para alertar sobre

a. a inércia do continente africano diante das injustiças sociais.

b. a persistência da Guerra enquanto houver diferenças raciais e sociais.

c. as acentuadas diferenças culturais entre os países africanos.

d. as discrepâncias sociais entre moçambicanos e angolanos como causa de conflitos.

e. a fragilidade das diferenças raciais e sociais como justificativas para o início de uma guerra.

Enem 2012

Quotes of the Day

Friday, Sep. 02, 2011

"There probably was a shortage of not just respect and boundaries but also love. But you do need, when they cross the line and break the law, to be very tough."

British Prime Minister DAVID CAMERON, arguing that those involved in the recent riots in England need "tough love" as he vows to "get to grips" with the country's problem families.

> Disponível em: www.time.com. Acesso em: 5 nov. 2011 (adaptado).

A respeito dos tumultos causados na Inglaterra em agosto de 2011, as palavras de alerta de David Cameron têm como foco principal

a. enfatizar a discriminação contra os jovens britânicos e suas famílias.

b. criticar as ações agressivas demonstradas nos tumultos pelos jovens.

c. estabelecer relação entre a falta de limites dos jovens e o excesso de amor.

d. reforçar a ideia de que os jovens precisam de amor, mas também de firmeza.

e. descrever o tipo de amor que gera problemas às famílias de jovens britânicos.

Studying for Enem

DONAR. Disponível em: http://politicalgraffiti.wordpress.com.
Acesso em: 17 ago. 2011.

Cartuns são produzidos com o intuito de satirizar comportamentos humanos e assim oportunizam a reflexão sobre nossos próprios comportamentos e atitudes. Nesse cartum, a linguagem utilizada pelos personagens em uma conversa em inglês evidencia a

a. predominância do uso da linguagem informal sobre a língua padrão.

b. dificuldade de reconhecer a existência de diferentes usos da linguagem.

c. aceitação dos regionalismos utilizados por pessoas de diferentes lugares.

d. necessidade de estudo da língua inglesa por parte dos personagens.

e. facilidade de compreensão entre falantes com sotaques distintos.

Enem 2013

After prison blaze kills hundreds in Honduras, UN warns on overcrowding

15 February 2012

A United Nations human rights official today called on Latin American countries to tackle the problem of prison overcrowding in the wake of an overnight fire at a jail in Honduras that killed hundreds of inmates. More than 300 prisoners are reported to have died in the blaze at the prison, located north of the capital, Tegucigalpa, with dozens of others still missing and presumed dead. Antonio Maldonado, human rights adviser for the UN system in Honduras, told UN Radio today that overcrowding may have contributed to the death toll. "But we have to wait until a thorough investigation is conducted so we can reach a precise cause," he said. "But of course there is a problem of overcrowding in the prison system, not only in this country, but also in many other prisons in Latin America."

Disponível em: www.un.org. Acesso em: 22 fev. 2012 (adaptado).

Os noticiários destacam acontecimentos diários, que são veiculados em jornal impresso, rádio, televisão e internet. Nesse texto, o acontecimento reportado é a:

a. ocorrência de um incêndio em um presídio superlotado em Honduras.

b. questão da superlotação nos presídios em Honduras e na América Latina.

c. investigação da morte de um oficial das Nações Unidas em visita a um presídio.

d. conclusão do relatório sobre a morte de mais de trezentos detentos em Honduras.

e. causa da morte de doze detentos em um presídio superlotado ao norte de Honduras.

National Geographic News

Christine Dell'Amore
Published April 26, 2010

Our bodies produce a small steady amount of natural morphine, a new study suggests. Traces of the chemical are often found in mouse and human urine, leading scientists to wonder whether the drug is being made naturally or being delivered by something the subjects consumed. The new research shows that mice produce the "incredible painkiller" – and that humans and other mammals possess the same chemical road map for making it, said study co-author Meinhart Zenk, who studies plant-based pharmaceuticals at the Donald Danforth Plant Science Center in St. Louis, Missouri.

Disponível em: www.nationalgeographic.com. Acesso em: 27 jul. 2010.

Ao ler a matéria publicada na *National Geographic*, para a realização de um trabalho escolar, um estudante descobriu que

a. os compostos químicos da morfina, produzidos por humanos, são manipulados no Missouri.

b. os ratos e os humanos possuem a mesma via metabólica para produção de morfina.

c. a produção de morfina em grande quantidade minimiza a dor em ratos e humanos.

d. os seres humanos têm uma predisposição genética para inibir a dor.

e. a produção de morfina é um traço incomum entre os animais.

Enem 2014

A Tall Order

The sky isn't the limit for an architect building the world's first invisible skyscraper.

Charles Wee, one of the world's leading high-rise architects, has a confession to make: he's bored with skyscrapers. After designing more than 30, most of which punctuate the skylines of rapidly expanding Asian cities, he has struck upon a novel concept: the first invisible skyscraper.

As the tallest structure in South Korea, his Infinity Tower will loom over Seoul until somebody pushes a button and it completely disappears.

When he entered a 2004 competition to design a landmark tower, the Korean-American architect rejected the notion of competing with Dubai, Toronto, and Shanghai to reach the summit of man-made summits. "I thought, let's not jump into this stupid race to build another 'tallest' tower," he says in a phone conversation. "Let's take an opposite approach – let's make an anti-tower."

The result will be a 150-story building that fades from view at the flick of a switch. The tower will effectively function as an enormous television screen, being able to project an exact replica of whatever is happening behind it onto its façade. To the human eye, the building will appear to have melted away.

It will be the most extraordinary achievement of Wee's stellar architectural career. After graduating from UCLA, he worked under Anthony Lumsden, a prolific Californian architect who helped devise the modern technique of wrapping buildings inside smooth glass skins.

HINES, N. Disponível em: http://mag.newsweek.com. Acesso em: 13 out. 2013 (adaptado).

No título e no subtítulo desse texto, as expressões *A Tall Order* e *The sky isn't the limit* são usadas para apresentar uma matéria cujo tema é:

a. Inovações tecnológicas usadas para a construção de um novo arranha-céu em Seul.

b. Confissões de um arquiteto que busca se destacar na construção de arranha-céus.

c. Técnicas a serem estabelecidas para a construção de edifícios altos na Califórnia.

d. Competição entre arquitetos para a construção do edifício mais alto do mundo.

e. Construção de altas torres de apartamentos nas grandes metrópoles da Ásia.

Studying for Enem

Disponível em: http://wefeedback.org. Acesso em: 30 jul. 2012.

A internet tem servido a diferentes interesses, ampliando, muitas vezes, o contato entre pessoas e instituições. Um exemplo disso é o *site* WeFeedback, no qual a internauta Kate Watts:

a. comprou comida em promoção.

b. inscreveu-se em concurso.

c. fez doação para caridade.

d. participou de pesquisa de opinião.

e. voluntariou-se para trabalho social.

Masters of War

Come you masters of war
You that build all the guns
You that build the death planes
You that build all the bombs
You that hide behind walls
You that hide behind desks
I just want you to know
I can see through your masks.

You that never done nothin'
But build to destroy
You play with my world
Like it's your little toy
You put a gun in my hand
And you hide from my eyes
And you turn and run farther
When the fast bullets fly.

Like Judas of old
You lie and deceive
A world war can be won
You want me to believe
But I see through your eyes
And I see through your brain
Like I see through the water
That runs down my drain.

BOB DYLAN. *The Freewheelin' Bob Dylan*. Nova York: Columbia Records, 1963 (fragmento).

Na letra da canção *Masters of War*, há questionamentos e reflexões que aparecem na forma de protesto contra:

a. o envio de jovens à guerra para promover a expansão territorial dos Estados Unidos.

b. o comportamento dos soldados norte-americanos nas guerras de que participaram.

c. o sistema que recruta soldados para guerras motivadas por interesses econômicos.

d. o desinteresse do governo pelas famílias dos soldados mortos em campos de batalha.

e. as Forças Armadas norte-americanas, que enviavam homens despreparados para as guerras.

Enem 2015

Horse or cow

  Prior to taking retirement and selling off his land, a farmer needed to get rid of all the animals he owned, so he decided to call on every house in his village. At houses where the man was the boss, he gave a horse; at houses where the woman was the boss, he gave a dairy cow.

  Approaching one cottage, he saw a couple gardening and called out: 'Who's the boss around here?'.

  'I am,' said the man.

  The farmer said: 'I have a black horse and a

brown horse. Which one would you like?' The man thought for a minute and said: 'The black one.' 'No, no, get the brown one,' said his wife. The farmer said: 'Here's your cow.'

TIBBALLS, G. *The book of senior jokes*. Great Britain: Michael O'Mara, 2009 (adaptado).

O texto relata o caso de um fazendeiro prestes a se aposentar e vender sua fazenda.

O aspecto cômico desse texto provém da:

a. constatação pelo fazendeiro da razão de sua aposentadoria.

b. opinião dos vizinhos referente à forma de se livrar dos animais.

c. percepção do fazendeiro quanto à relação de poder entre o casal.

d. agressividade da esposa relacionada a um questionamento inocente.

e. indecisão dos cônjuges quanto à melhor escolha a ser feita no momento.

First Footing

One of the major Hogmanay customs was "first-shooting". Shortly after "the bells" — the stroke of midnight when public clocks would chime to signal the start of the new year –, neighbours would visit one another's houses to wish each other a good new year. This visit was known as "first-footing", and the luckiest first-foot into any house was a tall, dark and handsome man – perhaps as a reward to the woman who traditionally had spent the previous day scrubbing her house (another Hogmanay ritual). Women or red heads, however, were always considered bad luck as first-foots.

First-foots brought symbolic gifts to "handsel" the house: coal for the fire, to ensure that the house would be warm and safe, and shortbread or black bun (a type of fruit cake) to symbolise that the household would never go hungry that year.

First-footing has faded in recent years, particularly with the growth of the major street celebrations in Edinburgh and Glasgow, although not the Scots love of a good party, of which there are a plenty on the night!

Disponível em: <www.visitscotland.com>. Acesso em: 23 nov. 2011.

A partir da leitura do texto sobre a comemoração do Ano-novo na Escócia, observa-se que, com o tempo, aspectos da cultura de um povo podem ser:

a. passados para outros povos.

b. substituídos por outras práticas.

c. reforçados pelas novas gerações.

d. valorizados pelas tradições locais.

e. representados por festas populares.

36 hours in Buenos Aires

Contemporary Argentine history is a roller coaster of financial booms and cracks, set to gripping political soap operas. But through all the highs and lows, one thing has remained constant: Buenos Aires's graceful elegance and cosmopolitan cool. This attractive city continues to draw food lovers, design buffs and party people with its riotous night life, fashion-forward styling and a favorable exchange rate. Even with the uncertain economy, the creative energy and enterprising spirit of Porteños, as residents are called, prevail – just look to the growing ranks of art spaces, boutiques, restaurants and hotels.

SINGER, P. Disponível em: <www.nytimes.com>. Acesso em: 30 jul. 2012.

Nesse artigo de jornal, Buenos Aires é apresentada como a capital argentina, que:

a. foi objeto de novelas televisivas baseadas em sua vida noturna e artística.

b. manteve sua elegância e espírito cosmopolita, apesar das crises econômicas.

c. teve sua energia e aspecto empreendedor ofuscados pela incerteza da economia.

d. foi marcada historicamente por uma vida financeira estável, com repercussão na arte.

e. parou de atrair apreciadores da gastronomia, devido ao alto valor de sua moeda.

Studying for Enem

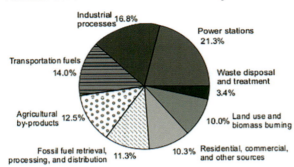

Disponível em: www.globalwaming.org. Acesso em: 31 jul. 2012 (adaptado).

A emissão de gases tóxicos na atmosfera traz diversas consequências para nosso planeta. De acordo com o gráfico, retirado do texto *Global warming is an international issue*, observa-se que:

a. as queimadas poluem um pouco mais do que os combustíveis usados nos meios de transporte.

b. as residências e comércios são os menores emissores de gases de efeito estufa na atmosfera.

c. o processo de tratamento de água contribui para a emissão de gases poluentes no planeta.

d. os combustíveis utilizados nos meios de transportes poluem mais do que as indústrias.

e. os maiores emissores de gases de efeito estufa na atmosfera são as usinas elétricas.

Disponível em: www.barhampc.kentparishes.gov.uk. Acesso em: 31 jul. 2012.

Uma campanha pode ter por objetivo conscientizar a população sobre determinada questão social. Na campanha realizada no Reino Unido, a frase "A third of the food we buy in the UK ends up being thrown away" foi utilizada para enfatizar o(a):

a. desigualdade social.

b. escassez de plantações.

c. reeducação alimentar.

d. desperdício de comida.

e. custo dos alimentos.

Language Reference

Unit 1

Subject-Verb Agreement

Em geral, na língua inglesa, seguimos a regra básica de concordância verbal: sujeito no singular concorda com verbo no singular, e sujeito no plural concorda com verbo no plural.

He buys fresh food on weekends.

We need to go shopping for clothes.

No entanto, alguns casos podem causar dúvida quanto à flexão do verbo. Veja:

- Quando o sujeito é seguido de preposição + objeto, essa estrutura não interfere na concordância do verbo.

  *The **parts** of the car **were** all damaged in the accident.*

  *My **opinion** about the students **hasn't** changed at all.*

- Dois sujeitos no singular unidos por *or, either/or, neither/nor* concordam com o verbo no singular.

  ***Either** Chris **or** Henry **is** coming to pick us up tonight.*

  *My mom **or** my dad **calls** me every day.*

- Sujeitos compostos ligados por *and* concordam com o verbo no singular quando considerados uma unidade.

  ***The bed and breakfast** they offer **is** the best service around here.*

  ***One and one equals** two.*

- Algumas vezes, o sujeito é separado do verbo por expressões como *as well as, along with, besides* etc, mas essas expressões não são parte do sujeito em si e, portanto, não interferem na concordância.

  ***The chair**, as well as the stool, **is** the cause of her backache.*

  ***The student**, along with the teacher, **is** supposed to arrive on time for the exam.*

- Quando o sujeito é composto por expressões que indicam porções, porcentagens e frações como *a lot, some, all, the majority, half, none, more, a third of* etc, o verbo concorda com o substantivo que as segue.

  ***All of the fruit is** ripe.*

  ***All of the books are** for sale.*

- Em frases iniciadas com *here* ou *there* em que o verbo antecede o sujeito, a concordância também acontece em número.

  ***There was** no **excuse** for your late arrival.*

  ***Here are** my sincere **apologies**, honey.*

- Para distâncias, períodos de tempo, quantias em dinheiro etc, quando considerados como unidades, o verbo concorda no singular.

  ***Ten months was** the longest period I'd been away from my country.*

  ***A hundred dollars is** a price I cannot afford.*

Language Reference | 169

Language Reference

1. Read the following news release. Then complete the sentences with the verb forms from the box. Finally, identify the subject that corresponds to each verb form.

| are | does not appear | finds | is | stresses | was |

Media centre

WHO: Number of people over 60 years set to double by 2050; major societal changes required

News release

30 SEPTEMBER 2015 ¦ GENEVA - With advances in medicine helping more people to live longer lives, the number of people over the age of 60 ♦ expected to double by 2050 and will require radical societal change, according to a new report released by the WHO for the International Day of Older Persons (1 October).

"Today, most people, even in the poorest countries, ♦ living longer lives," says Dr Margaret Chan, Director-General of WHO. "But this is not enough. We need to ensure these extra years are healthy, meaningful and dignified. Achieving this will not just be good for older people, it will be good for society as a whole."

Longer lives not necessarily healthier lives

Contrary to widespread assumptions, the "World report on ageing and health 2015" ♦ that there is very little evidence that the added years of life are being experienced in better health than ♦ the case for previous generations at the same age. "Unfortunately, 70 ♦ yet ♦ to be the new 60," says Dr John Beard, Director of the Department of Ageing and Life Course at WHO. "But it could be. And it should be".

While some older people may indeed be experiencing both longer and healthier lives, these people are likely to have come from more advantaged segments of society. "People from disadvantaged backgrounds, those in poorer countries, those with the fewest opportunities and the fewest resources to call on in older age, are also likely to have the poorest health and the greatest need," says Dr Beard.

The Report ♦ that governments must ensure policies that enable older people to continue participating in society and that avoid reinforcing the inequities that often underpin poor health in older age.

[…]

Extracted from <www.who.int/mediacentre/news/releases/2015/older-persons-day/en/>. Accessed on January 4, 2016.

2. Use the following prompts to write sentences about the text in activity 1. Write them in your notebook.

a. More and more people / expected to live longer by 2050

b. There / no evidence / people over 60 are living healthier lives

c. Some older people / experiencing longer and healthier lives

d. The majority of people from poor countries / less chance of living longer and healthier

3. Make subjects and verb forms agree to complete the quotes.

a.

Subjects	Verb Forms
Our inner lives	has
Age	are

" ♦ no reality except in the physical world. The essence of a human being is resistant to the passage of time. ♦ eternal, which is to say that our spirits remain as youthful and vigorous as when we were in full bloom. Think of love as a state of grace, not the means to anything, but the alpha and omega. An end in itself." (Gabriel García Márquez, Colombian writer)

Extracted from <www.goodreads.com/quotes/240375-age-has-no-reality-except-in-the-physical-world-the>. Accessed on February 19, 2016.

b.

Subjects	Verb Forms
Things	is
The great thing about getting older	aren't

"   ♦ that you become more mellow. ♦ as black and white, and you become much more tolerant. You can see the good in things much more easily rather than getting enraged as you used to do when you were young."
(Maeve Binchy, Irish novelist)

Extracted from <www.brainyquote.com/quotes/authors/m/maeve_binchy.html>. Accessed on May 31, 2016.

Unit 2

Order of Adjectives

Quando um substantivo é qualificado por dois ou mais adjetivos, devemos posicioná-los em uma ordem específica: adjetivos que expressam opinião devem preceder aqueles que expressam fatos.

*That's a **beautiful old** house.*

*My friends run a **nice Italian** restaurant in the suburbs.*

*The school is in an **interesting**, **pleasant** neighborhood.*

Dois ou mais adjetivos que expressam fato podem, no entanto, qualificar um mesmo substantivo. Nesse caso, eles obedecem à seguinte ordem:

Tamanho	Forma	Idade	Cor	Nacionalidade	Material
big	flat	new	black	American	gold
small	round	young	green	Brazilian	metal
tall	square	old	red	South African	wooden

Leia os exemplos a seguir.

*Who's that **tall young** man over there?*

*I don't need such a **large square glass** table. I'll buy a **small wooden** one.*

Observe que adjetivos que modificam de uma mesma maneira os substantivos (como os dois adjetivos que expressam opinião em *interesting, pleasant neighborhood*) são separados por vírgula. Por outro lado, adjetivos que modificam substantivos de diferentes maneiras (como um adjetivo que expressa opinião e um que expressa nacionalidade, como os dois adjetivos em *nice Italian restaurant*) não são separados por vírgula.

1. Read the critics' reviews of the movie *Central Station* and find the nouns that are preceded by two or more adjectives. Then identify the adjectives that correspond to the nouns you have found.

    a. Central Station tells a familiar story, but it makes use of its setting in an original and thoughtful way.
Full Review | June 3, 2014
Peter T. Chattaway
Patheos

Language Reference 171

Language Reference

b. What separates and elevates Walter Salles' film above the familiar neo-realist type of melodrama is the stylized visual style and Fernanda Montenegro's stunning performance.
Full Review | August 9, 2010
Emanuel Levy
EmanuelLevy.Com

c. A richly tender and moving experience.
Full Review | Original Score: A-

d. It's not just a strong, heartfelt drama. It's a film that transcends its national boundaries.

January 23, 2002

Louis B. Hobson

Jam! Movies

e. The film was too much stuck in its sentimentality and had an uninspiring and a contrived plot that kept me from warming up to the story.

Full Review | Original Score: C

Adapted from <www.rottentomatoes.com/m/central-do-brasil-central-station/>.
Accessed on January 4, 2016.

Adverbs

Advérbios modificam verbos, adjetivos ou outros advérbios. Em inglês, formamos grande parte dos advérbios acrescentando *-ly* a adjetivos ou substantivos.

Leia alguns exemplos e observe as alterações gráficas.

careful ⟶ *careful**ly***   *easy* ⟶ *easi**ly***

quick ⟶ *quick**ly***   *simple* ⟶ *sim**ply***

week ⟶ *week**ly***   *fantastic* ⟶ *fantastical**ly***

true ⟶ *tru**ly***   *full* ⟶ *ful**ly***

Leia as frases abaixo.

*Dan walks very **quickly**. I can never catch up with him.*

*I'm sure you can do the test **easily**. Go for it!*

*I **truly** love my profession.*

1. Identify the adverbs in the reviews of the movie *Elite Squad* and then answer: which is the only adverb that modifies a verb?

a. An impressive film (shame about the superficial and reactionary reviews)
★★★★★★★★★★
Author: Kit Collis from United Kingdom
24 October 2008

172　Language Reference

Elite Squad is an impressive and enjoyable film. It is well directed, well acted, and well worth watching.

There has been a lot of criticism of Elite Squad for being fascist. Such a perspective is disappointingly superficial. Too many critics have failed to distinguish the narrative perspective from the ideological perspective of the film. Although an admittedly reactionary and authoritarian BOPE member, Captain Nascimento, narrates it, the film's primary criticisms are regarding low pay for police, systemic corruption, and, the middle class's irresponsible consumption of drugs. As for any feeling that the brutal violence is justified that a viewer may be left with, this has more to do with the fact that in certain extreme circumstances desperate times call for desperate measures.

Extracted from <www.imdb.com/title/tt0861739/reviews?start=10>. Accessed on January 4, 2016.

b. Amazingly good... and horrifying

★★★★★★★★★★

Author: lurple from United States
12 November 2007

Tropa de Elite is an amazingly good film; by turns brutally real and horrifyingly hilarious.

It claims to be based on a true story and I find that sadly believable. The main plot revolves around the captain of an elite police unit trying to find a replacement for himself, while dealing with the birth of his child and the horrendous stress of his job, and a mission to clear out a dangerously violent slum.
There are no wholly good people in the movie, and it's frighteningly easy to compare some of what goes on to things happening in the USA (and other places) today. That said, the system of government and policing portrayed comes across as so amazingly inept and awful that it's almost like something straight out of a nightmarish sci-fi dystopia.
If I had to compare it to other movies, it comes off as a cross between Brazil, Office Space, and Full Metal Jacket. Not for the weak of stomach, and you may find yourself greatly disagreeing with the ideals of various groups portrayed (which I believe is part of the point), but I would be enormously surprised if this movie doesn't make you think and give you something to talk about.

Extracted from <www.imdb.com/title/tt0861739/reviews?start=0>. Accessed on January 4, 2016.

Unit 3

Conditionals

Em períodos compostos por uma oração principal (*main clause*) e uma oração subordinada condicional (*conditional clause*), podemos usar diversas combinações de tempos verbais. Veja algumas delas nos exemplos abaixo.

Conditional Clause	Main Clause
If you press this key,	the computer shuts down.
If I don't understand what he says,	I will ask him to speak slowly.
If you have any questions,	raise your hands.

Language Reference

If + Simple Present + Simple Present

Essa combinação é empregada quando nos referimos a uma condição que expressa leis naturais, verdades universais, fatos ou conclusões lógicas.

*If you **leave an** ice cream out of the fridge, it **melts**.*

*My little sister **cries if** we **pretend** to take away her dolls.*

*What **happens if** one **mixes** blue and yellow?*

If + Simple Present + Simple Future / can / may / might

Essa estrutura se aplica a uma ação ou situação que pode acontecer no futuro.

*If the weather **isn't** sunny, the children **won't swim** in the pool.*

***Can** you call me **if** Alan **drops by**?*

*We **may / might** travel in July **if** we **get** our visa.*

If + Simple Present + Imperative / Should

Essa combinação é utilizada para dar ordens, sugestões ou instruções.

***Buy** the book **if** it **interests** you!*

*If you **aren't** happy with your career, **don't hesitate** to change!*

*If she **doesn't believe** me, she **should** ask her father about that.*

Observações:

- A ordem das orações não altera seu sentido nem a combinação de tempos verbais. Porém, quando a oração condicional vem em primeiro lugar, usamos vírgula para separá-la da oração principal.

  *If my team **wins** the game, we **will celebrate**.*

  *We **will celebrate** if my team **wins** the game.*

- As conjunções *whether*, *unless* e *as long as*, entre outras, também podem ser usadas em orações condicionais.

  *Please let me know **whether** or not you will visit us on the holidays.*

  ***Unless** you study really hard, you won't get good grades.*

  ***As long as** you follow the guidelines, there won't be any mistakes.*

1. Read a passage from the news article *Violence and women in Brazil: What happens indoors stays indoors*, published on the English newspaper *The Independent*. Pay attention to the underlined sentence and choose the best answer to the question that follows.

   > [...]
   > In a society fuelled by machismo, there is quite a lot of resistance from the police and this is an issue we continue to work hard to combat. But we continue our battle to reaffirm the importance of public policies that can guarantee a full life for

all women and effectively prevent gender-based violence. I really believe that through our work we can open up the eyes of fellow citizens around the country to fight for women's rights. As church community members become aware of the violence suffered by their women, there will no longer be silence and I hope the perpetrators will be condemned. <u>If we can end the silence and denial, we will be victorious in the fight against violence against women</u>.

Extracted from <www.independent.co.uk/voices/comment/violence-and-women-in-brazil-what-happens-indoors-stays-indoors-8809947.html>. Accessed on January 4, 2016.

What does the sentence express?

- an order

- a future possibility

fuelled (UK) / fueled (US)

2. Now read part of a blog post and identify the sentences that express conditions. Then answer: do they express future possibilities as well? Explain.

What can you do when someone you know is experiencing DV?

Posted on 26 March 2013

What can we do when we know (or suspect) that a friend, family member, colleague, neighbour or somebody we know is experiencing domestic violence or family violence?

If you feel that someone you know is at risk, approach them about the abuse in a sensitive way. If a friend tells you that they are being abused, listen to them, believe them and take them seriously.

[…]

Extracted from <thesilenceofdomesticviolence.blogspot.co.uk/2013/04/what-can-you-do-when-someone-you-know.html>. Accessed on January 4, 2016.

3. Now complete the following text with the sentences from the box.

1. Even if your loved one stays with their partner, it's important they still feel comfortable talking to you about it.

2. If they break up with the abusive partner, continue to be supportive after the relationship is over.

3. If they do choose to leave, they may feel sad and lonely when it's over, even though the relationship was abusive.

4. If your friend or family member is undergoing the serious and painful effects of dating abuse, they may have a very different point of view than you.

Language Reference 175

Language Reference

> ## Get Help For Someone Else
>
> **Help a Friend**
>
> Watching a friend go through an abusive relationship can be very scary and you may feel like you're not sure how to help them. The decision to leave can only be made by the person experiencing the abuse, but there are a lot of things you can do to help your friend stay safe.
>
> **What Do I Need to Know?**
>
> ♦. They may have heard the abuse was their fault and feel responsible. Even after realizing that there's abuse, they may choose to stay in the relationship. As a friend, try to be there for them because although they may not show it, they need you more than ever.
>
> ♦ They may get back together with their ex many times, even though you want them to stay apart. Remember that it may be difficult for your friend to even bring up a conversation about the abuse they're experiencing.
>
> **What Can I Do?**
>
> - Don't be afraid to reach out to a friend who you think needs help. Tell them you're concerned for their safety and want to help.
> - Be supportive and listen patiently. Acknowledge their feelings and be respectful of their decisions.
> - Help your friend recognize that the abuse is not "normal" and is NOT their fault. Everyone deserves a healthy, non-violent relationship.
> - Focus on your friend or family member, not the abusive partner. ♦
> - Connect your friend to resources in their community that can give them information and guidance. Remember, loveisrespect.org can help.
> - Help them develop a safety plan.
> - ♦
> - Even when you feel like there's nothing you can do, don't forget that by being supportive and caring, you're already doing a lot.
> - Don't contact their abuser or publicly post negative things about them online. It'll only worsen the situation for your friend.
>
> [...]

Extracted from <www.loveisrespect.org/for-someone-else/help-a-friend/>. Accessed on January 4, 2016

Unit 4

Past Continuous

Usamos o *Past Continuous* quando nos referimos a ações em progresso no passado. Para formarmos o *Past Continuous* usamos o passado do verbo *to be* (*was / were*) + verbo principal + *ing*.

Observe alguns exemplos na tabela abaixo.

Affirmative	Negative	Interrogative
I **was listening** to music at the gym.	I **was not / wasn't listening** to music at the gym.	**Was** I **listening** to music at the gym?
You **were doing** the dishes while I was eating.	You **were not / weren't doing** the dishes while I was eating.	**Were** you **doing** the dishes while I was eating?
He **was studying** abroad when his dad died.	He **was not / wasn't studying** abroad when his dad died.	**Was** he **studying** abroad when his dad died?
She **was carrying** an umbrella when I met her.	She **was not / wasn't carrying** an umbrella when I met her.	**Was** she **carrying** an umbrella when I met her?
It **was raining** a lot when classes finished.	It **was not / wasn't raining** a lot when classes finished.	**Was** it **raining** a lot when classes finished?
We **were jogging** at the beach when she broke her foot.	We **were not / weren't jogging** at the beach when she broke her foot.	**Were** we **jogging** at the beach when she broke her foot?
You **were preparing** breakfast very early in the morning.	You **were not / weren't preparing** breakfast very early in the morning.	**Were** you **preparing** breakfast very early in the morning?
They **were asking** questions when the director came in.	They **were not / weren't asking** questions when the director came in.	**Were** they **asking** questions when the director came in?

Short Answers – Affirmative and Negative

Para formarmos as respostas curtas (*short answers*) no *Past Continuous*, usamos *was / were* para respostas afirmativas e *wasn't / weren't* para respostas negativas.

	Short answers	
	Affirmative	**Negative**
Was she reading a magazine?	Yes, she was.	No, she wasn't.
Were you playing cards?	Yes, I was.	No, I wasn't.

Duas ações em andamento simultâneo no passado podem ser unidas por *while*.

Observe.

While he **was eating** dinner, she **was writing** in her diary.

It **was raining while** we **were working** out at the gym.

Past Continuous and Simple Past

Em geral, o *Past Continuous* é associado ao *Simple Past* para indicar que uma ação mais longa, ou em progresso, é interrompida por outra, mais curta. *While*, *when* e *as* são frequentemente usados para unir tais orações. Veja os exemplos abaixo.

I ***was waiting*** for the bus when I ***saw*** Tom.

What ***happened*** while you ***were walking*** to school?

As they ***weren't working*** in the building at the time, they ***didn't witness*** the accident.

Language Reference 177

Language Reference

1. Read part of the feedback Kirsten has written about the medical volunteer program she has participated in Ghana. Then complete the sentences with either the Simple Past or the Past Continuous of the verbs *teach* and *work*.

Name: Kirsten

Nationality: UNITED STATES

Age: 20

Destination: Ghana

Program Type: Medical

Date: Jul 2015, 4.

I participated in the medical volunteer program in Ghana, where I volunteered at Asokwa Children's hospital. They rotated me around the different departments of the hospital: emergency ward, taking vitals, pharmacy, and lab, so I got to experience a little bit of everything. It was definitely a great learning experience, and I honestly feel like I got more out of it than I was able to contribute. Because I didn't have any medical training, I couldn't always be of help but after I got more acquainted with the place and the people, I began making a lot of friends and trying more and more to offer up help. I was actually very grateful I ♦ in the hospital, because there were a lot of nursing students my age who were also working there. They were very nice to me, and ♦ me some of the local language, took me to try local foods, helped me understand what I was supposed to be doing, and just befriended me in general. One girl actually invited me to her house, and when I was there she had her friend give me a few henna tattoos. It was such a great experience, and I am still in touch with many of the people I worked with.

Extracted from <www.lovevolunteers.org/node/194/feedback/kirsten-0>. Accessed on January 4, 2016.

2. Read the text in activity 1 once again and answer the following questions. Write full answers.

   a. Where did Kirsten volunteer?

   b. Why couldn't Kirsten help too much at the beginning?

   c. Who taught her some of the local language?

   d. Who did she stay with?

   e. Where did her Ghanaian friends volunteer?

   f. What did Kirsten and her Ghanaian friends do on weekends?

3. Go back to activity 1 and read the sentences you completed with the Simple Past and the Past Continuous. Reflect on them and answer: how do the usages of both verb tenses differ?

178   Language Reference

4. Read the text below and pay attention to the sentences in bold. Use your own words to write what you infer from them. Each sentence must include a verb in the Simple Past and a verb in the Past Continuous.

> **Name**: Rebecca
> **Nationality**: NEW ZEALAND
> **Age**: 21
> **Destination**: Cambodia
> **Program Type**: Teaching and Assisting in Schools
> **Date**: Jan 2013, 4 weeks.

Over summer I was placed at a school in Phnom Pehn, Cambodia teaching a Grade Three class of 36. The bright walls, cheerful kids and incredible teachers quickly made me fall in love with the place. I taught my class about nouns, adjectives and verbs, we learnt about singular, plural and negative form, occupations, appearances, clothing and directions. **Seeing most of the class succeed and grasp these lessons was hugely exciting, while trying to manage to find time to help those who were falling behind was difficult and pushed me to think outside the box.**

My highlights over the months are countless, they include seeing the kids faces light up when I brought out stickers, and watching their scheming and creative attempts to try and sneak more. It was discovering that unlike in New Zealand, these students loved to be tested, and it was seeing their marks improve over the month. It was receiving artwork and letters from them, and spending my evenings answering their questions. It was the million high fives I got as I walked up to class each day, and the multiple times I was asked 'what is your name?' and 'are you married?'. It was playing volleyball, yoyo or hacky sack with the boys in their break, and riding home with a few of the girls after school. **It was getting to know each child personally, and striving to spend a bit of time talking one on one. It was the class party on my last day, and seeing their smiles when the pizza finally arrived after a week of excited anticipation**. Saying goodbye was heartbreaking, and I cannot wait to visit them again.

For a country with such a sad and recent history, it was amazing to see the sense of determination to learn, a determination to catch up with the rest of the world and make up for lost time. Given their history it wouldn't have surprised me if Cambodians were cold, hard and broken, but instead in the month I was there I found myself living amongst the most gentle, generous and friendly people I have ever come across. I cannot wait to return to Cambodia, and in particular to return to the school and to my class.

The opportunity to teach exceeded my expectations. Love Volunteers was exceptional, while their prices reasonable and far cheaper than anywhere else.

Adapted from <www.lovevolunteers.org/node/428/feedback/rebecca>. Accessed on May 31, 2016.

Language Reference 179

Language Reference

Unit 5

Past Perfect

Usamos o *Past Perfect* quando nos referimos a uma ação que aconteceu antes de outra ação no passado. Para formarmos o *Past Perfect* usamos o passado do verbo *to have* (*had*) + verbo principal no particípio passado.

Leia alguns exemplos na tabela abaixo.

Affirmative	Negative	Interrogative
I **had lost** my job when she started working there.	I **had not / hadn't lost** my job when she started working there.	**Had** I **lost** my job when she started working there?
You **had worked** hard on the project before you were fired.	You **had not / hadn't worked** hard on the project before you were fired.	**Had** you **worked** hard on the project before you were fired?
He **had heard** of that band when he saw it on TV.	He **had not / hadn't heard** of that band when he saw it on TV.	**Had** he **heard** of that band when he saw it on TV?
She **had written** the letter before she left.	She **had not / hadn't written** the letter before she left.	**Had** she **written** the letter before she left?
It **had been** the coldest day before the end of the winter.	It **had not / hadn't been** the coldest day before the end of the winter.	**Had** it **been** the coldest day before the end of the winter?
We **had arrived** before mom.	We **had not / hadn't arrived** before mom.	**Had** we **arrived** before mom?
You **had** already **gone** home when she called.	You **had not / hadn't gone** home when she called.	**Had** you **gone** home when she called?
They **had done** the shopping, so they decided to watch a movie.	They **had not / hadn't done** the shopping, so they decided to watch a movie.	**Had** they **done** the shopping when they decided to watch a movie?

Short Answers – Affirmative and Negative

Para formarmos as respostas curtas (*short answers*) no *Past Perfect*, usamos *had* para respostas afirmativas e *hadn't* para respostas negativas.

	Short answers	
	Affirmative	**Negative**
Had he been there?	Yes, he had.	No, he hadn't.
Had you come before?	Yes, I had.	No, I hadn't.

É comum usarmos *after, before, when, by the time* etc., quando usamos o *Past Perfect* e o *Simple Past* para evidenciarmos qual ação passada aconteceu primeiro. Veja os exemplos a seguir.

180 **Language Reference**

After the party **had finished**, I decided to sit down and rest.

Had you **sold** your car **before** you bought the motorcycle?

When her husband arrived, she **had** already cleaned the garage.

By the time Helen answered the phone, he **had called** her at least three times.

1. The text below has been published on the Understanding Slavery Initiative (USI) website, whose aim is to support the teaching and learning of transatlantic slavery and its legacies through the use of museum and heritage collections. Read the text and identify the verb forms that indicate actions that happened before other actions in the past.

On the eve of the transatlantic slave trade

In most parts of Africa before 1500, societies had become highly developed in terms of their own histories. They often had complex systems of participatory government, or were established powerful states that covered large territories and had extensive regional and international links.

Many of these societies had solved difficult agricultural problems and had come up with advanced techniques of production of food and other crops and were engaged in local, regional or even international trading networks. Some people were skilled miners and metallurgists, others great artists in wood, stone and other materials. Many of the societies had also amassed a great stock of scientific and other knowledge, some of it stored in libraries such as those of Timbuktu, but some passed down orally from generation to generation.

There was great diversity across the continent and therefore societies at different stages and levels of development. Most importantly, Africans had established their own economic and political systems, their own cultures, technologies and philosophies that had enabled them to make spectacular advances and important contributions to human knowledge.

The significance of the transatlantic slave trade is not just that it led to the loss of millions of lives and the departure of millions of those who could have contributed to Africa's future, although depopulation did have a great impact. But just as devastating was the fact that African societies were disrupted by the trade and increasingly unable to follow an independent path of development. Colonial rule and its modern legacy have been a continuation of this disruption.

The devastation of Africa through transatlantic slavery was accompanied by the ignorance of some historians and philosophers to negate its entire history. These ideas and philosophies suggested, that among other things, Africans had never developed any institutions or cultures, nor anything else of any worth and that future advances could only take place under the direction of Europeans or European institutions.

Adapted from <www.understandingslavery.com/index.php?option=com_content&view=article&id=306&Itemid=151>. Accessed on January 4, 2016.

Language Reference 181

Language Reference

2. Choose the statements that are true according to the text in the previous activity.

a. Some African societies were already highly developed before 1500.

b. Many of these societies had difficulties in solving agricultural problems because they could not count on advanced techniques.

c. All African societies had a lot of knowledge stored in books.

d. Africans have made amazing advances and have contributed a lot to human knowledge.

e. The slave trade devastated Africa and as a consequence, African societies could not follow an independent path of development.

3. Choose the correct alternative to complete the text below.

African Influences in Modern Art

During the early 1900s, the aesthetics of traditional African sculpture became a powerful influence among European artists who formed an avant-garde in the development of modern art. In France, Henri Matisse, Pablo Picasso, and their School of Paris friends blended the highly stylized treatment of the human figure in African sculptures with painting styles derived from the post-Impressionist works of Cézanne and Gauguin. The resulting pictorial flatness, vivid color palette, and fragmented Cubist shapes helped to define early modernism. While these artists ◆ nothing of the original meaning and function of the West and Central African sculptures they encountered, they instantly recognized the spiritual aspect of the composition and adapted these qualities to their own efforts to move beyond the naturalism that ◆ Western art since the Renaissance.

[…]

The Stylistic Influences of African Sculpture

Modernist artists were drawn to African sculpture because of its sophisticated approach to the abstraction of the human figure, shown, for example, by a sculpted head from a Fang reliquary ensemble (1979.206.229), and a reliquary by an Ambete artist (2002.456.17). The provenance of the Fang work includes the collection of London-based sculptor Jacob Epstein, who ◆ Vorticist associations and was a longtime friend of Picasso and Matisse; the Ambete reliquary was once owned by the pioneering Paris dealer Charles Ratton and then by Pierre Matisse, a son of the artist.

The Fang sculpture exemplifies the integration of form with function that ◆ a centuries-old tradition of abstraction in African art before the European colonial period. Affixed at the top of a bark vessel where remains of the most important individuals of an extended family were preserved, the sculptural element can be considered as the embodiment of the ancestor's spirit. The representational style is therefore abstract rather than naturalistic. The abstract form of the Ambete piece goes even further to serve its function. Because the figure is the actual receptacle for the ancestral relics, the torso is elongated, hollow, and accessible from an opening in the back. The exaggerated flatness of the face in these reliquaries, and its lack of affect, typify elements of African aesthetics that ◆ frequently evoked in modernist painting and sculpture.

[…]

Extracted from <www.metmuseum.org/toah/hd/aima/hd_aima.htm>. Accessed on May 31, 2016.

a. had known / had defined / had / created / were

b. knew / defined / had / had created / was

c. knew / had defined / had / had created / were

4. Read another passage from the text *African Influences in Modern Art* and complete it with the verb forms from the box.

> had observed   had visited   moved   worked

[...]

Modernism in America

Matisse and Picasso were key figures in the spread of interest in African-influenced modernism among the avant-garde in the United States. In 1905, the American artist Max Weber ♦ to Paris and studied painting with Matisse. By 1908, Weber, a frequent guest at the Sunday evening salons hosted by Gertrude Stein and her brother Leo, ♦ Picasso in his studio, where he may have viewed Picasso's extensive collection of African art. After returning to the United States, Weber wrote to photographer Alfred Stieglitz about the African influences that he ♦ in the work of Picasso and other Paris-based modernists; and Weber's own paintings featured mask forms rendered in an increasingly abstract style. Stieglitz later presented the first Picasso exhibition in the United States at his small gallery, named "291" for its Fifth Avenue address, and then ♦ with Mexican artist Marius de Zayas on a 1914 exhibition which was among the first in the United States to present African sculpture as art. A 1923 exhibit at the Whitney Studio Club, a precursor of the Whitney Museum in New York, was among the earliest to present Picasso's paintings together with African sculptures.

[...]

Extracted from <www.metmuseum.org/toah/hd/aima/hd_aima.htm>. Accessed on May 31, 2016.

Unit 6

Direct and Indirect Speech

Usamos o discurso direto para reproduzir o que alguém disse usando exatamente as mesmas palavras, que colocamos entre aspas. Observe.

The woman said, "I am your best friend now."

She told her father, "We didn't have time to deposit the check yesterday."

No discurso indireto, por outro lado, reportamos o que uma pessoa disse com nossas próprias palavras. Para tanto, em geral é necessário alterar o tempo verbal, os pronomes e as expressões de tempo e de lugar. Veja.

The woman said (that) she was my best friend then.

She told her father (that) they hadn't had time to deposit the check the day before.

Observe as mudanças em relação aos verbos na tabela a seguir.

Language Reference 183

Language Reference

Direct Speech	Indirect Speech
Simple Present He said, "I **need** to buy cat food."	Simple Past He said (that) he **needed** to buy cat food.
Present Continuous She said, "I**'m doing** my homework."	Past Continuous She said (that) she **was doing** her homework.
Present Perfect They said, "We **have met** before."	Past Perfect They said (that) they **had met** before.
Simple Past You said, "I **didn't ask** about Jen."	Past Perfect You said (that) you **hadn't asked** about Jen.
Will We said, "We **will** tell him the truth."	Would We said (that) we **would** tell him the truth.
Can / May I said, "I **can** help you with that." He said, "I **may** not arrive for lunch."	Could / Might I said (that) I **could** help you with that. He said (that) he **might** not arrive for lunch.
Must She said, "I **must** wear my uniform."	Had to She said (that) she **had to** wear her uniform.
Imperative They said to us, "**Calm down**." The director said to the students, "**Don't be** late again."	Infinitive They told us **to calm down**. The director told the students **not to be** late again.

Observe que *could, might, would* e *should* não sofrem alterações.

*He said, "I **could** give you a hand." (Direct Speech)*

*He said (that) he **could** give me a hand. (Indirect Speech)*

*She said, "This **might** be difficult." (Direct Speech)*

*She said (that) that **might** be difficult. (Indirect Speech)*

Na tabela abaixo, observe as mudanças em relação às expressões de tempo e de lugar.

Direct Speech	Indirect Speech
a week / a month / a year ago	a week / a month / a year before
last week / month / year	the week / month / year before
next	the following
now	then / at that time
today	that day
tomorrow	the next day / the following day
tonight	that night
yesterday	the day before / the previous day
here	there

Para transformarmos uma pergunta do discurso direto para o indireto, usamos a oração na forma afirmativa, fazendo as devidas alterações quanto ao tempo verbal, aos pronomes e às expressões de tempo e lugar. Quando não há uma *wh- question*, usamos *if* para reportar o que foi perguntado.

Veja os exemplos abaixo.
He asked, "What time is it?"
He asked what time it was.
They asked, "Where will you travel to next month?"
They asked where we would travel to the following month.
He asked his son, "Did you do the laundry this morning?"
He asked his son if he had done the laundry that morning.

Nos exemplos acima, observe ainda que os pronomes demonstrativos *this* e *these* são alterados para *that* e *those* quando no discurso indireto.

1. Read part of a report by *Voice of America*, a multimedia international broadcasting service, and then do the activities that follow.

News / Africa

False Report on Zimbabwe President Sparks Social Media War In Kenya

AFRICA

November 09, 2015

Ndimyake Mwakalyelye

WASHINGTON DC – By Monday, the storm of words set off by a false quote originated by Kenyan newsmagazine, *The Spectator*, but fueled by social media, including the group Kenyans on Twitter or KOT, and then the respected *New York Times*, that Zimbabwe President Robert Mugabe called Kenyans thieves, had died down after the quote turned out to be a hoax.

However, while some were enraged by the statements, which *The Spectator* reportedly said it made up for satirical purposes, some questioned the authenticity of the outrageous claims quoting Mr. Mugabe warning Zimbabweans to be on high alert when visiting Kenya, because "stealing was in their [Kenyans] blood," and that he was sure the universities even offered a degree called, "bachelor of stealing!"

Kenyan resident Judith Murugi, however, gave President Mugabe the benefit of the doubt.

"From what I've read about him and the speeches I've heard from Mugabe, I think it's a lot of speculation or twisting words around, so as to create some sort of conflict but I don't think that Mugabe would actually say something like that," she said.

Following revelation that the quote was a hoax, anger initially directed at President Mugabe and Zimbabwe then turned to the so-called social media hypers such as KOT, and then the reputable *New York Times* that helped spread the false quotes worldwide.

Zimbabwe's state-run *Herald* Newspaper quoted Presidential Spokesperson George Charamba reproaching Jeffrey Gettleman, the East Africa correspondent for the *New York Times* for not verifying the quote before publishing it.

Charamba reportedly said, "I find it incredible that Mr. Gettleman can insert a quote he attributes to my President in his story, and then seek to check its veracity only later."

[...]

Extracted from <www.voazimbabwe.com/content/false-quote-on-zimbabwe-president-sparks-social-media-tension-between-ya-and-zimbabwe-/3050234.html>. Accessed on January 4, 2016.

Language Reference 185

Language Reference

a. What do the extracts below report? Read them again and explain.

> "From what I've read about him and the speeches I've heard from Mugabe, I think it's a lot of speculation or twisting words around, so as to create some sort of conflict but I don't think that Mugabe would actually say something like that,"

> "I find it incredible that Mr. Gettleman can insert a quote he attributes to my President in his story, and then seek to check its veracity only later."

b. Rewrite the words said by Judith Murugi and George Charamba in the extracts above.

2. Choose the alternative that correctly rephrases the cartoon lines using indirect speech.

a.

Extracted from <www.cartoonstock.com/cartoonview.asp?catref=forn4869>. Accessed on May 31, 2016.

- The man told the woman if she sent those people $50 they'd show her how to make money off the net!
- The man told the woman to send those people $50 and they will show her how to make money off the net!

b.

Extracted from <lowres.cartoonstock.com/law-order-online_scams-banking_details-internet-online-scam-mlyn1667_low.jpg>. Accessed on May 31, 2016.

- The man was astonished because they have been the victims of cyber-crime… Someone on the other side of the world will pay all their bills.
- The man was astonished because they had been the victims of cyber-crime… Someone on the other side of the world had paid all their bills.

c.

"I know those big money deals from *Nigeria* are a scam, but this e-mail is from *New Guinea!*"

Extracted from <lowres.cartoonstock.com/law-order-con-scam-scammer-email_scam-email_con-rman15241_low.jpg>. Accessed on May 31, 2016.

- The man said he knew those big money deals from Nigeria are a scam, but added that that e-mail is from New Guinea!
- The man said he knew those big money deals from Nigeria were a scam, but added that that e-mail was from New Guinea!

d.

"You're not how I imagined you'd look from your avatar, Conan."

Extracted from <lowres.cartoonstock.com/computers-avatar-online_dating-dates-couples-conan-tcrn842_low.jpg>. Accessed on May 31, 2016.

- The woman told Conan that he was not how she had imagined he'd look from his avatar.
- The woman told Conan that he was not how she imagined he'd look from his avatar.

Unit 7

Reflexive Pronouns

Reflexive Pronouns são usados quando:
- o sujeito e o objeto da oração são iguais.
  *Alex hurt **himself**.*
  *Take care of **yourselves**!*

Language Reference

- queremos enfatizar o agente de uma ação.

    I **myself** will take care of the drinks for dinner.

    The director **herself** invited me for the meeting.

    The students planned the graduation ceremony **themselves**.

- têm o sentido de sozinho(a), sozinhos(as), sem ajuda. Nesse caso, os pronomes reflexivos são precedidos pela preposição *by*.

    I like to go to the movies **by myself**.

    My notebook is out of order: it turns on and off **by itself**.

A cada pronome pessoal corresponde um pronome reflexivo.

Observe a tabela.

	Subject Pronouns	Reflexive Pronouns
Singular	I	myself
	you	yourself
	he	himself
	she	herself
	it	itself
Plural	we	ourselves
	you	yourselves
	they	themselves

1. Identify the reflexive pronouns and the subjects they correspond to.

"Whoever said 'We have nothing to fear but fear itself' ought to have a look at my credit card bill."

188 Language Reference

2. Read two extracts from an OECD's (Organisation for Economic Co-operation and Development) document entitled *Financial Education in Schools* and complete them with reflexive pronouns.

a. FINANCIAL LITERACY: A CORE LIFE SKILL

[…] Financial education can make a difference. It can empower and equip young people with the knowledge, skills and confidence to take charge of their lives and build a more secure future for ♦ and their families. Supporting financial education can be viewed by the main public, private and civil stakeholders as a critical long-term investment in human capital.

b. THE IMPORTANCE OF STARTING YOUNG AND AT SCHOOL

[…] " "For each of us, financial literacy is key to living our daily lives with dignity. It is also "a gift" that each of us has to give to him or ♦, in order to be a dignified citizen of the world." Ardian Fullani, Governor, Bank of Albania" […]

Extracted from <www.oecd.org/daf/fin/financial-education/FinEdSchool_web.pdf>. Accessed on December 26, 2015.

Passive Voice III

Como já visto antes, a voz passiva é normalmente usada quando a ação é mais importante do que o agente, quando falamos de uma verdade universal ou quando não é importante mencionar ou não sabemos dizer o que ou quem realizou a ação.

Para formarmos a voz passiva, usamos o verbo *to be* no mesmo tempo verbal da voz ativa, acrescido do particípio passado do verbo principal. Assim, o sujeito da voz ativa torna-se o objeto da voz passiva e vice-versa. Para mencionarmos quem ou o que realizou a ação, usamos a preposição *by*.

Veja:

Active voice: J. K. Rowling wrote the Harry Potter series of books.

Passive Voice: The Harry Potter series of books was written by J. K. Rowling.

Nesta unidade estudamos a voz passiva no *Past Perfect* tense. Observe.

Active Voice	Passive Voice
The firemen **had warned** them of the danger.	They **had been warned** of the danger (by the firemen).
She **hadn't baked** the chocolate cake before the guests arrived.	The chocolate cake **hadn't been baked** (by her) before the guests arrived.
Had Jarrod **sold** the apartment when he moved out?	**Had** the apartment **been sold** (by Jarrod) when he moved out?

1. Read the quotes below and extract the parts that contain Passive Voice structures in the Past Perfect tense. Then turn them into active voice.

a. "They had been corrupted by money, and he had been corrupted by sentiment. Sentiment was the more dangerous, because you couldn't name its price. A man open to bribes was to be relied upon below a certain figure, but sentiment might uncoil in the heart at a name, a photograph, even a smell remembered."

Graham Greene. *The Heart of the Matter.* Extracted from <www.goodreads.com/quotes/416558-they-had-been-corrupted-by-money-and-he-had-been>. Accessed on January 4, 2016.

b. "Imagine the world of mobile based on Nokia and Motorola if Apple had not been restarted by a missionary entrepreneur named Steve Jobs who cared more for his vision than being tactical and financial." (Vinod Khosla, American businessman)

Extracted from <www.brainyquote.com/quotes/quotes/v/vinodkhosl529623.html#fHWly3TffiAFBlbR.9>.Accessed on January 4, 2016.

Language Reference 189

Language Reference

Unit 8

Verb Tense Review

Simple Present

Usamos o *Simple Present* para falar de fatos, opiniões ou ações rotineiras.

*This hotel **doesn't offer** free Internet access.*

*I **wake up** at 6 o'clock, **take a shower**, and **get dressed** to go to school.*

Present Continuous

Usamos o *Present Continuous* para falar de ações que estão acontecendo no momento da fala.

***Is** Brenda **using** the computer in her room now?*

*We **aren't eating** our lunch, we**'re preparing** it.*

Present Perfect

Usamos o *Present Perfect* para nos referirmos a ações que aconteceram em algum momento indeterminado do passado e que normalmente têm influência no presente ou continuam até o presente.

*My parents **have** never **been** to Curitiba.*

***Has** your teacher **corrected** the tests yet?*

Simple Past

Usamos o *Simple Past* para falar de ações que ocorreram e tiveram fim em determinado momento do passado.

*I **finished** high school in 2018.*

***Did** you **visit** your relatives last month?*

Past Continuous

Usamos o *Past Continuous* para falar de ações que estavam em curso no passado.

*Dora **was cleaning** her bedroom while her little sisters **were sleeping**.*

*What **were** you **doing** when I called you?*

Past Perfect

Usamos o *Past Perfect* para falar de ações que aconteceram antes de outras ações no passado.

*The teacher handed in the tests we **had done** the week before.*

*I **hadn't bought** the tickets when you told me about the weather forecast.*

Simple Future

Usamos o *Simple Future* para falar de previsões ou para expressar decisões tomadas no momento da fala.

*My soccer team **will win** the national championship this year.*

*Uncle Sam is inviting me out but I **won't go** anywhere tonight. I'm awfully tired!*

1. Read part of the graduation speech below, pay attention to the verb forms in bold, and identify the meaning they express.

> "If you had asked me a year ago where I saw myself today, I probably would have told you something along the lines of "getting ready to leave Washington and travel across the country to create a new

beginning for myself and never come back." But here I am today, in a much different circumstance. After a crazy year of failure and success and ups and downs, I somehow found myself committing to a college in Seattle, just 30 minutes away from my house. I**'ve lived** in Washington my whole life, in 3 different houses all within about 15 minutes of each other. So naturally, when the topic of college came up, I **wanted** to get out. I had been here for almost 18 years. My sights were set on leaving. But a few months ago, my sister and I **were driving** through downtown Seattle. I was looking around at this city that I **had grown up** so close to my whole life. And as I gazed out across Lake Union and up toward Capitol Hill, I realized that I didn't really know this city at all. I had always assumed I knew it because I had driven through it so many times; but in reality, I didn't know of the secret back roads, the little coffee shops, the underground restaurants; all I knew were the Space Needle and the sports teams and the Science Center. Seattle was familiar to me, but I didn't really have a good understanding of all that the city is. And I wonder if I've done that with people. If they've become familiar to me – if I assume I know them because I see them five days a week. I wonder if I only know people's space needles and sports teams, but not their back roads and hidden coffee shops. It seems as if I know people's main productions but not their behind the scenes. I wonder if I really know people at all sometimes.

[…]

Remember that sometimes you **will want** to get away – from people, a city, a job, but no matter where you go or how far you travel, you will always carry yourself with you. You can't escape how you feel or who you are.

Remember that failure **builds** character, although it takes time. When you first fail, there's nothing very romantic or satisfying about it. […] But as you go on and reconstruct yourself, you come back with a little more fight than before. You can empathize with other people a whole lot easier. You become a little more – well – human.

So let's just go out there and be human and fall down and marvel at the unknown and not feel the need to be these big superheroes. Let's go out there and be beautiful and gutsy and stubborn and spunky. Let's just go out there and – with hearts full and arms open – just simply live."

Congratulations class of 2015. We did it!

Thank you!

Extracted from <www.heraldnet.com/section/gradspeeches?SchoolSearch=Archbishop%20Murphy%20High%20School&FirstNameSearch=Sam%20&LastNameSearch=Byrne>. Accessed on April 25, 2016.

2. Read the text again and answer: what is the predominant verb tense in the first part of the speech? How do you explain that?

3. Use the verb forms from the box to complete the text below.

| are doing | grab | marched | remember | 's done | were writing | will become |

In a Blink of an Eye, High School Is Over

Published 11:04pm Tuesday, May 10, 2016

Boom – just like that high school is over. I read a post expressing that message.

"That's how it happens," I said to myself. "Suddenly, it ◆ and you are standing at the door of a new reality."

There are a lot of seniors about to stand in that doorway over the next few weeks. One moment high school is your world. Whether you love it or not, it's the place you know well. Then they hand you a diploma, and that familiar place becomes a memory.

Language Reference 191

Language Reference

Of course, this doesn't hit you until some time passes. No, graduation is excitement and looking forward to possibilities. Finally, adulthood is within reach and with it the freedom that is a teenager's dream.

I remember feeling that way as I ♦ out those double doors of the high school auditorium. Standing in the late spring evening, I felt a rush of anticipation at the thought of moving beyond the days of bells and study hall, lockers and lunchrooms.

What I didn't consider was it was also the end of other things. There would be no more recess when we laughed and talked about the drama going on in our lives. Pep rallies on Friday afternoons were over. Days of seeing the faces that were part of my life since elementary school were history.

When we took off our caps and gowns, we began journeys that carried us away from each other, writing an ending to years of being a group of people known as the class of such and such a year. Again, we didn't give this much thought as we ♦ that ending.

Now, years later reading that message about the end of high school brought a rush of memories, recollections of my final days at Opp High School. There was the push to get signatures in my last yearbook. I ♦ tears as we hugged after class day and following Baccalaureate and graduation night.

We vowed to stay in touch, to remain a class of friends forever. Some of us saw each other from time to time, maybe in the grocery store or at some community event.

And, there were reunions when part of the class returned to visit and remember together. However, in the years since that last day as a class, we never were all together again in one place.

The internet and Facebook make it easier to rekindle friendships and catch up on where classmates live and what they ♦. It also a way to share the sadness when we hear about one of us reaching the end of his or her journey.

Still, looking at online pictures or reading email messages doesn't replace talking face-to-face with friends. It's not the same as looking into the eyes of someone who knew you when lost your baby teeth and then as you struggled through pimples.

Yes, for the Class of 2016 high school is almost over. Some day you will feel like BOOM it was over in the blink of an eye.

So, enjoy these last days. Look into the faces of the people who are in your class. Even the ones you don't know well ♦ a memory you treasure. They are part of your history.

True, high school is often a hard and awkward time. It is a mix of fun, confusion and growing pains. And no matter what your experience during those years, happy, sad, good or bad, you remember this time in your life forever.

All of us who grabbed diplomas and stepped bravely into what lies beyond high school wish you well on your journey.

One final word from a former high school student — cherish the memories of these precious days, but don't attempt to live in them for the rest of your lives. High school is a nice memory, but there are more memories to make beyond graduation.

So move on with courage. ♦ life and run with it. We are cheering you on.

Nancy Blackmon is a former newspaper editor and a yoga teacher.

Extracted from <www.andalusiastarnews.com/2016/05/10/in-a-blink-of-an-eye-high-school-is-over/>. Accessed on May 31, 2016.

Audio Scripts

Track 2, page 20, activity 2

People who live on their own can become very self-centered. They can't see any other view but their own. And they suffer from that. The person who says, "No, uhm…that's what I think, and I'm sticking to it." I think, "You poor things. You're not opening the door." (0:00 - 0:25)

Transcribed from <www.abc.net.au/health/features/stories/2014/02/14/3944120.htm>. Accessed on September 23, 2015.

Track 3, page 20, activity 3

I'm Beryl Francis Newton. I'm over 100 years old, and for the last 70-odd years, I have lived in Maleny.

We were married in 1938, and we were together for nearly 60 years. He died when he was 89 and I was 83, so we had a very good time together.

Since that time, I have been lucky enough to live on my own, with the help of outside help. And I handed in my license. Yeah, they didn't ask for it, but I thought that's a…it's quite fair enough uh… at 97.

Isolation depends on yourself. I have never felt isolated. (0:26 - 1:30)

Transcribed from <www.abc.net.au/health/features/stories/2014/02/14/3944120.htm>. Accessed on September 23, 2015.

Track 4, page 21, activity 4

"Knock, knock, Beryl. Hello."

Daniele is my carer. She comes Monday, Wednesday, and Friday to shower me. She comes on Tuesday to sit and read letter and gossip.

"Do you want these shoes?"

She's the one who looks around and sees that my slippers are where I need them. She's the one that'll go and take the clothes off the line and folds them up and puts them away in my … drawers and so on and so…

"Alright, I'll be back in a minute, Beryl."

Sometimes she gets a bit bossy. And sometimes, she says, "Beryl!" And then my face sort of folds into a…

"Is it inside?"

"It is."

And people are kindly. People are very kindly. They make allowances for old ladies, if the old ladies are sensible enough to know when to take things.

"No men to impress."

"No."

"But I can impress ladies."

"Yes."

Sometimes people passing by… the lady across the road, if she sees both doors open…

"Come in, dear."

She'll slip across to say "How are you?" because she's got two youngsters.

"Come in."

"I just came to ask you…"

"Come in!"

And generally speaking, at most times I can talk to anybody. It doesn't matter whether they're my little great grandson or an old, old, old, old woman like me. I think… I think it's because I'm… I want to know about them. I want to know what they feel like and how they manage. Now, I don't ask them that question, but I can see by the way they answer me.

"Beryl, uhm…You're going to the hairdresser today, aren't you?"

"Yes."

"Are you gonna wear that lovely blue shirt of yours?"

"Yes, dear."

"So, we'll get that organized before you go today."

"Good morning, Beryl."

"Good morning."

"What are you doing this week? What's happening?"

"Keeping appointments."

"I'm just ringing on behalf of Beryl Newton. She'd like to cancel her meals on Wheels for today."

Audio Scripts

Am I happy? Well, no. You can't be happy all the time. It isn't that way. But you can be contented and make it so. You don't have to be happy all the time. And you won't be.

"What do you think? 65?"

"Yeah."

"About… about 65." (1:31 - 4:21)

Transcribed from <www.abc.net.au/health/features/stories/2014/02/14/3944120.htm>. Accessed on September 23, 2015.

Track 5, page 35, activity 3

SS: It strikes me that one… one danger, perhaps, that you have is that football is important in your movie.

WS: Right.

SS: It's one of the escape routes that poor Brazilians have to try and make it.

WS: Right.

SS: Uhm, and yet football is almost a… a cliché now when one thinks of Brazil. It's become stereotypical.

WS: Right. (0:00 - 0:17)

Transcribed from <www.youtube.com/watch?v=jI5IBoebVTw>. Accessed on April 28, 2016.

Track 6, page 35, activity 4

SS: You could also argue perhaps that the wider issue of favela poverty and ways of getting out, including crime, have become stereotypical because of the number of movies made about these subjects. Do you… do you worry about that?

WS: I agree on both points actually, and what interested me here in *Linha de Passe* was exactly the reverse angle of what you see. You know, when you open the papers, either in Brazil or in the U.K, you have the stories of the Robinhos and Ronaldos, the very few, uhm, young kids coming from Brazil, breaking the line of poverty, who ended up making it. But what about the two million kids who try to make it? Those stories are never told. And that's what interested us here. Uhm, now jumping to the second part of your question, it is true that the representation of Brazil became biased in cinema due to the number of films that explore the theme of, uhm, gang warfare in… in our streets.

SS: And one film many people will have seen around the world is *City of God*…

WS: Yes, of course…

SS: Which you produced.

WS: Yes, and that was a very important film because it let us know that that phenomenon existed in the heart of our cities. And that was not in Brazilian television. That was not in the Brazilian newspapers. Nobody knew about that, so… Fernando…

SS: Could you remind the people who haven't actually seen the movie, it basically portrays, in the most graphic way, gang violence in one of Rio's favelas. I mean, it…it looks beautiful. It is an amazing film to watch, but it is also imbued with…with violence, corruption…

WS: Right.

SS: It's a pretty grim picture.

WS: Yes, and it's, it's a very grim picture. And it's done by a very talented director who was, I think, very faithful to that reality, Fernando Meirelles. And it was co-directed by Kátia Lund, also a very talented director. But once Fernando did that film, he drifted to other territories and, uh, didn't insist on that, on that uh specific subject matter. And then other films came and came and came, and what you have is a certain representation of Brazil in which you could think that all the kids in our suburbs carry AK-47s. And they do not. And this is why we also wanted to do this film is to show that, you know, the youth can have aspirations, uh, in Brazil as they have in any other latitude. That it's about reinventing another future. It's about refusing what destiny has in line for you and actually reinventing oneself. And that is something that we carry in Brazil constantly. I mean, that desire to reinvent the country, I think is…is utterly Brazilian. It's part of our, uhm, I think, national desire. We're part of this. (0:18 - 2:53)

Transcribed from <www.youtube.com/watch?v=jI5IBoebVTw>. Accessed on April 28, 2016.

194 Audio Scripts

Track 7, page 35, activity 5

SS: Well, uh, we'll talk politics in a second because it…it definitely is a part of of of your take on Brazil, I think. But, before we do that, I just wonder whether there is a danger that when you say you want to get away from the clichés…

WS: Right.

SS: Whether it be the violence, uh, or Carnaval, or whatever…

WS: Right.

SS: The danger is you lose the audience because what you produce is, is bleak. And you could argue, it's depressing.

WS: Right.

SS: If you're just looking at ordinary people's lives in an ordinary, poor suburb…

WS: Right.

SS: That, that isn't necessarily entertaining.

WS: Yeah, well, it depends a lot on the point of view, like uhm…I see Mike Lee films or uh Ken Loach's films, and I don't, I don't think that they are depressing. Uh, although, sometimes what they represent is bleak, uh, there is such humanity in the characters.

SS: Well, I'll tell you what…I tell you what

WS: of those two filmmakers that I, I completely fall in love with, with…

SS: I, I…

WS: With those films.

SS: I'm so interested in the comparisons you drew. It makes me want to play, uh, the second clip that we have of your movie because you mentioned Mike Lee, for example. He's famous for making these sort of interior dramas wi…you know, literally ki, kitchen sink sort of movies where it is people's relationships that really matter.

WS: Right.

SS: Let's look at another clip where you get to that sort of level.

WS: Absolutely. (3:00 - 4:08)

[…]

Transcribed from <www.youtube.com/watch?v=jl5lBoebVTw>.
Accessed on April 28, 2016.

Track 8, page 54, activities 2 and 3

911. Operator 911. Where's the emergency?

127 Bremier.

OK, what's going on there?

I'd like to order a pizza for delivery.

Ma'am, you've reached 911. This is an emergency line.

Yeah, uhm, a large with half pepperoni, half mushrooms.

Uhm, you know you called 911. This is an emergency line.

Do you know how long it'll be?

OK, ma'am, is everything OK over there? Do you have an emergency or not?

Yes.

And you're unable to talk because…

Right, right.

Is there someone in the room with you? Just say yes or no.

Yes.

OK, uhm… it looks like I have an officer about a mile from your location. Are there any weapons in your house?

No.

Can you stay on the phone with me?

Um um… No. Uh…see you soon. Thank you. (1:00)

Transcribed from <www.youtube.com/watch?v=rTJT3fVv1vU>.
Accessed on October 10, 2015

Track 10, page 68, activity 3

Hi, my name's Sarah Pitcher. I'm 18 years old. I'm in Fiji right now. Who would've thought? I'm in a little town called Navidula, which is about three hours from Suva. As you can see, it's raining right now. But, when there's sunny days, it's amazing, and even when it's raining, it's still beautiful.

At Navidula District School I spend four days: Monday, Tuesday, Wednesday, Thursday. I spend a day with each class… uhm, from Class 1 to Class 8, and I teach either English or sports or pretty much whatever else they need me to do. I type exams and I mark exams. Uh… my computer literacy

Audio Scripts

skills are very highly valued here. And we have one school computer… uh, one school computer that's very old. So, I use my laptop most of the time. And most of the kids have never seen a computer, never touched a computer. (0:00 - 0:57)

Transcribed from <www.lattitude.org.au/index.php?nodeId=153>. Accessed on December 10, 2015.

Track 11, page 69, activity 4

Uh, there's 123 students overall. Uhm, very cheeky, very loud, but very fun. Most of them speak English… from Class 2 and up speak English, uhm, obviously the older they get, the better they get. Uh, Class 7 and 8 speak English very well. And if I talk slowly, they'll understand everything I say. Although their vocabulary is, uhm, pretty limited.

Uhm, I also spend a day in, uhm, Korovou Town. On Fridays I go to the environmental center there.

I'm pretty much just trying to educate nearby schools, nearby villages to try and get them to be resourceful and, uh, decrease waste and improve waste management and pretty much just take care of the rivers and the animals and everything around here.

I live on the school compound with the head teacher, a Fijian man and his Indian wife, who's also a teacher. Uh, I have two little brothers here, two little Fijian brothers. Uh, they go to school here, so I teach them sometimes. Uh, at home… so, this is my home just behind me, we wake up in the morning and my Indian mother cooks us breakfast. We usually have roti and curry, something like that. We go to school, kind of, whatever time we feel like. There's not much of a time basis here, which is kind of funny. Uh, we teach for a while. I go and help out whatever I'm doing and then come back home in the afternoons. After school if it's sunny or even if it's rainy, we go and play. We go jump off the bridge, jump in the river, climb some trees, ride some horses.

I hadn't had any teaching experience before. At first, it can be a bit intimidating. You stand up in front of the class and they're all quiet, they're all really shy with you at first 'cause they're afraid that they'll say something wrong in English and you'll know that it's wrong and you might make fun of them. By now, you get to know them, you get to know which ones are the cheekiest and you know how to discipline them and they respect you and it… it's so much fun when you get to know all their names and you can joke with them and have fun and really appreciate what the Fijian children are like.

Uh, when I first came here, I was a bit worried, like I guess anybody would be when they're coming to a new place on their own. Uh, but as soon as I got here I felt straight at home. You've got… everybody is your family, everywhere you go they'll say, they'll introduce themselves but they won't tell you their name. They'll say call me "grandma" or "nanda" (grandma), or call me "nei", which is "auntie", or call me "nana", which is "mum". So, everyone is your family and they treat you like their family. They'll… they're constantly looking after you, they're constantly concerned for you, so you don't need to be concerned about yourself 'cause you know everyone else is worrying about you anyway. (0:58 - 3:40)

Transcribed from <www.lattitude.org.au/index.php?nodeId=153>. Accessed on December 10, 2015.

Track 13, page 88, activity 2

Inside Africa, I'm Errol Barnett. This week's journey is about all of us. You know, it's widely believed that us modern-day humans originated here, in Africa. But have you ever wondered how scientists know that for sure? I've always wondered if we're from Africa, why do we all look so different today and how did we get to a point where we've populated every corner of the globe? Well, my mission this week is to have the experts answer those questions. And I'll even have my own DNA tested, looking back thousands of years to see where my ancestors link up in our human family tree. (0:00 - 0:36)

Transcribed from <www.youtube.com/watch?v=EnWTi8SrUOs>. Accessed on December 18, 2015.

Track 14, page 88, activity 3

Paleoanthropologist Ron Clarke is among an elite few who've been unlocking these discoveries.

"What do all of these findings mean?"

"Well, you…you know, what makes us human is that we analyze our surroundings. We want to know how things work. How, why, where. And so, one of the big questions is how did we become human?"

"How far back are we going in time?"

"Here, we go back to around three million years ago."

"Wow!"

"And of course, in East Africa, the fossils go back much further, to beyond four million years. But we don't have those preserved at that age here."

"Well, I want to, you know, take that time travel trip with you. We're at the location of your most famous discovery. So, can we head inside and take a look around?"

"Sure."

"Great."

Professor Clarke leads me into the Sterkfontein Cave, which is currently owned by the University of the Witwatersrand, also known as Wits University. But more than a century ago, this was an active limestone mine. Unwittingly, miners blasted away rock containing some of the oldest fossils in the world. But it also allowed for Ron's predecessors to dig deeper into our past.

"Now, my research tells me that there is no other cave in the world like this one. Why is that?"

"That's true. We have a great number and variety of fossils relating to our ancestors that date from about three million years ago up until a hundred thousand years ago."

"All right here."

"All right here. And I'm going to show you one of the deepest and oldest."

In the 1890s, miners handed over fossil remains to scientists, but it would take generations and many experts to make sense of what's here. In 1936, Professor Raymond Dart and his students realized a skull from this region, dubbed the Taung Child, was from a previously undiscovered living being. A kind of half ape, half man called *Australopithecus*. It sent shock waves throughout the scientific world. A decade later, Dr. Robert Broom found a

more complete *Australopithecus* skull in this cave, nicknamed "Mrs. Ples," adding to the excitement. (1:16 - 3:40)

Transcribed from <www.youtube.com/watch?v=EnWTi8SrUOs>.
Accessed on December 18, 2015.

Track 16, page 103, activity 2

16 years ago, fresh out of college, a 22-year-old intern in the White House, and, more than averagely romantic, I fell in love with my boss, in a 22-year-old sort of way. Back then, in 1995, we started an affair that lasted, on and off, for two years. And at that time, it was my everything. Overnight, I went from being a completely private figure to a publicly humiliated one. I was patient zero. The first person to have their reputation completely destroyed worldwide via the Internet. (0:00 – 0:55)

Transcribed from <www.dailymail.co.uk/news/article-2993054/
Monica-Lewinsky-says-worlds-cyberbullying-victim.html>.
Accessed on December 19, 2016.

Track 17, page 103, activity 3

16 years ago, fresh out of college, a 22-year-old intern in the White House, and, more than averagely romantic, I fell in love with my boss, in a 22-year-old sort of way. Back then, in 1995, we started an affair that lasted, on and off, for two years. And at that time, it was my everything. Overnight, I went from being a completely private figure to a publicly humiliated one. I was patient zero. The first person to have their reputation completely destroyed worldwide via the Internet.

When I ask myself how best to describe how the last 16 years has felt, I always come back to that word: shame. That's what happened to me in 1998 when public Monica, that Monica, that woman, was born – the creature from the media lagoon. I lost my reputation. I was publicly identified as someone I didn't recognize. And I lost my sense of self, lost it, or had it stolen because in a way it was a form of identity theft.

Today, I think of myself as someone who – who the hell knows how, survived. Believe me, denial can be pretty useful still, but these days I need it less and less and in smaller and smaller doses. But having survived myself, what I wanna do now is

Audio Scripts

help other victims of "The Shame Game" survive too. I wanna put my suffering to good use and give purpose to my past. (0:00 - 2:16)

Transcribed from <www.dailymail.co.uk/news/article-2993054/ Monica-Lewinsky-says-worlds-cyberbullying-victim.html>. Accessed on December 19, 2016.

Track 18, page 122, activities 2 and 3

Narrator – From an early age, children observe people interacting with money.

Asher Buck – Even from as young as four years old they're learning about money they're learning to bank money, they're learning how they can earn it, save it and put it towards something else.

Narrator – Talking to children about money and good money management will encourage future, healthy financial habits.

Shannon Foy – If we start teaching kids at a very early age, then they will just build and build and build on these skills to become MoneySmart people in the future.

Narrator – We know financial literacy is part of school communities. Kids interact with money at school, in the canteen, planning for excursions, organising ticket sales and fundraising. Financial literacy is part of the school curriculum and students find it really interesting and love learning about it.

Bevan Ripp – MoneySmart Teaching has provided a real context for their teaching and as a whole school we believe that kids need to have a skill set around financial literacy, that's going to carry them to, you know, adult lives.

Paul Clitheroe – When students were asked, 80% thought it was important to learn about money management at school and schools are the logical place for young people to learn about money. This is essential learning, it supports equity and economic participation.

Kim Dixon – The MoneySmart Teaching program is embedded at Wingham High School across every faculty in our school.

Student – I think it gives you a much bigger understanding of what it's like to have a job.

Student 2 –To not just think that, "oh yeah, I can just get money off my parents." It's not that easy and it does take a lot of work.

Paul Clitheroe – If the leadership team in schools understand the importance of kids being financially literate and promote being MoneySmart in their school believe me, the whole school community will benefit.

MoneySmart! (Kids shouting)

Narrator – Are the schools in your community MoneySmart? (0:00 - 2:07)

Extracted from <<www.moneysmart.gov.au/tools-and-resources/videos/ video-why-should-schools-be-moneysmart>.>. Accessed on December 19, 2016.

Track 20, pages 136 and 137, activities 3 and 4

Good morning, esteemed faculty and families of my fellow graduates. It's an honor to be standing up here today. I know we all think that we are immortal. We are supposed to feel that way. We're graduating, but like our brief four years in high school, what makes life valuable is that it doesn't last forever. What makes it precious is that it ends. We know that now more than ever, and I say it today of all days to remind us that time is luck. So don't waste it living someone else's life, make yours count for something. Fight for what matters to you, no matter what, 'cause even if we fall short what better way is there to live? It's easy to feel hopeful on a beautiful day like today, but there will be dark days ahead of us too. There will be days where you feel all alone, and that's when hope is needed most. No matter how buried it gets or how lost you feel you must promise me that you will hold on to hope. Keep it alive. We have to be greater than what we suffer. My wish for you is to become hope. People need that. And even if we fail, what better way is there to live? As we look around here today and all of the people who helped make us who we are, I know it feels like we are saying goodbye, but we will carry a piece of each other into everything that we do next. To remind us of who we are and of who we are meant to be. I've had a great four years with you. I will miss you all very much. (0:00 - 2:17)

Adapted from <www.allreadable.com/d9e4Etaf>. Accessed on December 29, 2015.

Extra Resources

Unit 1

Take a look at the list of 44 wisdoms a wise old lady has written to celebrate growing older.
<www.theagepage.co.uk/the_age_page/2013/12/be-eccentric-now-dont-wait-for-old-age-to-wear-purple.html>. Accessed on September 21, 2015.

Read about how loneliness can affect our lives and what to do to overcome social isolation.
<www.abc.net.au/health/features/stories/2014/02/14/3944120.htm>. Accessed on September 21, 2015.

DOCTER, Pete. *UP*. 2009. 96 minutes.
The animated film shows that heroes don't have to be young.

Unit 2

Watch Fernanda Montenegro's interview for the *Late Show with David Letterman* on CBS.
<www.youtube.com/watch?v=ixc7IJuDRaY>. Accessed on September 28, 2015.

Get to know the latest movie news through clips, interviews and comments.
<www.euronews.com/programs/cinema>. Accessed on October 2, 2015.

Salles, Walter. *Central do Brasil*. 1998. Duration: 115 minutes.
The movie tells the story of two very different characters that develop a strong, life-changing relationship.

Unit 3

Get to know about the Brazilian law that imposes stricter penalties for violence against women.
<time.com/3738529/brazil-violence-women-law-femicide/>. Accessed on October 11, 2015.

Take a look at this fact sheet about violence against women all over the world.
<www.who.int/mediacentre/factsheets/fs239/en/>. Accessed on October 11, 2015.

Learn about five types of domestic violence.
<www.weaveinc.org/types-domestic-violence>. Accessed on October 11, 2015.

Watch a video about domestic violence in Brazil and learn how *Programa Chapéu de Palha* has been helping women in Pernambuco.
Available at <www.youtube.com/watch?v=4t5jArJCvLg>. Accessed on October 11, 2015.

Unit 4

Read about Lattitude Global Volunteering – what they do and where they offer volunteering programs. You can also read stories or watch videos of people who have had this experience.
<www.lattitude.org.au>. Accessed on December 11, 2015.

Get to know about some volunteering organizations in Brazil and some other countries.
<www.voluntariado.org.br/default.php?p=principal.php >. Accessed on February 24, 2016.

Watch a three-minute video about someone who has decided to make a difference in many people's lives.
<www.huffingtonpost.com/2011/07/28/health-benefits-of-volunteering-helping-others_n_909713.html>. Accessed on February 24, 2016.

Unit 5

Read about African civilizations: Ancient Egypt, Great Zimbabwe, the kingdom of Kongo, the kingdom of Mali and others.
<www.britishmuseum.org/learning/schools_and_teachers/resources/all_resources/wealth_of_africa/african_civilisations.aspx>. Accessed on December 17, 2015.

Get to know about African arts and cultures worldwide.
<africa.si.edu/>. Accessed on December 17, 2015.

If you are curious about music in Africa, go to the following site.
<africa.si.edu/wp-content/themes/NMAfA/scripts/radio_africa/index.html>. Accessed on December 17, 2015.

Extra Resources

 Watch this 3:42-minute video in which the Senegalese musician Akon talk about his "lighting Africa" project, one that aims at bringing electricity to 600 million people across Africa.

<www.bbc.com/news/world-africa-34109620>. Accessed on December 17, 2015.

Unit 6

 Read the news article about Monica Lewinski and Bill Clinton's story published on March 2015. Her 2:16-minute video is also available on this page.

<www.dailymail.co.uk/news/article-2993054/Monica-Lewinsky-says-worlds-cyberbullying-victim.html>. Accessed on December 19, 2015.

Learn about different types of bullying and other facts concerning bullying.

<www.bullyingstatistics.org>. Accessed on December 19, 2015.

 Watch a 3:10-minute video made by End to Cyber Bullying (ETCB).

<www.youtube.com/watch?v=bfT2qqrqzgo>. Accessed on December 19, 2015.

Unit 7

 Get further information about ASIC MoneySmart Teaching at

<www.moneysmart.gov.au/teaching>. You can also watch the video whose recording you have already listened to. Accessed on December 27, 2015.

Read the whole news article *High school students' money skills tested* and get to know more details about the research done with the students in New Zealand.

<www.3news.co.nz/business/high-school-students-money-skills-tested-2015090307#axzz3vW925J1x>. Accessed on December 27, 2015.

Try some financial lessons and check out your personal finance skills.

<www.practicalmoneyskills.com/foreducators/lesson_plans/highschool.php>. Accessed on December 27, 2015.

 Watch a short video (2:49 min) about the financial literacy program at Maryland High School, USA, and check what students learn during these lessons and how they feel about it.

<www.voanews.com/media/video/financial-literacy-class-teaches-teens-money-skills/2619746.html>. Accessed on December 27, 2015.

Unit 8

 Read about life after high school and get to know some tips that can help you prepare for the new journey.

<kidshealth.org/teen/school_jobs/jobs/after_hs.html#>. Accessed on December 29, 2015.

This article reveals the increase in the number of foreign students studying at U.S. colleges and universities, especially students from China, Brazil and India.

 <www.ischoolguide.com/articles/34369/20151117/report-foreign-students-studying-u-s-colleges-significantly-increase-few.htm>. Accessed on December 29, 2015.

Take a look at this list of 10 Top Commencement Speeches *Time Magazine* has published and get to know important lessons renowned people such as Steve Jobs have taught to university students.

<content.time.com/time/specials/packages/completelist/0,29569,1898670,00.html>. Accessed on January 3, 2015.

Irregular Verbs List

Base form	Past	Past Participle	Translation
arise	arose	arisen	erguer(se), levantar(se)
awake	awoke	awoken	despertar
be	was, were	been	ser, estar
bear	bore	borne, born	carregar; suportar
become	became	become	tornar-se
begin	began	begun	começar, iniciar
bind	bound	bound	juntar, ligar, unir
bleed	bled	bled	sangrar
blow	blew	blown	assoprar, ventar
break	broke	broken	quebrar
bring	brought	brought	trazer
build	built	built	construir
burst	burst	burst	explodir
buy	bought	bought	comprar
catch	caught	caught	capturar, pegar
choose	chose	chosen	escolher
cling	clung	clung	segurar-se
come	came	come	chegar, vir
cost	cost	cost	custar
cut	cut	cut	cortar
deal	dealt	dealt	lidar
do	did	done	fazer
draw	drew	drawn	arrastar; desenhar
dream	dreamt/ dreamed	dreamt/ dreamed	sonhar
drive	drove	driven	dirigir, levar a
eat	ate	eaten	comer
fall	fell	fallen	cair
feed	fed	fed	alimentar
feel	felt	felt	sentir
fight	fought	fought	brigar, lutar
find	found	found	achar, encontrar
flee	fled	fled	escapar, fugir
fly	flew	flown	voar
forecast	forecast	forecast	calcular de antemão
forget	forgot	forgotten, forgot	esquecer
forgive	forgave	forgiven	perdoar
get	got	got, gotten	conseguir, obter
give	gave	given	dar
go	went	gone	ir
grow	grew	grown	crescer
hang	hung	hung	pendurar, suspender
have	had	had	ter
hear	heard	heard	escutar, ouvir
hide	hid	hidden	esconder
hit	hit	hit	atingir
hold	held	held	agarrar, segurar
hurt	hurt	hurt	machucar
keep	kept	kept	guardar, manter
know	knew	known	conhecer, saber

Irregular Verbs List

Base form	Past	Past Participle	Translation
lay	laid	laid	colocar ou ficar em posição horizontal; espalhar-se
lead	led	led	conduzir, liderar
leave	left	left	partir, sair
let	let	let	deixar, permitir
lie	lay	lain	deitar, estar deitado
light	lit	lit	iluminar
lose	lost	lost	perder
make	made	made	fazer
mean	meant	meant	significar
meet	met	met	conhecer, encontrar
pay	paid	paid	pagar
put	put	put	pôr
read	read	read	ler
rewrite	rewrote	rewritten	reescrever
rise	rose	risen	erguer-se; subir
run	ran	run	correr
say	said	said	afirmar, declarar, dizer
see	saw	seen	ver
seek	sought	sought	buscar, procurar
sell	sold	sold	vender
send	sent	sent	enviar, mandar
shoot	shot	shot	alvejar, atirar; filmar
show	showed	shown	exibir, mostrar
sing	sang	sung	cantar
sink	sank	sunk	ficar deprimido(a)
sit	sat	sat	sentar
sleep	slept	slept	dormir
speak	spoke	spoken	falar
spend	spent	spent	gastar (dinheiro); passar (tempo)
spread	spread	spread	espalhar
stand	stood	stood	ficar de pé; parar
steal	stole	stolen	furtar, roubar
strive	strove	striven	esforçar-se, tentar
swear	swore	sworn	jurar, prometer
take	took	taken	pegar, tomar
teach	taught	taught	dar aula, ensinar
tell	told	told	contar, dizer
think	thought	thought	pensar
throw	threw	thrown	arremessar, atirar
trust	trust	trust	acreditar, confiar
understand	understood	understood	compreender, entender
undertake	undertook	undertaken	experimentar, tentar
wake	woke	waken	acordar
wear	wore	worn	vestir
win	won	won	ganhar, vencer
write	wrote	written	escrever, redigir

Glossary

abruptly: repentinamente
abut: encostar
accomplishment: realização
achievement: conquista
addiction: dependência, vício
advantageous: vantajoso(a)
aid: ajuda, apoio, auxílio
alike: da mesma maneira
alleged: suposto(a)
alleviate: aliviar
amenable to: acessível à
amongst: entre, no meio de
anguished: aflito(a), angustiado(a)
appalling: espantoso(a)
aptitude: aptidão
assessment: avaliação
attempt: tentativa
avocado: abacate
barefoot: descalço(a)
be targeted: ser alvo(a)
be teased: ser provocado(a)
be trapped: ficar preso(a)
bear the brunt: sofrer as consequências
beaver: castor
befriend: fazer amizade
belief: crença
bereavement: perda
beseeching: suplicante
biopic (biographical picture): filme biográfico
bitterness: amargura
blame: culpar, responsabilizar
blaming: acusação
blazing: ardente
blend: combinar, misturar
boon: bênção
bother: preocupar-se
brass: bronze
bravura: executado(a) de forma brilhante
breach: violar (lei)
brighten: iluminar
bring about: ocasionar
brokerage: corretagem
budget: orçamento, verba
burden: sobrecarregar; carga, peso
burial: enterro, funeral

burst: estourar, rebentar
bury: enterrar
calibre: grandeza
camarilla: camarilha (conjunto de pessoas que cerca o Chefe do Estado e com ele convive intimamente, influindo diretamente em sua gestão)
carry out: executar, realizar
catchall: de caráter geral, genérico
catch up: alcançar, encontrar
charitable: de caridade
childish: infantil
children's wagon: carrinho de bebê
churn out: produzir rapidamente ou continuamente
claim: reclamar, reivindicar
clay: barro
clear out: limpar
coarse: inferior, ordinário(a)
cocoon: casulo
coercion: coerção
collectible: colecionável
come to terms: conviver com
commence: começar, iniciar
complaint: denúncia, queixa
concern: afligir, preocupar; preocupação
convey: comunicar, expressar, transmitir
cope: lidar
corn: milho
cornerstone: alicerce, pedra fundamental
counter: contrário(a), oposto(a)
court: área, pátio; corte de justiça, tribunal
crack: estalar; ruptura, rachadura
cradle: berço, local de origem
crane operator: operador de grua
cull: acabar com, exterminar
curse: desgraça, maldição
cushion: almofada
darned: consertado(a), remendado(a)
decisiveness: determinação, poder de decisão
deemed: considerado(a)
defeat: derrotar
defy: contestar, desafiar
delight: deleite, prazer
denying: negação
device: aparelho eletrônico
dig: cavar, escavar

Glossary

discharge: eliminação
disdain: desdém, desprezo
disperse: dispersar-se
disregard: desprezo
disseminate: disseminar
distill: destilar
distorted: deturpado(a), distorcido(a)
distress: aflição, angústia
dotted (with): salpicado(a) (de)
dream-catcher: apanhador(a) de sonhos
dust-bin: lata de lixo
ease: aliviar, atenuar
echo: ecoar, ressoar
elderly: idoso(a)
elective: matéria opcional
emptiness: vazio
enabled: habilitado(a)
engage: engajar, envolver
engraving: gravura
enroll: matricular-se
ensure: assegurar, garantir
entirety: totalidade
eradicate: exterminar
escalate: intensificar-se
exchange: trocar; intercâmbio
executive: executivo
expel: expulsar
expert: especialista
expertise: competência
failure: fracasso
faith: fé
farewell: adeus
farthing: tostão; um quarto de pêni (moeda inglesa)
fate: destino
fawn: fazer festa, sacudir a cauda demonstrando alegria (cachorro, leão)
feasibility: exequibilidade, viabilidade
feasible: exequível, possível
figure out: arquitetar, imaginar; concluir, perceber
fill in: preencher
financial literacy education: educação financeira
finding: descoberta
fit: ajustar-se
flame: chama
flourish: prosperar

flourishing: próspero(a)
foisted: empurrado(a)
formulaic: usado(a) muitas vezes nas mesmas situações
fortunate: afortunado(a)
fossil: fóssil
fractious: turbulento(a)
frame: fotograma, moldura
freshman: primeiranista(s)
fulfilled: realizado(a)
full-fledged: completo(a)
funding issue: problema financeiro
furthermore: além disso
gain: obter
gatekeeper: guardião
gather: reunir-se
gaze: olhar fixamente
give back: dar em retorno, retribuir
give up: abrir mão de, desistir; render-se
go down: dar-se por vencido
grab: prender, segurar
graduate: formar-se, graduar-se
grasshopper: gafanhoto
graze: pastar
greedy: ganancioso(a)
grudgingly: de má vontade
gruelling: cansativo(a), exaustivo(a)
guise: pretexto, disfarce
handful: punhado
harassment: assédio
hard-bitten: obstinado(a)
heap: grande quantidade
hearing issue: problema de audição
heartfelt: sincero(a)
highlight: destacar, ressaltar
hire: contratar
hoax: brincadeira, embuste
hooked up: conectado(a)
hop: pular, saltar
hostel: albergue, hospedaria
household income: renda familiar
hurdle: impedimento, obstáculo
hurricane: furacão
hype: propaganda ou promoção espalhafatosa, publicidade
idolized: idolatrado(a)

Glossary

illiterate: analfabeto(a)
impoverished: empobrecido(a)
in awe: em admiração
in-house: empregado fixo
indeed: de fato, realmente
inheritance: herança
injury: ferimento
intern: estagiário(a)
ivory: marfim
jail: prisão
jaw: mandíbula, maxilar
jeopardise: pôr em perigo
joyless: sem alegria, triste
joyously: alegremente
judge: juiz; julgar
jumbled: confuso(a), misturado(a)
jut: projetar-se, sobressair
keep an eye: ficar atento(a)
kick-started: iniciado(a)
knot: nó
lack of: falta de
landscape: paisagem
latter: último(a)
lawless: sem lei
leadership: comando, liderança
legacy: legado
legend: lenda
let loose: libertar
liar: mentiroso(a)
lick: lamber
life expectancy: expectativa de vida
life-threatening: (que) ameaça de morte
lifeblood: força vital
link up: conectar, ligar
literate: alfabetizado(a)
loan: emprestar (dinheiro); empréstimo
loathing: aversão
locker: armário com cadeado
lofty: altivo(a), imponente
lump of gold: pepita de ouro
lush: magnífico(a), suntuoso(a)
made up (one's) mind: decidir
mainstream: convencional, tradicional
make the most of: fazer o melhor uso, tirar o melhor proveito

malaise: mal-estar
manage: administrar; conseguir (fazer alguma coisa)
medication: medicamento
mend: consertar
merit: ser digno de, ser merecedor; virtude
mindset: mentalidade
mire: atoleiro, brejo
misconception: concepção errada
miser: avarento(a), sovina
mission: missão
misunderstanding: mal-entendido
movie buff: aficionado(a) por cinema
movie rating: classificação por faixa etária
murder: assassinato
nefarious: abominável, execrável
neglected: abandonado(a), negligenciado(a)
nest: ninho
nursery: berçário, creche
oddly paired: estranhamente unidos(as)
on display: à mostra
oohing: suspirar
outcome: resultado
outgrow: ultrapassar
overall: geral
overwhelmingly: predominantemente
pacing: ritmo
painful: doloroso(a)
pang: pontada
part: separar-se; divisão, separação
partnership: parceria
path: caminho
pathway: caminho
pattern: padrão
paw: pata
pay off: pagar
peer: colega
pelt: couro, pele de animal
pervasive: difundido(a)
pet: acariciar, cuidar (de animal de estimação)
pit of one's stomach: boca do estômago
pittance: ninharia, pequena porção
plague: praga
plight: condição, situação (geralmente má)
plot summary: resumo da trama
poignantly: pungentemente

Glossary 205

Glossary

polishing: polir
potter: ceramista, oleiro(a)
preconceived: preconcebido(a)
pregnancy: gravidez
pretzel: rosca salgada em forma de laço
prime: preparado(a)
privilege: privilégio
profitability: rentabilidade
provide: oferecer, proporcionar
psychoanalyst: psicanalista
pump: bomba de gasolina
punch line: ponto principal
purchase: compra
pursue: perseguir, procurar
put aside: pôr de lado
quell: acalmar
query: perguntar, questionar
random: aleatório
range: gama
rather than: em vez de
rattle: chocalhar
re-enact: reviver
reasonable: razoável
rebel: rebelde
rebellious: rebelde
refined: aprimorado(a), refinado(a)
regardless of: independentemente de
regret: arrepender-se
reliable: de confiança
remain: permanecer
render: dar, oferecer
repay: recompensar
restrain: conter, impedir
retirement: aposentadoria
revered: idolatrado(a), venerado(a)
reward: recompensa
rewarding: gratificante, recompensador(a)
roadblock: obstáculo
roam: andar a esmo, perambular, vagar
roar: rugir
rocking-horse: cavalinho de balanço
roll away: rolar
roof: telhado, teto
root: origem, raiz
routinely: rotineiramente
rumour: boato, rumor

run-of-the-mill: habitual
satire: sátira
scamper: disparar
scared stiff: assustadíssimo(a)
scattered about: espalhado(a)
scowl: olhar bravo ou zangado
seclude: afastar, excluir
self-esteem: autoestima
self-explanatory: óbvio
self-harm: automutilação
sensitive: sensível
setting: cenário
shape: moldar
shift: mover; mudança, substituição, turno
shoeshine boy: engraxate
shortcoming: deficiência, limitação
shot: cena de filme
skull: crânio
slam: rebater, criticar severamente
slave: escravo(a)
slip: escorregar
slit: abertura, corte
snap: morder, tentar abocanhar
sophomore year: segundo ano (escolar)
sovereign: independente
spark: despertar, deflagrar
spoilt brat: menino(a) mimado(a)
spot: avistar, reconhecer
spread: propagar
spread like wildfire: espalhar-se rapidamente
sprinkle: um pouco
staff: equipe (de trabalhadores)
staggering: assombroso(a)
stamp: bater o pé
startup: empresa nova/iniciante
steel: aço
steer: conduzir
stem: estancar, impedir
step up: aumentar
stiff: firme
stint: período
stock: ação (parcela em uma empresa)
stock market: mercado de ações
strata: camada social
strength: força, poder
stressful: tenso(a)

Glossary

strict: estrito(a)

strive: esforçar-se

strudel: tipo de torta de origem austríaca

struggle: lutar

stuff: coisas, mercadorias

stuffed: cheio(a)

stupid: tolo(a)

sue: processar

support: apoiar, sustentar

surrounding: ambiente circundante, arredores

suspicious: desconfiado(a)

swarm: fervilhar, lotar

swear: jurar, prometer

swindle: enganar, trapacear

swollen: inchado(a)

tabloid: tabloide (jornal)

tackle: enfrentar

take a part: escolher um papel (para representar)

take over: assumir

takeaway: comida para viagem

tale: conto, história

teasing: provocação

tend: tender

thorn: espinho

threat: ameaça

threshold: limiar

thrive: prosperar

throughout: ao longo

tight: apertado(a); dinheiro curto

time to part ways: momento de separar-se de alguém, de seguir caminhos diferentes

tofu: tipo de queijo japonês feito de leite de soja

toil: labuta; labutar

townscape: paisagem urbana

trade: negociar; negócio

traverse: atravessar

trend: tendência

tripod: tripé

twirl: rodopiar

two-way street: rua de duas mãos

unaware: inconsciente

undergo: passar por, ser submetido a

undertake: realizar

undesirable: indesejável

unfurl: desenrolar, abrir

unity: união

unlocking: desvendar

unnamed: anônimo(a)

unparalleled: incomparável

unreasonable: inadequado, irracional

unrivalled: incomparável

untouched: intacto(a), intocado(a)

untoward: desfavorável

up-to-date: atualizado(a)

uproar: alvoroço

urge: instar

utter: absoluto(a), total

vacant: vago, vazio

vanish: desaparecer, sumir

vault: cripta

venture capital: capital de risco

volunteer: voluntariar-se

volunteering: voluntariado

wad: maço

wardrobe: guarda-roupa

warehoused: armazenado(a), guardado(a)

wasted: desperdiçado(a)

welfare: bem-estar

wellness: bem-estar

whereas: enquanto, ao passo que

whisper: murmúrio, sussurro

whilst: enquanto

widely: amplamente

will: testamento, vontade

willpower: determinação, força de vontade

wing: asa

wire: corda, fio

wisdom: sabedoria

wisely: de forma inteligente

worship: adoração, veneração

worth: que vale a pena; valor (custo, preço)

worthless: inútil

yield: produzir, render

youth development charity: instituição de caridade para o desenvolvimento dos jovens

Bibliography

ABREU-TARDELLI, L. S.; CRISTOVÃO, V. L. L. (Org.). *Linguagem e educação*: o ensino e aprendizagem de gêneros textuais. Campinas: Mercado de Letras, 2009.

BEZERRA, M. A.; DIONISIO, A. P.; MACHADO, A. R. (Org.). *Gêneros textuais & ensino*. São Paulo: Parábola Editorial, 2010.

BRASIL/SEMTEC. *PCN+ Ensino Médio: Orientações educacionais complementares aos Parâmetros Curriculares Nacionais*. Volume 1: Linguagens, códigos e suas tecnologias. Brasília, DF: MEC/SEMTEC, 2002. Disponível em: <portal.mec.gov.br/seb/arquivos/pdf/02Linguagens.pdf>. Acesso em: 12 julho 2015.

BRASIL/SEMTEC. *Linguagens, Códigos e suas Tecnologias: Orientações Curriculares para o Ensino Médio. Capítulo 3. Conhecimentos de línguas estrangeiras*. 2006. Disponível em <http://portal.mec.gov.br/seb/arquivos/pdf/book_volume_01_internet.pdf>. Acesso em 12 julho 2015.

COPE, B. & KALANTZIS, M. Multiliteracies: The Beginning of an Idea. In: COPE, B. & KALANTZIS, M. (Eds.). *Multiliteracies: Literacy Learning and The Design of Social Futures*. London: Routledge, 2000. p. 3-8.

CROSS, D. *Large Classes in Action*. Hertfordshire: Prentice Hall International, 1995.

DIONISIO, A. P. et al. (org.) *Gêneros textuais & ensino*. Rio de Janeiro: Lucerna, 2002, p. 19-36.

Diretrizes Curriculares Nacionais da Educação Básica. Ministério da Educação, 2013.

FREIRE, Paulo. *Pedagogia da autonomia*: saberes necessários à prática educativa. São Paulo: Paz e Terra, 1996.

GRELLET, F. *Developing Reading Skills*. Cambridge: Cambridge University Press, 1981.

HEIDE, Ann & STILBORNE, Linda. *Guia do professor para a internet*: completo e fácil. Trad. Edson Furmankiewz. 2. ed. Porto Alegre: Artmed, 2000.

HOFFMANN, Jussara. *Avaliar para promover*: as setas do caminho. Porto Alegre: Mediação, 2001.

LAPKOSKI, G. A. O. *Do texto ao sentido*: teoria e prática de leitura em língua inglesa. Curitiba: Ibpex, 2011.

MARCUSCHI, L. A. "Gêneros textuais: definição e funcionalidade". In: DIONISIO, A. P. et al. (org.) *Gêneros textuais & ensino*. Rio de Janeiro: Lucerna, 2002, p. 19-36.

MARTINEZ, P. *Didática de línguas estrangeiras*. São Paulo: Parábola Editorial, 2009.

MOITA-LOPES, L. P. "Ensino de inglês como espaço de embates culturais e de políticas da diferença." In: GIMENEZ, T. *et al.* (Org.). *Perspectivas educacionais e o ensino de inglês na escola pública*. Pelotas: Educat, 2005.

_____. *Oficina de linguística aplicada*. Campinas: Mercado de Letras, 2000.

RAIMES, A. *Techniques in Teaching Writing*. New York: Oxford University Press, 1983.

RICHARDS, J. C.; RENANDYA, W. A. (Ed.). *Methodology in Language Teaching*: an anthology of current practice. New York: Cambridge University Press, 2002.

RODRIGUES, D. (Org.). *Inclusão e educação*: doze olhares sobre a educação inclusiva. São Paulo: Summus, 2006.

ROJO, Roxane; MOURA, Eduardo. *Multiletramentos na escola*. São Paulo: Parábola Editorial, 2012.

SCHNEUWLY, Bernard & DOLZ, Joaquim. *Gêneros orais e escritos na escola*. Campinas: Mercado das Letras, 2004.

SOUZA, Adriana Grade Fiori *et al. Leitura em língua inglesa*: uma abordagem instrumental. São Paulo: Disal, 2005.

TOMLINSON, B. *Developing Materials for Language Teaching*. Londres: Continuum, 2003.

VYGOTSKY, L. S. *Pensamento e linguagem*. São Paulo: Martins Fontes, 1993.

WALESKO, A. M. H. *Compreensão oral em língua inglesa*. Curitiba: Ibpex, 2010.